MORE FROM THE SAGER GROUP

The Swamp: Deceit and Corruption in the CIA
An Elizabeth Petrov Thriller (Book 1)
by Jeff Grant

Eat Wheaties: A Novel
by Michael Kun

#MeAsWell
by Peter Melhlman

Death Came Swiftly: Novel About the Tay Bridge Disaster of 1879
by Bill Abrams

High Tolerance: A Novel of Sex, Race, Celebrity, Murder... and
Marijuana
by Mike Sager

Miss Havilland: A Novel
by Gay Daly

The Orphan's Daughter: A Novel
by Jan Cherubin

Lifeboat No. 8: Surviving the Titanic
by Elizabeth Kaye

Into the River of Angels: A Novel
by George R. Wolfe

See our entire library at TheSagerGroup.net

DEATH *of a* Childhood

A MEMOIR OF 1989 AND THE "WHY NOT?" BALTIMORE ORIOLES

RYAN BASEN

Published in the United States of America.
Cover and Interior Designed by Siori Kitajima, PatternBased.com
Cataloging-in-Publication data for this book is available from the Library of Congress

ISBN-13
eBook: 978-1-958861-53-0
Paperback: 978-1-958861-54-7

Published by The Sager Group LLC
(TheSagerGroup.net)

DEATH *of a* Childhood

A MEMOIR OF 1989 AND THE "WHY NOT?" BALTIMORE ORIOLES

RYAN BASEN

THE SAGER GROUP

Artifex Te Adiuva

Putting gifts from my grandparents' and parents' vacations to good use, circa age 7 or 8.

CONTENTS

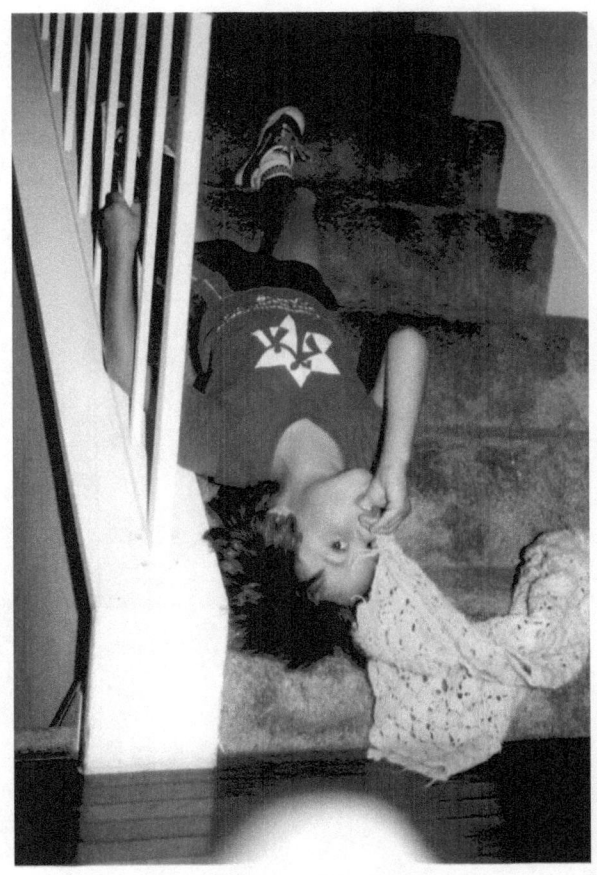

Lounging at home one summer day at age 6, on the staircase I used to jump from top to bottom.

AUTHOR'S NOTE

I never believed in Santa Claus or Hanukkah Harry. My light-sleeping and older cousins ruined the tooth fairy and the prophet Elijah for me, respectively, at early ages.

I did believe in miracles, however, especially of the sports variety. This is a story about how once upon a season, a Baltimore Orioles baseball team led by Mickey Tettleton, Jeff Ballard, Gregg Olson, and twenty-some other Major League players made a precocious preteen believe in miracles one last time—one last baseball season of pure joy before my world suddenly and unalterably changed.

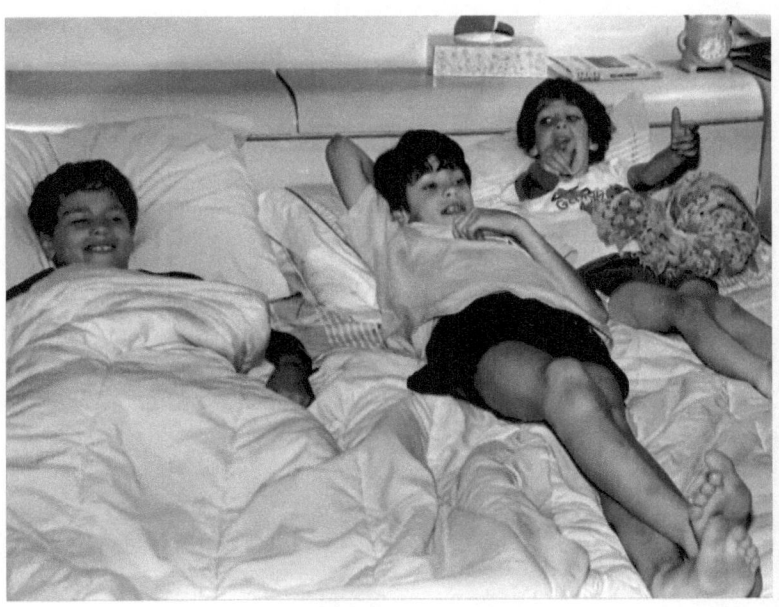

Watching TV in between my brothers Michael (to my right) and Tyler on our parents' bed, one summer morning in 1989.

INTRODUCTION

It was late in September 1989—a few months after I had stared at the TV trying to figure out why some "Teeee-an-an-men" Square kept interrupting sports broadcasts, and about a month before a radio broadcast reported the fall of the Berlin Wall to my school carpool. I was rooting against Notre Dame's serious national title defense as the college football season bloomed (I preferred Miami), while the defending NFL champion San Francisco 49ers were equally as annoying and successful. At eleven, I had recently thrown away my New Kids on the Block cassette while memorizing the words to Young MC's "Bust a Move." Teal and bright orange T-shirts were part of my regular rotation, and I certainly knew Bo (Jackson).

In my leafy Washington, DC, suburb of Rockville, Maryland, I was intensely following a classic race for Major League Baseball's (MLB) American League East division title. The chase had boiled down to two teams: the Baltimore Orioles, our adopted hometown team, and the Toronto Blue Jays, those annual chokers from some odd place up north. The O's were young, plucky upstarts who had captured the hearts of baseball fans nationally; the Jays were under-achieving veterans that nobody I knew rooted for. In our eyes the Jays were classic villains, trying to prevent what would be a remarkable, historic title for an O's team that had lost more than one hundred games only one season before.

During this final week of the regular season, the Orioles and Blue Jays had both won two of three games—against Milwaukee and Detroit, respectively. They matched each other, going win-loss-win across Monday-Tuesday-Wednesday. After those series' ended, Baltimore trailed Toronto by one game.

That set up a final series the last weekend of September between the O's and Jays in Toronto. The setting was modern: SkyDome, which had just opened a few months earlier, the first stadium in major American sports with a retractable roof. But the story was as traditional as century-plus-old MLB itself: A division race and a spot in the postseason would be decided over the mere final few days of a six-month regular season, with the loser's season ending suddenly. There were no wild card spots in 1989, no backdoors into the playoffs.

I keenly understood this scenario as the first game began just after seven thirty Friday night. Left-hander Jeff Ballard started on the mound for the Orioles against righty Todd Stottlemyre of Toronto, so we liked our chances. The twenty-six-year-old Ballard, in his third Major League season, had already won eighteen games during the season and was finishing strong. The twenty-four-year-old Stottlemyre, in his second season, had won seven games while splitting time between the rotation and bullpen. He had also pitched well in August and September, but had lost two of his last three starts.

I wore my black hat with a dignified-looking oriole on the front as my nine-year-old brother Michael, my father, and I sat at the kitchen table and stared at the small, boxy TV in the kitchen. We finished dinner as we watched O's outfielder Phil Bradley lead off the game by launching a Stottlemyre pitch deep into left-center field. The ball disappeared over the fence, giving the Orioles an early lead.

"Yes!" we screamed in unison. I probably pumped a fist too.

The 1–0 lead stood as my parents put my brother Tyler, four, to bed and disappeared for a while. Michael and I moved first to our living room downstairs, then upstairs to watch the later innings in my parents' bedroom. Now clad in my regular pajamas—old sweatpants with holes in the knees and the T-shirt I had worn since changing immediately after school—I stretched out my growing, thin legs toward the end of their king bed as we leaned our heads against pillows lining the headboard rising parallel to the wall. We stared down the broadcast as my parents eventually joined us.

Ballard held Toronto scoreless through seven innings, benefiting not only from his own masterful pitching, but also from stellar defense and key plays on the bases. Baltimore catcher Jamie Quirk threw out Pat Borders at second with two on and two out in the second inning, and the fleet Mookie Wilson was picked off first to end the third. Ballard escaped a bases-loaded jam in the fifth, getting Wilson to fly out to right with two outs. We celebrated these escapes with pumped fists and exclamations in unison.

But we groaned as the Orioles could not pad their lead with the bases loaded and two out in the fourth—with Quirk grounding out to first—and again when the Orioles stranded two more in the fifth, after Randy Milligan flew out to right with two outs.

At some point Michael went to bed in his room down the hall. My heart was pounding as I lay on the bed between my parents, the game now passing ten p.m. Even with a division title on the line, I knew my mother would not let me stay up to watch the end. Instead she would surely push me to get to bed soon, knowing I had to wake up for Rosh Hashanah services the next morning.

I hoped Mom would not notice the clock, but alas she never failed. On cue, "Ry," she muttered, not looking up from the day's *Washington Post* she was buried in, "almost bedtime." Her casual tone suggested she thought she was being generous.

"Can I stay up until the game is over?"

My father was silent, pretending to be too focused on the game so he did not have to give a response that would either infuriate Mom or infuriate me and force him to watch the rest of this tense game basically alone.

After a beat, my mother responded: "You can't be late for services tomorrow. And you need your sleep. Look at those bags under your eyes."

Her last point was indisputable. The bags were getting quite large. The advent of my puberty and suddenly having to rise earlier than usual for school that fall were depriving me of much-needed sleep. Throw in adjusting to a school day that was longer by one hour as well, and it was hard to argue with her logic.

"Noooooo!" I turned my head away from the TV momentarily to look straight at her. "I am not missing the end of this game!"

But she did not budge. So after the seventh inning, I trotted down our dimly lit, narrow hallway to my room and turned off the lights. I climbed onto my bed and lay on my stomach, resting my chin over the tops of my clasped, flat hands as I faced the hallway with my door mostly open. In the dark I could still see the moon on the Michael Jordan poster that adorned the entire height of the outside of my door. The young Bulls guard grasped the celestial object high in his right hand as he prepared to dunk it.

With my father still watching the game and the volume at a decent clip, I followed the action for a bit longer.

It has been more than thirty years, and I consumed some of the ensuing part of that game only via broadcast sound and visual reflections off my parents' bedroom window. But I will never forget what happened that night.

Or the next day.

Or that whole season, both on baseball fields and in settings encompassing the rest of my life.

It was a campaign that unfolded in a very different America over less than seven months, a small portion of a life now in its fifth decade. But the 1989 Baltimore Orioles were an unusual team remembered well by fans who followed them. And while their season progressed with the typical daily hum of an MLB year, it did so as my mostly carefree life started to morph considerably, leaving me a different foundation I have lived with ever since.

What impact did that baseball season, that year, have on me? Why, as an adult, did I feel not so much that I wanted to write this book—but like I had to? I knew I could only find the answers by doing so.

Here is a snapshot of what I discovered: I began the season as a precocious, careless fifth-grader on the verge of turning eleven. My beloved maternal grandmother and cat were still alive and well, I was still attending my longtime school with my closest friends, and I was not dealing with any health problems (beyond the untreated attention deficit hyperactivity disorder that only seemed to bother some adults—like I cared). I still believed in miracles, and the O's—up through that last September weekend in Toronto—only reinforced that sentiment.

They also hooked me like no baseball team before or after. When I started following baseball in 1986, I had not yet played organized ball. It was the '86 Mets who sucked me into the sport; they had Doc and Darryl and bench-clearing brawls, and they won 108 regular season games and a world title. By the start of the 1989 season, I was in my third year playing organized ball and was a burgeoning baseball junkie. It would take more than flash and winning to engross me.

The Orioles that year provided that "more." They had Cal Ripken Jr., who was the best shortstop in the game and played every day; what young baller does not want to play every day? They had closer Gregg Olson, who hated losing as much as me and my equally hyper-competitive friends. They had Billy Ripken, as solid fundamentally as they came; outfielders not much older than me throwing their bodies around as recklessly as I did; and a couple of stories impossible for anyone older than me to believe in, pitchers Ballard and Dave Johnson. Plus they had the division race, power hitter Mickey Tettleton and his Fruit Loops, and a hit song ("Why Not?").

I also still recalled this club so well and felt like I needed to research and write about them because I had related to them. Our stories often mirrored each other as that season ensued, and I saw a version of myself that I wanted to become in the baby faces of Ballard and Olson and Tettleton (among others). Like the callow O's, I embodied the innocence of youth for most of the season, especially its first half. We both hit hiccups during the season's third quarter, then recovered—only to be blindsided by the reality marking September, that month when hopeful summers come to die for preteens and often for young ballclubs.

The 1989 Baltimore Orioles hold a special place in many hearts, but if you are not among us, you are probably not familiar with their story. They are not the 1986 Mets or 1998 Yankees or 2004 Red Sox—big winners destined to be recalled by baseball fans forever. Spoiler alert: These Orioles did not capture an MLB title or even lose a World Series in dramatic fashion.

But their story deserves to be told, for my nieces and nephews and so many others who missed it—not to mention thousands who surely forgot about it as soon as the first pitch of the 1990 season. These O's oddly mimicked the fictional Cleveland Indians of the cult film *Major League* that debuted early in that 1989 season. But they were much more than a collection of young, lovable overachievers led by a couple of crafty veterans. Throughout a season in an era when there was little to watch on summer nights besides baseball and *Wonder Years* reruns, they became a new version of the 1969 Miracle Mets—one for my generation.

The Orioles threatened all season to become the first MLB team ever to win a division title one season after finishing last. They were a club mostly of misfits and rookies who set records and won in numerous walk-offs well past my bedtime. They were the best story in baseball that season, "the best story in baseball in years," announcer Bob Costas said before a mid-June broadcast, despite operating without much flare off the field.

These achievements set this club apart from more recognizable teams in baseball lore: These O's are remembered fondly by their fans despite not winning big and largely being devoid of characters and controversy. Whenever I reminisce, the first thing that comes to mind is when fans tossed Fruit Loops onto the field after Tettleton homers. Back then, Phillies fans threw batteries, Yankee fans candy bars, Red Sox fans nearly everything else—all in frustration. O's fans tossed boxes of sugar cereal—in joy.

They must have been a phenomenon because this team captured not just one but two major metro areas. They were (and still are) celebrated in Baltimore, sure, but they also connected in the Washington region at a level that no O's team had since the Washington Senators moved away nearly two decades earlier—even more than the 1983 MLB champion Orioles did.

That they have largely been forgotten nationally says more about our society than it does about them.

But when they were done, they left a deep, dark void that only widened over the next few years. As I look back at the events immediately preceding, during, and right after the 1989 MLB season through the lens of a tested, forty-something jaded former journalist, it's evident: Neither the O's nor I would end 1989 as the same people we had been when the year started. We were changed forever by that year, especially that baseball season.

Here are our tales, the intertwined stories of a boy and a boyish Major League Baseball team, both forced to suddenly grow up too soon.

Hanging with Pluto, Michael, and Tyler at Disney World, December 1988, while sporting one of the many Nike shirts I owned as a preteen.

Chapter 1

THE WINTER OF MY CONTENT(-EDNESS)

It was Hanukkah, December 1988, and our rowdy fifth-grade Hebrew school class was celebrating. Ms. P., our teacher, had asked us to bring in gifts to exchange during class, and I pulled a number scrawled on a scrap of paper out of a hat, looked down and realized I had drawn the last pick. By the time it was my turn, all that was left were colorful, silicon, twistable bracelets.

Let's just say they were not a gender-neutral gift, at least not in late-twentieth-century America.

Something inside of me suddenly broke. At first I was merely upset at the prospect of receiving bracelets instead of a new football or bags chock full of Hanukkah gelt. Then I thought about the other boys in my class seeing me with the bracelets. *And what if they told kids at school and in my neighborhood?* I wondered. *What if they told my cousins?*

I struggled to breathe, and it felt like a sharp object was piercing my chest. My hands and feet got very cold; my forehead was pounding. I felt terrified and anxious. I could sense tears building up in my eyes, so I focused exclusively on holding them back. Owning bracelets was bad enough. Crying while said bracelets sat on my desk, I thought, would be too much for me to ever live down.

Janie was sitting next to me. This patient, sweet-natured girl had an older brother and had attended school and Hebrew school with me for years. She noticed I was upset. "It's okay. They're just bracelets," she said, modeling them for me on her wrists.

But it was NOT okay. Not to a preteen boy who thought he did not measure up physically. I was skinny and weak in a culture that celebrated muscular and strong. I worried that my peers would see through the masculine, tough veneer I projected (playing a ton of sports, slinging my heavy bookbag over one shoulder, belching, and spitting) to the hypersensitive, sweet-natured boy who delighted in playing with his three-year-old brother and reading in bed next to his mother. Being seen with colorful bracelets could blow my cover.

I told Janie she could keep the bracelets and walked away with nothing from the Hanukkah exchange, but I was much happier for it. Within seconds after gifting Janie the bracelets, I was able to breathe again and felt relief overtake fear throughout my body.

Some twenty-five years later, while attending a cognitive behavioral therapy class, I flashed back and realized this episode was one of my earliest panic attacks, maybe the first. There have been many, many more.

At ten, my panic disorder was still largely dormant. But on that day in Hebrew school, it hammered me. I felt lucky the lasting damage was minimal; nobody teased me about the bracelets or said anything about my meltdown afterward.

I did not tell my parents or any other soul what happened, certainly not about the sheer terror I felt. It was too frightening for me to even try to comprehend, and there was no way I was going to admit to anyone that I was scared of anything or momentarily possessed flashy bracelets favored by the models in those annoying Benetton ads. Not even Mom.

Instead I reflexively buried the episode. For years. Once we got home, I forgot all about it as we lit another candle on the menorah and my brothers and I received Hanukkah gifts after dinner. I then maybe did some homework, watched some of the *Monday Night Football* game and went to bed as if nothing unusual had happened.

But I could not ignore major changes for much longer. While that was probably not my first panic attack, it was the first severe one I can recall—and it was a nasty harbinger of the major adversities I was going to face in 1989 and beyond. Winter had begun.

As I stood on the precipice of turning eleven in late 1988, I was never bored or boring. I adored team sports—playing, watching, and reading about them. I was always loud, sometimes funny, and often obnoxious. The dimple cratering my left cheek; my large, almond-shaped, hazel eyes; and dark brown, unkempt bushel of hair allowed me to get away with a lot. So did the smirk I often wore when I frequently pushed boundaries and buttons.

I still sometimes jumped clear down the eight stairs leading from the second story of our house to the hardwood foyer by the front door, landing with a crash that could (and did) wake up Tyler from naps. I was interested in having girls as friends again, but most of them found me and my habits disgusting—in addition to the posterizing, I also cracked my knuckles loudly, bit my nails, and never so much as glanced at myself in the mirror before leaving for school. "I once got busy in a Burger King bathroom" was a song lyric that I was still a year-plus away from simultaneously hearing and understanding. I almost certainly had ADHD, although it was never diagnosed.

I was being raised a Conservative Jew in an upper-middle class neighborhood by two working parents—including Mom, who balanced her part-time career as a public health consultant with serving as our primary caretaker, and my father, a full-time radiologist. Both had grown up in the area in religious households with strict, no-nonsense parents, including my sports-obsessed grandfathers, who encouraged my parents to play and follow team sports as they had growing up. My parents knowingly passed on these values to me and my two brothers.

As a relentlessly curious, extroverted kid, my life extended well beyond my family. I was getting into pop culture, obsessed with pop music, Michael Jordan's spectacular dunks, and Bo Jackson's ability to play two pro sports simultaneously and play them well. I only wore Nike sneakers and donned several Nike shirts per my rotation. I had ditched the short shorts Mom had been buying me for much of the 1980s for more stylish, baggier shorts. But I would not touch jeans or anything remotely nice, wearing shorts or sweatpants daily, along with an untucked T-shirt and sometimes an untucked sweatshirt.

My chosen garb hung off my very skinny frame as if I were intentionally aping the hip-hop culture spreading through the suburbs. (This was the year of Tone Loc.) I refused to wear a jacket unless there was a blizzard out, insisting I was warm enough without one even during cold winter days. (I think I was; when outdoors, I was usually too engaged in the moment to notice weather of any sort.)

That Mom was okay with me going into public looking like this spoke to how much I resisted her efforts to tame me and her recognition that she needed to pick her battles. But she fretted that people would see me and wonder if she was taking good care of me.

Like my parents and grandfathers, I was a compulsive sports fan, one armed with a cable package, my own subscription to *Sports Illustrated*, and the *Washington Post* sports section delivered to our driveway every day to share with my father. On vacations my parents would buy me *USA Today* so I could read its sports section.

Washington had the NFL's Redskins, NHL's Capitals, and NBA's Bullets—and the *Post* focused coverage on Maryland and Georgetown men's basketball just as much—but the area did not have an MLB team. The city had lost two versions of the Senators to relocation because of local indifference, consistent losing, and subpar ownership.

My parents grew up rooting for those Senators and still smarted from their moves. But Mom kept her old glove that she had used to throw the ball around with her father in our garage. A former standout high school athlete, she sometimes played catch with me in our front yard until I started throwing too hard. She was the only mother I knew who did this.

The Senators' moves happened years before I started following baseball. But despite broadcasting most of their games locally and reaching two World Series after the Senators ultimately left town following the 1971 season, the O's had not effectively replaced them as the DC area's home team. Some kids I knew rooted for the Chicago Cubs and Boston Red Sox. Like a few of my friends with New York roots, Michael, and my older cousin Brad, I still pulled for the flashy, brawling, winning New York Mets.

The Orioles were everybody's second-favorite team, mostly because they had Cal Ripken Jr., and were the only team within driving distance. They played at Memorial Stadium in northern Baltimore, which was still a hike for us, especially on weekdays. But due to my father's knowledge of Baltimore's roads from his residency at Johns Hopkins Hospital, and his willingness to jeopardize our safety to get there as quickly as possible, we could make it in an hour most weekends.

Not that we attended too many O's games before 1989. What adult wanted to drive squirrely kids an hour to see a terrible, fading team?

That first year I followed MLB, 1986, I tracked the Orioles as intently as I watched the Mets—at least until September, when the once-proud franchise began to crater. Legendary manager Earl Weaver had come out of retirement that season, after the Orioles failed to win the division for two straight seasons following their 1983 World Series title. That had marked their third championship and sixth World Series appearance in eighteen seasons, and they won at least ninety games that year for the sixteenth time dating to 1964. Even in 1984 and 1985, they finished above .500.

The O's figured to still be contenders in 1986, with cornerstones including first baseman Eddie Murray, Ripken, and a deep pitching staff. Weaver guided them to a 59–47 mark by early August, two and one-half games behind the first-place Red Sox, rebounding from a ten-game deficit only three weeks earlier. They were second in a seven-team division with one-third of the season left.

As my interest in baseball bloomed, I watched day games, early innings of night games, and replays of night games on weekend mornings—reading daily about the O's in the *Post*. Murray homered and Ripken doubled in a run during the first game I ever attended, a 4–3 win over the Yankees that June. (You just don't forget stuff like that; I recall being in line at the concourse when Murray homered.) My sudden yet sincere dedication was poised to pay off as the O's surged later that summer.

Then the O's launched a nosedive that would embarrass even the 1899 Cleveland Spiders or 1962 Mets. They lost exactly three of every four remaining games, going 14–42 to finish the season last in the AL East. A team with a winning percentage above .500 for nearly all of four months played at a .250 clip for the final two months of the season.

After the season, Weaver retired again, for good. Cal Ripken Sr., the father of Billy and Cal Jr., and a long-time coach in the O's system, took over. But the O's went 67–95 in 1987 and after that season, general manager Hank Peters was fired after twelve years running the club.

Roland Hemond replaced him. The former long-time GM of the Chicago White Sox, Hemond had spent the previous two years as a special assistant to MLB commissioner Peter Ueberroth. Frank Robinson, a Hall of Fame outfielder with the O's and Cincinnati Reds in the 1960s and 1970s, was named assistant GM.

When the O's started the 1988 season 0–6, Hemond fired Ripken Sr. He was replaced by Robinson, who had managed the Cleveland Indians and San Francisco Giants over eight seasons in the 1970s and 1980s, never finishing higher than third in the division.

Robinson fared little better than Ripken Sr., with an aging, disgruntled core that openly feuded with ownership. It was an all-time horrible team, like if the *Bad News Bears* mated with the 1993 Mets. The O's set a record by losing their first twenty-one games. Billy Ripken, the second baseman, was immortalized on the cover of *Sports Illustrated* to mark the occasion in late April, in an issue published just before the streak ended. Seated in the dugout and photographed from the side, his left eye was closed as he leaned his forehead into a bat. "0–18" the headline blared. "THE AGONY OF

THE ORIOLES." The O's finished the season 54–107 and the season-opening losing streak is still a record.

"There wasn't the same investment in the farm budget and there was a slow erosion of talent coming out of the minors," explained Baltimore sportscaster Keith Mills, discussing the franchise's deterioration in the book *A Season to Forget* about the 1988 team. "The team lost scouts and player development people. . . .

"The Orioles then tried to get into the free agent market aggressively for the first time ever and missed really badly on a lot of players," he continued. "The players they brought in were either injured, past their prime, underperformed." All three descriptions could have referred to outfielder Fred Lynn alone, for example.

The 1988 season was embarrassing, but it served a purpose: Management awoke to the idea that the team needed a massive reconstruction. This was a veteran club built to chase a title that could not win a single regular season game until the penultimate day of April. So the O's spent the second half of the season and the ensuing offseason rebuilding for the first time in almost three decades.

With his immense popularity, steadiness and relative youth, Cal Ripken Jr., twenty-eight, was the only key veteran retained. This was important for more than just baseball reasons. Thousands of other kids and I idolized Cal. He stood six foot four, possessed a powerful arm and range, could hit for power (largely unheard of for the likes of Dickie Thon and Spike Owen playing shortstop in the late 1980s), and played every . . . single . . . day. He had already won a championship and an AL MVP award, projected a pristine off-field reputation, and was a Maryland native. That meant something even to Washington-area residents because, like true Marylanders, we also spent summers vacationing at Delmarva beaches and time in Baltimore for school and family day trips.

We looked at Cal as one of us. In fact Cal was a major reason why I drank milk, because of his ubiquitous milk ads that ran during local broadcasts throughout my childhood. I also learned to appreciate the mental aspects of baseball by reading about his preparation and adjustments, and watching him between pitches when we attended games.

As the 1989 season beckoned, though, it seemed Cal was a saint for sticking around. The O's were early in what looked to be a massive rebuild. Ripken was the only star worth watching, though a few young phenoms could possibly debut at some point that year, especially on the pitching staff.

It was shaping up to be yet another losing season, potentially with more losses than even 1988. With the Mets coming off another division title, the Capitals' season, and another hotly contested college basketball campaign well underway, during the winter the O's were not on the radar for me and my fellow sports-obsessed friends. Not even trading the disgruntled Murray, who had been the O's starting first baseman since before we were born, got much of our attention.

We were, of course, often preoccupied. Even at ten, life for us was far from just pop music, sports, and sweats. That was how our parents wanted it. They shared great expectations for us, as if they had plotted together at Hofberg's Deli or Theo's Pizza one afternoon while we were all at Hebrew school or other religious schools. We were fast-tracked. So I, for example, was enrolled in Center for Talented Youth (CTY) math classes on Saturday mornings, had weekly piano lessons and a weekly paper route I shared with Michael, and was expected to do well in school. All while attending Hebrew school twice weekly and playing on organized teams every season (that last one was my choice). Did I mention I was ten?

My parents set a tone, adorning the walls of our guest bedroom with their numerous diplomas and awards. Mom feared not doing everything in her power to help us achieve what they had. So she drove me. And drove me. And drove me more. In between that, she made plans for my brothers and me. "I'm doing this for you!" was a common and loud retort, her eyes bulging and voice straining when I tried to get her attention while she was on the phone.

Over one Thanksgiving break when I was eight or nine, my cousin visited from New Jersey. Mom interrupted his studying in a quiet room away from family to make a point. "Do you remember your cousin Peter?" she quipped, knowing damn well that I did not as she nudged me into the room. "He goes to Princeton. Maybe one day if you work as hard as he does, you can go there too."

I rolled my eyes and walked back into the kitchen, looking for more whipped cream or Cake Mate to inhale directly out of the bottle/tube. College seemed a loooooong time away.

Still, by late 1988, I was very close with Mom. The roots of my insomnia were already embedded in me. I sometimes lay awake at night for a few minutes, concerned about a school assignment or some other problem. Then I realized Mom would help me fix it, no matter what it was. So I went back to listening to broadcasts of games featuring the Orioles, Redskins, or Capitals on the clock radio that sat by my bed, usually falling asleep before the games ended.

As the year approached its end, I was a very happy kid. I didn't understand why I was supposed to want more out of life.

My attitude was partly because of the support I felt not just from family but from several close friends. I spent much of my free time hanging with my brothers, cousins, and a group of other boys in my grade at school. By fifth grade, we were—cliché alert—like brothers. I had known most of them since kindergarten and all of them since second grade, when Adam moved down from New York. We played football or basketball during recess; competed on some of the same rec flag football, basketball, and baseball teams; went to the same baseball camp for a week or two each summer; slept at each other's houses enough to call mothers by their first names. (But not most of our fathers. No way.) My cousin Melissa, fifteen, babysat a couple of them.

But by late 1988 our bonds were being tested, another harbinger of the shitstorm to come. We were in our last year of elementary school together, after the school board changed our school, Ritchie Park, from a K–6 school to K–5 beginning that academic year. The board had redrawn the boundaries a year earlier, moving our cohort from future Robert Frost Junior High (grades 7–8) and Thomas

Wootton High (9–12) students to Julius West Middle (6–8) and Richard Montgomery High (9–12).

Within weeks, the board's decision had impacted our lives. Some families started plotting moves into other school districts. Others played the system to keep their kids on the Frost–Wootton track. Still others enrolled their kids in Bullis, a nearby private school, including a few of my friends who were Ritchie Park mainstays.

These classmates soon told us they would be leaving Ritchie Park following that 1987–88 school year. When my friend Dave informed me one morning in our fourth-grade homeroom as we hung up our bookbags, I froze and stared at him, my mouth agape. I must have thought we would all be together forever because I could not remember a time when we were not. I certainly did not want us to be driven apart; a lot of my self-confidence was derived from their affirmation.

Dave probably sensed my disappointment. "Are you mad or sad?" he asked.

I could not muster an answer; I was both. This kid who cracked me up by calling everyone by nicknames he made up when it was his turn to call roll, who seemed more interested in making me a better baseball player than I was . . . he was leaving us?

These changes made for an auspicious start to the 1988–89 school year. In the span of a summer, those of us who returned to Ritchie Park morphed from being a large cohort of fourth-grade nothings walking the same upstairs hallways as seemingly much larger fifth- and sixth-graders . . . to a smaller group of undisputed princes and princesses of the school. It made me feel like something of a big shot. Suddenly I was among the oldest kids at a school I had been attending for almost six years, a place where I had usually looked up (literally and figuratively) at my older cousins and their friends, as well as my friends' older siblings. Like many of my classmates, they were all gone, sprinkled across different schools spanning our corner of Montgomery County and even Northwest DC.

At first it was eerie not seeing so many of them. I had no idea if I would join their exodus, but ominous seeds had been planted.

For the most part, though, I really enjoyed school that year. I was always with friends and every one of our recess football games felt like the Super Bowl. My friend Ross and I played a continuous paper football game every afternoon at my desk as the rest of our class packed up to depart.

Despite the school board move, many things did not change, helping me maintain a sense of security at Ritchie Park. Michael and I kept walking to school every day with the three oldest boys from the neighboring Gromley family. Steve was in my grade and had been one of my closest friends since before kindergarten. Like me, he was the oldest in an all-boy family with big eyes and a bigger heart. We competed in cracking each other up. Steve's brother Sean and Michael were also in the same grade and had been friends for just as long.

We usually walked to school and back daily without parental supervision, which made me feel even more like a little king as we cruised through the first half of the year. We typically arrived around 8:45, meeting Ross, Adam, and our other friends who rode the bus from other neighborhoods a short drive away. This gave us about ten precious minutes to hang out in front of the building before the bell rang and drew hordes of kids darting inside and scampering off to our respective homerooms.

My homeroom teacher was a fifty-something veteran named Bernice, a disinterested woman out of patience with squirrely boys. She once threatened to literally sit on Ross; she split up Ross, our friend Craig, and me after we had been noisily sitting together for only a week or two.

She eventually moved me to the back of the room on my own. This did not bother me much at first, after I realized I could quietly scribble projected baseball statistics or other thoughts into a small journal, blowing off her boring lessons. But my separation began to grate on me. When I asked to return to the rest of the class midway through the school year, however, she blew me off.

My history and math teacher, Gary, was hardly better. He delighted in teasing the girls about their singing and clothes, put his hands on their shoulders, and stacked *Jeopardy* teams on test prep days to make sure the teams with his favorite female students won. That latter trend drove me nuts.

Mom was frustrated too, but on a much more macro level than *Jeopardy* days in history class. After hating my ditzy third-grade homeroom teacher, dealing with the school board switcheroo, and now meeting our fifth-grade teachers, Mom's trust in the system was fading. My parents did not want to move, so she was seriously pondering whether to keep me in public school.

I was blissfully unaware of Mom's thinking as I careened through the school year, enjoying some routines I had long grown accustomed to and spending every day with most of my close friends.

Several moments from that winter stand out, however, demonstrating how much was changing around me and how much I was evolving myself. My world and I were still quite innocent and childish most of the time, but the following events hinted at the massive changes coming.

Start with the childish stuff. I was embracing my burgeoning reputation as a low-level troublemaker in school. In the past I usually behaved—when I could control myself. But now I seemed determined to carry the mantle of my departed classmates, who had set a high bar. In the fall I was issued detention for the first time, if not the first time I deserved it, for body-checking a classmate into the wall while we were walking down the stairs. Later I was sitting in our classroom when a patrol reported the incident to Bernice, who prepared to discipline me. I expected only a mild punishment; I had done far worse over the past couple of years without being disciplined much by the school (though my parents were much stricter).

This time, however, our principal Robert happened to walk into the room and catch the end of the discussion. He raised his eyebrows when he heard what happened and that I was involved. "That's detention," he said, loud enough for it to suddenly and powerfully sink in, sending fear cascading through my body. Nobody in the class dared make a sound. I immediately was gripped by two equally strong sentiments: I was terrified what my father was going to do to me, and I felt it was blatantly unfair for the principal to give me detention when my teacher was about to let me off much easier.

I kept my thoughts to myself. Robert was a towering man with a booming voice and big round eyes that could turn menacing on a dime. We feared him. So I accepted my punishment and spent an hour on a couple of Friday afternoons sitting in the school office doing homework.

But as December began, I apparently was not over what I perceived to be such an unfair punishment. Holiday songs had emerged on the radio, including my two favorites: "The 12 Pains of Christmas" and "Grandma Got Run Over by a Reindeer." One afternoon my class was preparing to leave the cafeteria and had to wait for the younger grades to clear out. I was getting bored and "Grandma" popped into my head. Only instead of singing "Grandma" as the protagonist, I created a new one: "Robert Got Run Over by a Reindeer." I came up with most of a verse and shared it with a few friends. We all laughed. Ross sang the chorus so loud in his natural falsetto voice that I feared Robert, who was standing close enough, would hear.

On the walk home I took out a piece of paper and scribbled down what I had come up with so far. Steve and I completed the verse and added another one, with me writing more as we walked. By the time I got home, we had written most of a full song.

When I walked into our house, I proudly displayed it to Mom. She tried to express some disapproval by giving me a serious look but did not seem too upset. After spending more than a year unsuccessfully fighting the school system (and longer protesting the Vietnam War in college), it must have given her some solace to see her son invoking the same spirit.

It was around that time that I almost harmed another educator: Ms. P. Hebrew school was a big part of my life and a setting for some memorable moments that school year—beyond the bracelet panic attack—moments that in hindsight marked both my enduring childhood and nascent transition into early adolescence.

I loathed Hebrew school. My feelings were rooted in my inability to take it seriously, even though Michael and I and many of our friends usually attended three days each week for two lllllooooooonnnnnngggg hours at a time.

Despite often goofing off in class, I was also savvy enough to realize it was a complicated situation for my parents. In fourth grade I had been upset that I would have to spend a warm, sunny afternoon there. I was lounging on my parents' bed staring out the window with a baseball game on TV in the background. It was just before our carpool arrived when Mom walked in and reminded me that I had to leave soon.

"Mom," I looked into her eyes earnestly, "why do I have to go to Hebrew school?" At all, I meant.

She had been expecting such a question but not until I was older, so she had no response prepared yet. She froze, then picked up the phone sitting on her nightstand and dialed my father at work. She sat down on the bed next to me and kept her eyes fixed on me. Leaning in, I could hear the phone ringing in her ear.

"Yes, Dr. Basen please," she said into the receiver. Pause. "It's his wife." There was another pause and then she said: "Your son just asked me why he has to go to Hebrew school."

My father did not need to be told which son she was referring to. As he responded, I could hear his voice but not make out his words. Mom nodded and then handed me the phone. I heard the unmistakable sound of my father's gruff, masculine voice on the other end. But there was a hint of levity as he spoke: "Why do you have to go to Hebrew school? Because I had to go and your mother had to go."

"Okay," I said softly into the phone. His response made sense. I often had to do things because my parents did them when they were kids; familial expectations were drilled deep into my head. So I handed Mom the phone and prepared for another fun-filled two hours of flicking my watch wristband, watching the clock move far too slowly, and lip-synching prayers I had not bothered to learn despite three years of consistently practicing them.

My fifth-grade Hebrew school class generally went smoothly—even if one moment I acted like a clueless boy, the next a maturing young adult.

Ms. P., a fiftyish woman, was a patient teacher who let us have some wins. She was generous with recess, always allotting at least fifteen minutes and taking us outside whenever possible. She often watched the other boys and me play football, until one afternoon when my ignorance shocked her.

As my team came to the line of scrimmage on offense, the bell rang, signaling recess was over. I was playing quarterback: "Last play!" I called out. "Everybody go deep!" I dropped back, waited a couple of seconds and heaved the ball as far and high as I could toward the mess of bodies at the end of the field. As the ball fluttered through the air, I called out: "Haaaaaaaailllll Maaaaaaaarrrrrrryyyyy!"

Ms. P. was walking toward us as the play unfolded, preparing to usher us all inside. When she heard my yell, she gasped. "Raziel! What did you say?" she asked me a few seconds later, as we were jogging past her toward the building's entry.

"Hail Mary," I casually replied, staring straight ahead and oblivious to any non-football connotations of the phrase as I kept moving.

"That is a Catholic prayer," she responded. "Where did you hear that?"

I shrugged. "It's a football play." Without glancing at her, I walked back inside with my classmates.

About a week later, just before winter break, Ms. P. asked us to write short essays during class. We had to select our "tzedakah heroes" and write a few hundred words about them.

I rolled my eyes and groaned along with many classmates, then got to work. I chose Mom, without much thought. Whenever we grew out of clothes and toys, or other items became expendable, she would donate them to Goodwill or another charity. I did not think she was doing anything heroic, but I needed a tzedakah hero so she would have to be it. It helped that she was still largely a god in my eyes.

I wrote a couple of hundred words about what she did and why it made me proud. That part was genuine. I also threw in a couple of sentences about how her efforts taught me to think of others, which may or may not have been true, but I had a word count to meet. I then turned in the essay and did not give it another moment of thought.

Until after winter break. One afternoon we were discussing a service our grade would be hosting for the synagogue on a Friday night later in January. Ms. P. informed us that a handful of students had been selected "with the honor of" reading their essays during the service. I was largely ignoring Ms. P. until she read off the list of the students who had been selected: "Mordecai, Yonatan, Raziel . . ."

Words shot out of my mouth before I could think. "No way!" I protested. "Why do we have to do this?!"

"These are lovely essays," she replied, in the warm, gentle tone she had perfected to calm our group. "We don't have time for everyone to read theirs, but we have chosen the best ones."

Whatever satisfaction I felt from being told I had written a good piece was easily usurped by the dread I had of getting up before the whole grade and our families to read my essay. My sentiment was affirmed when I found out that, in addition to my parents, Michael and Brad would also be attending our service.

I coped with this impending doom by ignoring it. I never told Mom or anyone outside Hebrew school that I would be speaking, nor did I spend any time preparing. In addition to using this denial tactic, I did not care enough about the speech to practice anyway. It would be the largest crowd I had ever spoken in front of, surpassing the thirty or so kids I had given presentations to several times in school. But I did not worry because I never allowed it to build up in my head. By ten, I had become quite good at that.

The day of the service came. I dressed in slacks and tucked in a button-down shirt, sitting with my classmates in rows near the bema. If they gave us any indication when we would read our essays, I don't recall. Perhaps I was still in denial. But soon it was time.

"Our fifth-graders each wrote an essay about their tzedakah heroes recently," the principal addressed the audience. "We have selected a few of them to read. Now we would like to invite them up here."

The principal soon called my name. I quickly rose and marched up to the bema with a copy of my essay, avoiding eye contact with anyone. I could hear Michael giggling (Mom got there early to get everyone front-row seats) as I set up and launched into the essay. I focused on a dark space in the crowd as I looked up and read aloud, only glancing in brief spurts at my speech, just as Mom had taught me when I prepared for other presentations. "My tzedakah hero is my Mom . . . " I began. The room fell quiet. All eyes on me.

After a couple of minutes, I finished the essay without a hiccup and briskly walked back to my seat.

When the service ended, we dispersed to our families. Michael started laughing again as soon as I approached them. Brad greeted me with a wide grin: "Your mom was CRYING during your speech," he said.

"Oh my G-d!" I responded, completely clueless and a bit worried. "Was I that bad?"

As a ten-year-old boy learning to bury his emotions—as our culture and my teachers, coaches, and father had been subtly and overtly instructing me to do for years—I did not understand. *Why had she cried over watching me deliver a speech calling her my hero?*

Before we left the synagogue, I hugged Mom tight.

As the winter continued, so did my deep-seated relationships, reinforcing my senses of security and stability.

Our cousins and older neighbors were too busy partying with Spuds MacKenzie to babysit us, so Michael and I celebrated New Year's Eve while my parents were out by reading to Tyler, watching movies and highlights from "The Fog Bowl," and coming up with new nicknames for Freddy, our plump, beloved eighteen-year-old cat. Michael and I were still up when they got home after midnight, with Freddy lounging on the foot of the bed.

Several weeks later, my parents took a midwinter vacation for a few days. On the Sunday morning that they came home, I awoke fairly early. Mild light shone through the bottom of my bedroom blinds as I looked up and saw Mom. She was sitting on the edge of my bed facing me as I lay on my back, most of my body still submerged under the covers. Her face was glowing as she rubbed my chest over my T-shirt and stared directly into my eyes.

I was comforted to see her too; even a few days apart were a lot for us. I smiled softly and stretched, still feeling sleepy.

Then, as she moved her hand to massage my forehead and hair, her facial expression suddenly showed concern. "Oy, you're burning up. I think you're coming down with something."

"Hmmm," I responded lightly. "I don't feel sick."

Mom vanished and returned quickly with a thermometer, inserting it into my mouth and then pulling it out. "One-hundred-and-three!" she said flatly, frowning.

I went back to sleep, a state that I stayed in for much of the next few days as I battled a fever.

By Thursday I was feeling well enough to return to school, but Mom still kept me out. Before I went to bed Thursday night, my father barnstormed the kitchen and saw me snacking on leftover pizza and watching a hockey game.

He too stared into my eyes, but with a less loving look than Mom had provided a few days earlier. "You might be able to fool your mother," he snarled. "But you are healthy enough to go to school tomorrow. I wasn't born yesterday, you know!"

Mom kept me out of school Friday anyway, and my basketball game Saturday.

The following Monday I returned to school. It had been over a week since I had seen any of my classmates. We had a field trip first thing in the morning downtown and loaded onto buses. The bustle of a bus full of my fellow elementary schoolers was something I had become very accustomed to over the years. But that morning it felt like too much. I retreated toward the back, finding an empty seat and scooting toward the window, hoping nobody would see me.

Adam soon spotted me, darted over and sat down next to me. "Where have you been?!" he wondered, looking right at me.

With that I was jolted right back into school mode.

Late in February, as pitchers and catchers were reporting to MLB spring training, my friends helped me cope with another incident that kept me out of school and marked another change in my life. After a couple of years of bumpers and rubber bands polluting my mouth, it was finally time for me to get braces.

Jack, my orthodontist, was a short, impatient baby boomer who cornered much of the Rockville-Bethesda pediatric market. It is unclear to me to this day whether he actually liked working with kids.

I had been seeing him for three years. Now, not quite eleven and still a few months shy of graduating from elementary school, glistening silver brackets would physically signal my unofficial entree into adolescence. I already had a mouth full of adult teeth; they were perhaps the only part of me that even closely resembled an adult, after my parents had a specialist yank my final two baby teeth to expedite the process.

I lay in the chair for what seemed like most of the morning as Jack and his assistant slapped the brackets on me, putting me in a protracted state of mild agony as they placed tiny, shiny marks of adolescence onto the adult teeth of a squirmy child.

My parents graced me with the day off from school, figuring getting braces would be enough drama for one day. I was grateful I did not have to go to school that afternoon, but now I needed to plot how I would hide this monstrosity from my classmates. I was the first one of my friends, the first kid I knew in my grade, to get braces. For some reason, that was a big deal to me.

And, for some reason that I could not grasp then, I was beginning to dislike standing out.

My plan was simple: I would tell Steve, whom I could trust to keep his mouth shut. Then I would keep my mouth literally shut all morning as we loitered outside the school, make it to my seat in homeroom, and go from there. What did "go from there" mean? Who knows. But if I could just make it past the morning crush without anyone noticing . . .

That night, the phone rang. Mom picked up, calling me from the kitchen where she was sitting at her desk. "Ryyyyy . . . phone! It's Ross!"

I picked it up.

"Yo. Why weren't you in school today?" I detected a hint of concern.

"Oh, uh . . .," I paused. "Don't tell anyone," I continued, "but I got braces today. My parents let me skip the rest of the day."

"Oh. Okay. I thought maybe you were sick again."

I went to sleep sure that my secret was safe. The next morning, I showed Steve. He agreed to keep quiet, as planned, and we walked with our brothers to school. As we trotted up to the front of the school building, our friends were already standing there. I walked up clenching my mouth shut.

Ross smiled wide and turned to me: "Basen! Do you have something to show everyone?"

I instantly lost my composure. My mouth reflexively opened into a broad smile, the braces lightly reflecting the light on this overcast morning.

A couple of kids chuckled. "Let me see! Open wider so I can see!" somebody called out.

I tried closing my mouth, to no avail, instead smiling wider as they inspected my teeth. Once again, as had been the norm for so many years, I did not feel at all anxious being the center of attention. At least not with this crew.

Playing Monopoly in my family basement at my eleventh birthday party. I'm wearing my Capitals tee-shirt. To my left (moving clockwise) are my cousin Brad and Michael. To my right (counterclockwise) are my friends Ross, Brett, Steve, Adam, and Craig.

Chapter 2

MARCH: NO MAD-
NESS ... YET

arch unofficially marks the start of baseball season, with MLB
spring training launching into full swing as the month begins.
As I oiled up a new glove and read every baseball preview I
could find, it began with a bang for me too.

At some point that winter, Mom had come to me with an
idea. "What do you want to do for your birthday this year?" she
began.

My birthday was still several weeks away, which meant I was
nearly several weeks away from thinking about it. But I knew
instantly what I wanted: "Sleepover party."

"How about a sleepover, but with an activity?" she replied.

I stared at her, waiting impatiently for her to continue.

"Like what if we went to a Caps game?"

I had never even thought to ask.

So she went about planning the party. My birthday was not until
early April, but Mom planned it for the first weekend of March.

After school that Friday, a bunch of my classmates and I played
basketball on the blacktop. As we prepared to go home afterward,
Ross approached me: "What are you up to now?"

"I don't know," I replied. "Want to come over?"

He nodded.

"Let me ask my parents."

We found a quarter (likely buried in my bag when I lost it on a chocolate milk day) and a pay phone just outside the school gym. I dialed our number and hoped Mom or Michael would pick up.

Whammy! "Hello?!" I heard my father's voice on the other end.

"Dad," I hesitated, "can Ross come over?"

What followed was some awkward diatribe about homework, my Centers for Talented Youth math class the next morning and my impending sleepover party the next night. About a year earlier Dad had made me sign a contract promising to do my homework on a Sunday night if friends came over that day. Now he was trying to leverage the freedom of a ten-year-old's Friday afternoon to get said ten-year-old to make other promises I knew I would never keep—because he would not follow through. I just had to grind through the conversation.

Finally he stopped talking. I jammed the phone back into the receiver with a loud ding and turned to face Ross, standing next to me. "Yeah, you can come over."

"Oh. Okay cool. I thought for a second I wasn't allowed to."

"Why?"

"You looked like, like he said no."

After my math class and basketball game the next day, it was finally time for my party. Craig was one of the first to arrive, charging down the basement stairs and tackling me. Others came shortly thereafter. As snow flurried outside, we played basketball on our makeshift hoop in the basement, started Monopoly, switched to Nintendo, and watched a couple of movies.

The Caps' game was scheduled for Sunday afternoon and my parents planned to feed us breakfast beforehand, so they wanted us to go to bed at a reasonable time. But getting Brad, Michael, and ten preteens to go to sleep proved challenging.

Finally, well after midnight, Mom came downstairs for the third or fourth time, sitting on a concrete slab facing us. "Okay!" she said, quickly shushing everyone with her mere presence. "I am going to sit here until you are all quiet and go to sleep."

Most of my friends had known her for years, so they knew better than to test her. A few peeps could be heard, but eventually we fell asleep.

A few weeks later we gathered at Brett's house for his sleepover party. It was well past midnight as we lay in sleeping bags spread out across his living room floor, doing whatever we could to keep from going to sleep.

Brett's mother entered the room. "I am going to do exactly what Shelly Basen did," she said. And so she sat there, on a ledge, scarcely moving or making a sound, waiting for us to get quiet and fall asleep.

Mike, a friend of Brett's older brother, Kevin, was also there. He knew me fairly well as Brett's friend for a few years. He must have known that my friends typically called me "Basen." But he obviously did not put two and two together: "Who the fuck is Shelly Basen?" he wondered aloud.

Steve and I looked at each other and tried really hard not to laugh. Everyone giggled, trying to muffle themselves as Brett's mother continued to sit there stoically.

"No, seriously," Mike continued, "who the fuck is Shelly Basen?"

The Sunday of my sleepover, we gulped down bowls of sugared cereal and headed for the Capital Centre in Landover. We filed into our seats together in the dimly lit upper level and watched the Caps score one goal in each period to secure a 3–0 victory over Vancouver.

Besides enjoying the win, we also left clutching wooden sticks. It was Stick Day, meaning the first thousand or so kids under fourteen got street hockey sticks with replica autographs from the entire Caps team baked in.

As we walked through the parking lot toward our cars, I saw a stone on the ground in front of me and instinctively wound up for a slapshot. But Adam was standing behind me and I clipped him in the face. I immediately felt horrible. First I had nearly injured Steve while roughhousing at his sleepover party back in August, now this.

Adam's reaction did little to make me feel better. He wasn't that hurt and was rather used to my often-careless behavior. But

Adam could oscillate between being a hyperactive preteen like the rest of us and the wise man who, throughout our childhoods and into college, always seemed to possess a bit more maturity. He just stared at me like his father sometimes did during baseball practice (he was one of our assistants), not saying anything as I beat myself up inside.

I soon recovered. When we arrived back at our house most of my friends left, but Ross stuck around for a while. His mom showed up to pick him up with his two brothers, roughly the same age as mine. Ross, Michael, and I were pitching to each other in the front yard as they pulled up and climbed out of a maroon Dodge Caravan. His mom addressed me—"Hi Ry!" she shouted in her usual chipper, projected high-pitch voice—and then walked inside. For a good while she talked to Mom as we continued to play in the yard, now with Ross's brothers as well.

The next morning it was rainy and cold out, so Mom offered to drive Michael and me to school. I did not want the weekend to end. As I climbed into the back of her car, I whimpered: "Why do we have to go to school today?"

"Honey, you just had an incredible weekend," Mom said, "but you have to get back to normal at some point."

It was then that I saw a plastic B. Dalton bookstore bag on the ground. Feeling it with my hand, I could tell there was a large book inside. "Mom, what's this?"

"I don't know. Maybe one of your friends left it in the car yesterday."

We had been so busy, I had never bothered to open my gifts in front of my friends. One present was indeed still sitting in the car, unwrapped. I pulled the book out and recognized immediately what it was: *The 1989 Elias Baseball Analyst*, a large baseball encyclopedia. There was a note attached; it was from Ross.

Other kids in my class, even friends, sometimes gave me shit for being so obsessed with sports statistics.

Not Ross.

The gift was not only thoughtful, it was also timely. As March began, watching preseason baseball games joined basketball and hockey in my regular winter rotation.

In previous years, I was quite familiar with the O's roster by early March. But despite my ridiculous knowledge and the new presence of the *Elias* book, in March 1989 I could name very few players besides Cal and Billy Ripken.

And I knew of Billy mostly because of his brother and because he was nationally infamous, at least among kids my age. His notoriety was due not just to that *Sports Illustrated* cover shot, but also because he posed for a 1989 baseball card with the nickname "Fuck Face" scrawled on the handle of his bat. The card had just been issued by the Fleer Corporation, which then whitewashed the nickname from production—making the early runs of this "error card" valuable and Billy possibly the second most-known Oriole.

The rest of the roster as they reported to camp?

I knew of Randy Milligan, the first baseman, and outfielder Mike Devereaux from their splashy new Upper Deck rookie cards. Both were considered fringe Major Leaguers, not necessarily building blocks.

Milligan had been discarded by two teams in 1988 alone: the Mets, who drafted him in 1981 but ultimately chose Dave Magadan over him to platoon with aging star Keith Hernandez; and the Pirates, who traded Milligan to Baltimore in November with their own logjam at first. Both the Mets and Pirates had been contenders in 1988; they saw no room for Milligan on their big-league clubs in 1989. He had a combined eighty-three Major League at bats in his career and was already twenty-seven as the season began.

Devereaux only joined the Orioles on March 12, when the Dodgers shipped him for reliever Mike Morgan. Devereaux had ninety-seven Major League at bats over two seasons in LA, and would turn twenty-six early in the season. He was part of a crowded Dodger outfield and also deemed expendable.

But he, Milligan, and many other discarded players would now get a shot to start with the rebuilding O's. Of the thirty-eight rostered players in camp, twenty-six had less than two years of

Major League experience. Their team lacked a single pitcher who had won even fifteen games in a season. Outside of the Ripken brothers, Phil Bradley, and hurler Dave Schmidt, virtually everyone else was fighting for a starting job, roster spot, or both.

By the end of camp, however, many legitimately earned roles on the team. Rookies Pete Harnisch, twenty-two (a first-round pick in 1987), and Bob Milacki, twenty-four (a second-round pick in 1983), were slated to start the season in the rotation, along with the veteran Schmidt, the ever-promising Jose Bautista, and Jeff Ballard. Only Bautista and Ballard had been mainstays in the rotation in 1988; both had struggled.

Gregg Olson, twenty-two, the club's 1988 first-round pick, did not allow an earned run in exhibition play. He was slated to share the closer's job with Mark Williamson, who moved to the bullpen permanently after starting ten games in 1988. After San Diego drafted him at twenty-two in 1982, it had taken Williamson five years to make his Major League debut. The O's acquired him in a package for starter Storm Davis following the 1986 season, but he struggled in both 1987 and 1988. Nobody knew what to expect from Williamson in 1989, but Olson at least had coaches and management salivating.

Like Olson, much of the roster had been assembled only over the past year. Juan Bell was being touted as another young prospect to build around. Bell was one of the players acquired when Baltimore finally traded Murray, to the Dodgers. The twenty-one-year-old middle infielder, younger brother of Blue Jays star outfielder George Bell, was the centerpiece of the three-player package the Orioles received in that December deal.

Just before the trade deadline in July 1988, the O's had acquired prospects Brady Anderson, a twenty-four-year-old fleet outfielder, and Curt Schilling, a twenty-one-year-old right-handed pitcher, by trading former ace Mike Boddicker to the Red Sox. Both were expected to contribute at some point in 1989.

In April 1988, Baltimore had signed catcher Mickey Tettleton after Oakland cut him a week earlier. He was penciled in to share catching duties with veteran Bob Melvin, after posting decent power numbers (and only power numbers) in part-time duty in 1988. He also had platooned for the A's dating to his Major League debut in 1984 and was twenty-eight entering the season. Melvin was a solid defensive player who was traded to Baltimore in January for veteran catcher Terry Kennedy, an All-Star as recently as 1987—but one whose defense was rapidly declining. Prospect Chris Hoiles rounded out Baltimore's catching options, after Detroit traded him for the aging Fred Lynn in August 1988.

(That's correct: The 1988 team that started 0–21 included Cal Ripken, Eddie Murray, Fred Lynn, and Mike Boddicker. Only Lynn was past his prime.)

Then there was Bradley, a journeyman outfielder who had often been surfacing in my baseball card packs since I had started collecting two years earlier. The Phillies became the second team to give up on him in consecutive years, even though he was just thirty and had hit around .300 and stolen at least twenty bases annually for much of his career. They traded him to Baltimore in December for reliever Ken Howell (whom Baltimore had acquired as part of the Murray trade) and a pitching prospect.

In the offseason Baltimore also signed veteran utility infielder Tim Hulett, who had not played in the majors in 1988.

Top organizational prospects in outfielder Steve Finley and third baseman Craig Worthington nailed down starting jobs as rookies. Finley, twenty-four, was a late-round pick in 1987 who began the 1988 season in Single-A before ascending through the Oriole ranks. Also twenty-four, Worthington was Baltimore's first-round pick in 1985.

Young veterans Joe Orsulak, Larry Sheets, and Jim Traber—all decent hitters—were among the few returnees to the big league club. So were utility infielder Rene Gonzales and the Ripken brothers.

With so many castoffs and inexperienced players, nobody thought the team would succeed. Experts with the *Post*, *Sports Illustrated*, and ESPN nearly unanimously picked the Orioles to finish last again. They were a three hundred–to–one shot to win the World Series.

Taken together, as I scanned the roster when the Orioles broke camp late in March, my reaction was fairly similar to the question posed by a construction worker perusing (he would not have used that word) the Cleveland Indians preseason roster in a scene from the 1989 movie *Major League*: "Who are these fuckin' guys?"

That flick would be released in theaters April 7, just after the regular season started. Although it was about a fictionalized version of the Indians, it would serve as a harbinger of a season for a real struggling team playing in a decaying rust belt city.

But that city wasn't Cleveland.

By 1989, in addition to reading nearly every line of box scores and other stats in the *Post*, I was regularly reading the works of several great sportswriters. The *Post* had columnists Mike Wilbon and Tony Kornheiser, and national guys such as Frank Deford and Rick Reilly wrote for *SI*, which I read as meticulously as the *Post* sports section.

The dean of baseball writers was the *Post*'s Thomas Boswell. A veteran scribe, his pieces would come to define much of the 1989 season and thus paint a detailed portrait of one of the most remarkable stories in baseball history.

His perspective of the 1989 O's did not start out too nicely. He previewed the club in a *Washington Post Magazine* feature published a week before the season started, entitled "Bad Baseball":

"THEY'RE BACK," Boswell wrote. "The team that, with enough ill luck, could break every major league record for futility this season."

About two weeks before *Major League* rolled out in theaters, Boswell unintentionally (I think) alluded to a killer line from the movie: "The plan is to go with youth. But this spring the Orioles also called in a platoon of emergency veterans, most of whom had been presumed dead for years," he wrote. "Some of them had been out of the majors so long when they reported to camp that they should have been given an autopsy instead of a physical. Now is the time for all good Oriole fans to realize that this season could be even more amazingly bad than 1988."

But while "they show teasing promise of being the most fascinatingly atrocious team in at least a generation—yet maybe, just maybe, they could fool everybody and be the most improved team in baseball in 1989," he countered. "At least the Orioles have reason for hoping they've got 'the right ones.' The greatest pleasure, or pain, in watching the Orioles this season will come from observing the development, or the destruction, of Harnisch, Olson, Milacki, and Schilling. Also, three of the better players anywhere in AAA last season—outfielder Steve Finley, third baseman Craig Worthington and shortstop Bell—will surely be force fed. Unfortunately, none is a sure thing."

That they had committed to an organization-wide rebuild gave us a reason to watch, at least. So that was an improvement over 1987 and '88.

"The names most closely associated with The Fall are all gone: the late owner Edward Bennett Williams (who died in August 1988), general manager Hank Peters and farm director Tom Giordano. Nobody left in the Oriole clubhouse blames anybody else for the sorry state of affairs," Boswell wrote. But: "NO MATTER HOW WELL THE ORIOLES rebuild, even if their fondest hopes are realized for their young players, this team will lose, and lose badly, for the next two to three years."

"Anyone, especially any child, can root for a champion. What's tough about loving perfection? Miss Universe always gets a date. It takes conviction, maybe even a smidgen of character, to root for Herb Plews or Billy Ripken," he concluded.

Apparently my friends and I had conviction, then. We already knew we had plenty of character; hadn't many of our coaches and parents told us that over the years? We indeed rooted for Billy Ripken—at least in the field, where he could play. Maybe not so much at the plate, where he hit .207 in 1988 in 512 official at bats. Fuck Face was mostly on his own there.

"The Orioles all know the long arduous schedule they are on. Baltimore's new stadium will be ready by 1992. The Orioles are expected to be worthy occupants by then," Boswell wrote. "In a sense, a season without expectations is a less obsessive and, perhaps, more gently enjoyable experience than the nightly agonies of following a team that's 'in contention.' "

We were in for nightly agonies, for sure. But nobody thought in March that they would occur because the 1989 Baltimore Orioles were actually in contention.

As the O's marched through camp in Florida, my class took a memorable trip south of our own. Every fifth-grade class at Ritchie Park used to take a two-day jaunt to Williamsburg, Yorktown, and Jamestown in Virginia per our American history curriculum. My class went on a cold, sunny Thursday and Friday, just as March Madness was kicking off on the day before St. Patrick's Day.

I was excited. A couple of weekdays on the road with my friends and outside the classroom sounded amazing. I usually loved field trips no matter where we went, mostly because they did not involve me sitting on my ass for hours inside a classroom and they featured my friends and me pushing boundaries. This time I was especially eager because we would be going overnight and Mom had volunteered to be one of the chaperones.

I awoke around four or five in the morning that Thursday. As I showered, Mom smiled at me through the translucent sliding door separating me and her getting ready in my parents' bathroom. Even without Michael to compete with for the hallway bathroom I shared with my brothers, I still chose my parents' bathroom to shower in. I dressed in sweats, threw my bags into Mom's silver Audi station wagon, plopped into the front seat, and turned on Q107 (one of the two pop stations I frequently listened to) as Mom drove us to school, parking near the buses that awaited us.

The first day started uneventfully, except for two girls screaming at each other while we waited to order lunch. Mom had always wanted a girl but knew that was unlikely now because she and my father did not want another child. At this moment she thought to herself, *Maybe it's good I only have boys.*

Things soon turned more dramatic. We had been promised a pool party at the hotel after dinner. Our two buses were filled with students, a handful of parent chaperones, our teachers, and our principal when they pulled into the hotel parking lot well behind schedule. Robert stood at the front of our bus. "Because we are running late," he said, "we will have to skip the pool party."

Suddenly I forgot all about his scary eyes and the threat of detention. I leapt out of my seat and joined (started maybe?) a growing chorus of impatient, pissed off fifth-graders. Our voices, some still quite high, hit a crescendo near the end of our cry: "We want a POOL party! We want a POOL party."

We kept chanting for what seemed like several minutes, as the adults met and talked at the front of the bus. Most of us had been together for six years, so they knew us well. To paraphrase a Tom Petty song that would be released a month later, we would not back down.

We got our pool party.

After overrunning the pool, we changed in our rooms and prepared for another shindig. Ross ostensibly (but really his mom) was hosting a post-party in his mom's room. I was there maybe fifteen minutes. It was loud and uncontrolled; there were candy and soda everywhere. I swear somebody was dancing on a table to "Walk the Dinosaur," which had surged to number twelve on the Billboard US chart that week.

Suddenly the door swung open. It was Robert. He was pissed. "Party is over! Everyone back to your rooms and get to sleep! Now!"

We scurried like the sugared-up preteens that we were, dashing back to our rooms. There we stayed for the rest of the night, eventually dozing off as Mom and the other chaperones sat outside their rooms in the hallway for a while to prevent any more madness.

The next morning as we walked downstairs to breakfast at the hotel, I begged Mom for fifty cents. "They have USA Today," I exclaimed, pointing at the metal newspaper rack just outside our hotel. I bought the paper, handed most of it to Mom and took the sports section over to sit with my friends. We opened the section up to face the entire March Madness tournament bracket, printed across the fold to cover two full pages, examining results from the night before and the schedule of upcoming games. "Georgetown plays tonight," Brett smirked. "They're going to destroy Princeton."

(Georgetown indeed won but almost became the first top seed to lose to a number sixteen seed.)

We spent the rest of the day touring a battlefield at Yorktown and walking around the cobblestone streets of Jamestown. Mom gave me ten dollars to spend at the gift shop; I chose a copy of the Declaration of Independence and pocketed the change to save for candy and baseball cards.

That night, we got back to school around eight. We had just one week left until spring break, about two weeks until the Major League regular season began, and three weeks until our youth baseball games started. It was chilly and dark as we pulled into the parking lot. The adults and some of my classmates were exhausted.

Not me. I was giddy. The weekend beckoned. Baseball season was almost here. In fact, preseason practices for our youth season started that weekend.

I was instantly hooked by baseball in large part because of those swashbuckling, brawling, winning Mets of 1986. But it was not until a year later that I began playing the sport on an organized team. After two full spring seasons, a few weeks of summer baseball camps, and practicing with Michael in our front yard for hours (to the point that all the grass died in the spots where we stood to pitch and hit), I had gradually improved. But I was still relying too much on my natural athleticism and had not developed the skills I needed to excel. I had never tried to pitch or play catcher, hated chasing fly balls, and often swung so hard I mistimed the "speed" of youth league pitching. In short, I was a very average recreational league player.

But by the spring of 1989, I knew the game cold. On previous summer nights I often flipped between four games at once—thanks to a cable package that included WWOR, which broadcast Mets games; Cubs games on WGN; Braves games on WTBS; and Orioles games on Home Team Sports and DC Channel 20. I also religiously read about the sport and played strategic games, including Statis Pro Baseball, Strat-O-Matic Baseball, and *MicroLeague Baseball*. As a third- and fourth-grader, I was probably better suited to help coach my team than play on it.

But by fifth grade I believed in my athletic abilities. I held my own in flag football and basketball leagues (sometimes even standing out), and during our competitive recess games earlier in the school year, and had legitimately earned awards at camps the previous summer. My confidence was soaring as the spring baseball season began, even if I still did not expect to be one of my team's top players.

Our first Rockville Baseball Association (RBBA) practice that year was at the Potomac Woods upper field next to my neighborhood, the last season we would play there before aging out. Clad in black sweatpants, I walked over on a windy, cold Saturday afternoon after we returned from terrorizing Virginia, carrying my new black-and-green metal Easton bat (thirty-one inches long, twenty-five ounces heavy). Along with my cat, Freddy, the bat was my other baby. I also had my dark brown Louisville Slugger glove. Unlike some of my teammates who were dressed (appropriately) in hoodies, I opted merely for a T-shirt.

We had lost Dave and Neal, arguably our two best players from a year earlier. But we had gained an advantage: After playing the past season as a team of solely fourth-graders in a league for fourth- and fifth-graders, most of our team had returned as fifth-graders. Everyone had improved. We had all grown, watched more baseball, played more strategy games. We also had played some the previous summer at those camps and made regular visits to the indoor batting cages in winter.

It was no longer snowy, cold, or wet most days and, with our basketball season ending in early March, I soon adjusted my nightly routine. Instead of shooting at the year-old hoop on my driveway, Michael and I returned to pitching to each other in the front yard nearly every chance we got. Mom even installed a new floodlight to cover much of the yard, giving up on her hope that we would come to our senses and stop playing in the dark.

My anticipation was growing. Baseball was my favorite sport and this season was building up in my head. Unlike basketball season or the previous baseball season, when I was content just to get some playing time on a team with friends, I now wanted to be on the field as much as possible. I also wanted to win every game badly. Losing, even dropping a pickup football game at recess, felt crushing.

Many of my teammates felt the same way. Following several more practices, we were itching to go. Our league featured twenty or so teams, including a handful that we thought were more talented than us. After going 5–9 the year before, nobody discussed winning a title. But we were determined to at least make a playoff run and beat our rivals. (Yes, we had more than one rival.)

Opening day, for both our club and the O's, was fast approaching.

Interrupting our flow just before the seasons began was spring break, which spanned the last week of March and beginning of April. My family stayed in town. One night our parents shipped us off to Leisure World in nearby Olney to see our maternal grandparents— Brad, me, and Michael.

We were very close with Mom's parents, who were now in their seventies and retired, but still healthy and vibrant. My maternal grandfather, known as "PopPop Eddie" to us, had been a standout high school athlete in multiple sports, including baseball, while growing up in the Philadelphia slums as a first-generation American in the 1920s and early 1930s. Like many in the Greatest Generation, he carried (and passed down) a lot of emotional baggage. Still, he found solace in sports and his wife of fifty-plus years, Freda.

PopPop Eddie was charged with spending the next day with his three exiled grandchildren. While we always saw him at family get-togethers and he often quietly attended our games, it was rare for us to bond with him. But that day he took us to the driving range, where I relished smashing golf balls as hard as I could, trying (unsuccessfully) to outdrive my older cousin. We then went to his condo complex's gym, where I tried to lift as much weight as possible at each machine, gritting my teeth and groaning loudly as I moved maybe a few plates.

My grandfather's neighbors at the gym were not thrilled. Eventually he had enough of their dirty looks and took us to Burger

King, ordering a Whopper. "Now I know," he said after taking a bite out of the burger, "why they call it the Whopper."

I turned and stared at him through his large-framed glasses as he spoke. My grandfather was literally a man of few words. He had survived the 1918 pandemic, Great Depression, World War II—and an LBJ presidency (as a top government economist, he knew and loathed Lyndon Johnson). But he never spoke of any of those eras to me.

Instead, I got tales of the 1920s Yankees' Murderers Row and Connie Mack's Philadelphia Athletics. Sixty years later he could still recall the lineups from these fabled teams. One day he watched Brad and me play MicroLeague Baseball, which featured all-time teams. "Urban Shocker," he deadpanned, referring to the former Yankee pitcher. "I remember him." From growing up without even a radio, to watching his grandchildren play a baseball game on a computer, he saw a lot of shit.

While he passed his love of baseball onto my eager-to-please mother when she was growing up, he must have really enjoyed regaling and watching his grandsons. By 1989, sports had become our bond. Now that I was older and had ditched theater camps for sports camps, we always had something to talk about. We were just getting close. It seemed like there was still plenty of time . . .

PopPop Eddie eventually steered his royal blue Cadillac ("the blue bomb") to my parents' house to drop us off. The week and month soon ended. On one hand I wanted the break to last forever, as always. But there were some slow days, and I did not do slow very well. Another afternoon when Michael and I were shipped to my paternal grandmother's house in Wheaton, we stood in the backyard and stared and laughed at a partially deflated football on the ground. After trying to play with it for a few minutes, we gave up.

It was time for baseball season to start already.

Sitting in the lower bowl at RFK Stadium in Washington, DC, to take in the Orioles' final exhibition game of the 1989 season, on the afternoon of Sunday, April 2—my eleventh birthday. To my left are Brad, Michael, my father, PopPop Eddie, and my Uncle Jeff.

Chapter 3

APRIL: BASEBALL! BASEBALL! CATCH THE FEVER NOW!

I awoke on the morning of Sunday, April 2, the final day of spring break, feeling pure excitement. That afternoon our nuclear family would be joining Brad, my aunt, and my uncle at the Orioles' final exhibition tune-up, against St. Louis. The O's were making their annual sojourn to RFK Stadium, where they played their last exhibition games to help them win over the skeptical Washington market.

The Cardinals were only two seasons removed from their most recent World Series and third of the decade and still had stars Ozzie Smith, Willie McGee, and Vince Coleman. So I quickly showered, retrieved some of their cards from my collection, grabbed a Sharpie from Mom's desk, and prepared to leave early for the game.

It was my eleventh birthday. Mom had promised we could get there early to chase autographs. As far as I can remember, this game presented my first chance to beg for autographs live. I had only been to two MLB games before and was frothing for some signatures to join my standard card collection. The Cardinals played in the National League, so this would be my only chance to see them on the season (unless by some miracle the O's and Cardinals met in the World Series).

But Michael was not cooperating. For whatever reason, he picked that morning to throw a fit. As the rest of our family prepared to leave, he locked himself in his bedroom and refused to come out.

What is going on?! I wondered, merely annoyed at first. He was usually so well-behaved. What could possibly have bothered this happy eight-year-old so much that he was going to piss away a chance to nab autographs just to mope?

As the minutes ticked by, I could sense that opportunity slipping away. Something else was slowly disappearing inside me. I charged upstairs to his room and banged hard on his door with my fists. "Open up! Let's go! Open the hell up!" I screamed.

He did not respond. At all.

By the time we finally got Michael over himself, it was too late for us to make the game in time to chase autographs. I pouted as I trudged off to my father's car, slamming the door just before we drove to a nearby Metro station and headed downtown.

But as we filed into our seats in the stadium's lower bowl along the first-base line, I settled into the game in southeastern DC. It was a cool afternoon as more than thirty-seven thousand fans packed RFK, the Senators' stadium for ten years and the Nationals' future home for two years. (The Redskins played there too, until 1997.)

Midway through the game, a boy and girl about my age were sitting a row in front of us as the public address announcer called out a St. Louis batter: "Now batting, catcher Tom Pagnozzi."

"Pagnozzi?" the boy said. "That sounds like the sound you make when you sneeze." He mimicked a sneeze and yelled out: "Pagnozzi!"

The girl laughed in response.

I sneered at them and scoffed, as Mom caught my eye: "Dorks!" I said loud enough for anyone to hear.

Mom smiled, suppressed a chuckle, and looked at me: "Do you know who Tom Pagnozzi is?"

"Of course," I replied. "He's one of their catchers. I have his rookie card. I think Michael does too."

In the bottom of the tenth, with the score tied 6–6 and two outs, Milligan was on third. Anderson hit an infield grounder and just beat it out, scoring Milligan to win the game.

We stood, clapped and cheered furiously, forgetting for a moment that the game meant nothing in the standings. I guess it meant something to us. "You know," my father said, turning toward me, looking down and grinning, "I have a feeling they'll be a lot better than people think this year."

My father often let his spontaneous emotions dictate his sports predictions, so I normally did not take them seriously, even as an elementary-schooler. But for some reason—unlike when he proclaimed the Caps future Stanley Cup champions every time they scored a playoff goal—this time I had an odd feeling that he could be right. To this day I can't explain it, but I felt joy and optimism shooting through my body. Unlike in 1987 and 1988, when we knew they were going to be terrible and even unwatchable, I was looking forward to watching the new-look O's. Maybe, just maybe, they would indeed surprise us all in 1989.

I smiled back at him, flung my jean jacket over my shoulder and prepared to head home.

After the game, reporters asked the O's about their opening day opponent, the Red Sox, who would be starting Cy Young Award-winner Roger Clemens against them the next day. To a man they were not fazed, they said. Finley confirmed to a reporter that he had never faced Clemens, "but I've seen a lot of him on television."

Several people told Devereaux that getting a single hit off Clemens as a team would be an achievement. "Can you believe that?" he told Ron Snyder years later for the book about the 1988 club. "We had not even played one game yet and people thought we were so bad that we would not get a hit on Opening Day. . . .[But] we were not the 1988 Orioles. We were our own team full of new, young players ready to make their own statement."

But many were so new to the O's, young and unproven, even Baltimore media had trouble introducing them to fans. That night, a

Baltimore TV station aired a season preview hosted by a local anchor and Jim Palmer, the former O's Hall of Fame pitcher-turned broadcaster. Tettleton was such an afterthought that a segment on the team's hitting did not mention him and the show spelled Olson's first name "Greg." A reporter interviewed fans around Baltimore and at the RFK games, aping the Abbott and Costello routine "Who's on First?" after Murray had manned the position for so long. Guesses ranged from "I don't know" to "McMillan," presumably a fan referring to Milligan.

In Rockville, I watched another baseball preview from my parents' bed as Mom read next to me. I watched the clock, hoping it would move more slowly. Every minute would take me closer to the end of my birthday, the end of spring break.

I did not want either to end, even if that ending also meant the beginning of baseball season. Did I subconsciously know this would be the last birthday I would celebrate while feeling so free (without the assistance of weed and/or alcohol)? Had I picked up on my older cousins not seeming to care nearly as much about their birthdays as my brothers, friends, and I did?

Eventually the clock hit ten o'clock. Bedtime.

But I could not let go. "Mom, can I stay up a little longer?" I said softly.

"Honey you have to go back to school tomorrow."

"Just thirty minutes."

"Fifteen."

"Twenty."

"Fine, but I want you in that bed by 10:20 sharp."

"Okay."

I felt vindicated but also a bit uneasy. Every minute would bring me closer to reality. When I awoke the next day, it would be back to rushing to and from school, back to homework, back to Hebrew school and piano lessons.

But at least something would be different that week: Baseball season was here. I had been waiting eagerly for my favorite sport to start, especially since the Super Bowl had ended football season more than two months earlier. College basketball games and regular season Caps games just did not completely fill that void.

I watched the numbers change on the digital clock sitting on top of my parents' TV. As it hit 10:20, without being asked, I hopped off my parents' bed and walked down the hall toward my bedroom, climbing into bed and shutting off the lights. I flipped on Q107 on the clock radio. Maybe the Fine Young Cannibals or Milli Vanilli greeted me.

I was asleep within minutes.

I used to keep piles of baseball cards in a corner of my bedroom, so-called "commons" that were not worth anything. Eventually so many piled up that when Freddy peed on them, they contained the smell for days until Mom finally noticed and forced me to clean them up.

The morning after my birthday, as I returned to my room from the shower, I saw a card in the pile sitting face up out of the corner of my eye. I walked over, knelt and looked closely at it. It was a 1987 Topps Dave Schmidt issue. Schmidt was wearing a navy White Sox jacket as he sat on the bench and looked away from the camera, hatless. (He played for Chicago in 1986.)

I picked up the card, looking at Schmidt and wondering what he was thinking as he prepared to start the season against the intimidating, dominant Clemens. Most of Boston's core had won the AL East in 1986 and 1988, and would win another AL East title in 1990.

Yet I had a good feeling about this game. I smiled to myself, put the card down and got dressed.

In Baltimore a few hours later, more than fifty-two thousand packed Memorial Stadium on a sunny early spring afternoon. The O's may have been picked by nearly everyone to finish last again, but they were treated like royalty on this day. O's fan and rock star Joan Jett sang the national anthem, reminding us it was still the eighties. President George H. W. Bush threw out the first pitch, while Red Sox great Ted Williams watched the game from a stadium box.

Baltimore's lineup featured few holdovers from 1988. Finley, Anderson, and Bradley started in the outfield. Batting eighth and playing third was Worthington.

Michael and I flipped on the game after school and were transfixed by Baltimore's new uniforms, which we had failed to notice in detail from a distance the day before. On their hats, the O's had replaced their customary cartoonish smiling oriole set against a white background with a sophisticated, realistic-looking bird on a plain black background. The unis looked snazzy too and, like all the new players, immediately differentiated the 1989 Orioles from the terrible Baltimore clubs of the recent past.

So did something else.

Steve Finley is a name known to many baseball fans. He played in nineteen Major League seasons, finally closing his career with the Rockies in 2007 at age forty-two. He finished with just over three hundred homers, stole at least twenty bases five times and was a perennial Gold Glove winner. He won a championship as a starting outfielder with the Arizona Diamondbacks in 2001 and started in another World Series with the San Diego Padres in 1998. He was a part of one of the worst trades in modern baseball history, which is how he eventually left Baltimore.

But in 1989, all that was years away. Finley was twenty-four on opening day (earning a $68,000 salary), a late bloomer who had surprised the O's by rising quickly through their minor league system. The six foot two outfielder from Union City, Tennessee, had been drafted in the thirteenth round in 1987 and signed with Baltimore two days later, after falling from the eleventh-round spot the Braves had selected him at a year earlier. Finley played in both Low-A and Single-A in 1987, then began the 1988 season at Single-A. He surged to Triple-A by the end of the season, yet was not called up to Baltimore in September despite the O's being well out of contention and committed to testing their prospects.

But the lefty's great offseason and spring cemented a spot on the big-league club as the 1989 season started, and he won a platoon starting job against right-handers, beating out Joe Orsulak and Devereaux among others.

So there he was stationed in right field when Boston's Nick Esasky led off the top of the third with a shot to deep right-center.

Finley chased it down on the warning track, extended his right arm and caught it just as his right shoulder collided with the wall. He never slowed down. After forcing his way into the lineup as a middling prospect, there was no way he was going to be denied catching that ball. Finley stayed in the game after being examined by a trainer, but Orsulak replaced him the next inning so the medical staff could get a further look.

Later, Anderson made a great running catch to save at least one run. The two rookies' defensive prowess set a tone for the season right away: The O's may not have the pedigree. They may not have much power, pitching depth, or a proven winning manager. But what they did have in abundance was speed and defense. The catches by Finley and Anderson, especially Finley's reckless determination, showed that this would be a team worth watching, a team that would scrap, a team that kids could learn a lot from and boast about. They also hinted that this team could win a bit.

Finley's catch remains one of the highlights of the season, a play O's fans still talk about today. He bruised and separated his shoulder, costing him three weeks of action. "I just knew I had to catch the ball," he told reporters afterward. "I didn't even think about the wall."

After he helped keep the game scoreless, the O's got more than one hit off Clemens, seizing a 1–0 lead through five innings.

Around then a neighbor pulled up on our driveway and honked softly, signaling it was time for Michael and me to limp off to Hebrew school via our carpool. We lowered our heads, turned off the TV, and found our bookbags, walking outside to climb into the car. As we filed out of our classrooms about two hours later, dashing madly toward the synagogue exits, rumors of what we missed cascaded around the hallways. "Yeah! Cal Ripken homered!" somebody said above the fray. Nobody knew the score.

I found my carpool outside and begged whatever poor parent was stuck with us that night to put on the radio broadcast. We soon found out that Ripken had indeed homered—and the O's had won, 5–4. The game ended just before Hebrew school did. It lasted nearly four hours and eleven innings. Schmidt pitched for six and one-third innings and held the Red Sox to the same amount of hits (seven) and runs (four) as Clemens.

In the bottom of the eleventh the game was tied 4—4. Tettleton walked and Milligan singled, moving Tettleton to third with one out. The Red Sox drew left fielder Mike Greenwell in, positioning him behind second base to essentially create a five-man infield. The two other Boston outfielders split the rest of the outfield.

Worthington stepped up for the first meaningful at bat of his career and hit a blooper into center. The ball fell in front of a diving Ellis Burks, Boston's center fielder, who had been positioned in left-center with the shift. Had Burks been playing in his usual spot, he may very well have caught it. Instead luck was already on the O's side this season, after it had taken luck a month the year before.

Tettleton marched home to clinch the walk-off victory. The crowd roared as the O's ran onto the field to mob each other. For the first time since June 5, 1987, the O's were above .500. It was a span of 270 games—or exactly one and two-thirds seasons. So what that they were only 1—0!

Afterward they displayed the bravado of a winning club. "This team is going to surprise a lot of people," Worthington said. "Teams might come here thinking we're going to lay down and die like last year. It's going to be different."

That statement would not prove to be hyperbole. "When you beat Roger Clemens and the Red Sox, you feel like you can do anything. It all just snowballed from there. There was energy and excitement on the team that was not there the year before," Ballard recounted to Snyder.

It was still light out and warm for early April when I got home, so Mom joined me on the driveway and challenged me to play one-on-one. I grinned and laughed as I saw her flail her arms at me, harking back to her own youth when she had ignored schoolyard taunts of "tomboy" to play ball with the boys at recess. We went nearly full speed at each other until the sun started to set and our family walked to the nearby strip mall to eat at a family friend's pizza place.

The O's had defeated Roger Clemens, my parents had promised I could stay up for all of that night's NCAA men's basketball national title, and I was nearly a full forty-eight hours away from my next Hebrew school class. I felt free.

As if MLB's opening day and the men's Final Four were not enough sports, that week the Caps kicked off what we hoped would be a championship postseason run. They closed the regular season by clinching their first Patrick Division title in their fifteen-year history, so I was sure this would be the season they finally at least reached the conference finals.

I should have known better. The first year I followed the Washington Capitals, 1986, we were also expecting them to contend for the Stanley Cup, the trophy awarded to the NHL champion. They had finished that regular season with the third-most points in the NHL and boasted a roster loaded with standouts. (My favorite was Scott Stevens, the physical defenseman with a blistering slapshot.) I figured they would easily beat the sub-.500 New York Rangers in the second round merely because they were better on paper.

We had watched much of the Caps' first-round sweep of the New York Islanders as a family on the day after games, popping in the VHS tapes I set up the night before. My father, who had been down since his father had died a couple of months earlier, seemed to be revived by watching these games with us; he often smiled and eagerly learned hockey nuances alongside me and Michael. Mom bought me a royal blue T-shirt that read "Stanley Caps" in block letters next to a picture of the Stanley Cup. I wore it proudly in school and was easily swept up as the region geared up for an extended playoff run.

My innocent theory about this series revealed itself to be sound when we attended Game Two of the Rangers series at the Capital Centre—my first playoff game as a fan in any sport—and the Caps won 8–1. It was an intoxicating experience, the arena was so loud and boisterous. Two days later they beat the Rangers in New York to take a 2–1 series lead.

Alas, they then lost the next three games and the series. During the decisive sixth game, I went to bed with the Caps trailing 1–0 after one period. My father awoke me the next morning. "Well baby, they lost," he said, with some pity in his voice.

I lay there for a few moments, stunned. The loss simply would not sink in. As a second-grader, I must have been too young to understand how they could have lost to such a seemingly inferior team. It just did not make any sense. Only that denial, combined with being too young and not yet invested enough, prevented me from suffering my first sports-related broken heart.

By 1989, though, the Caps had set a pattern of thrashing their fans' hearts. Each of the previous four seasons they had lost in the postseason to a team that finished behind them in the regular season standings. In addition to blowing that 2–1 series lead to the Rangers, they blew a 2–0 lead to the Islanders in 1985 and a 3–1 lead to the Islanders in 1987. They then lost to the Devils in 1988, with New Jersey scoring the series-winning goal late in Game Seven—in Washington, of course, after linesmen missed a blatant offsides on the Devils.

This mattered. While we were huge 'Skins and baseball fans, in my household and at school, the Caps rated just as high. They were not yet a regional phenomenon, so tickets were often available and cheap for regular season games, which meant my father could take me and Michael to a few games every year. It quickly became one of our things, along with Sunday afternoon trips to the local ice rink for me and Michael to skate around in the winter. Whatever vulgar language I did not learn from my father, cousins, in school and in camp, I learned in the cheap seats at the ol' Cap Centre. In the men's room there, I also learned how to confidently squeeze between menacing-looking adults, whip out my prepubescent penis and pee into a trough. (This was your only option if you wanted to go quickly and avoid missing too much game action. So for me, it was my only option.)

With the Caps' recent history and my entrée into preteen years, you would think I knew better when the 1989 playoffs started. Despite being one of the best teams in the league over the final four months of the regular season, including an eight-game win streak after acquiring veteran scorer Dino Ciccarelli to secure the division title in March, these loaded Caps promised nothing in the postseason.

But my father only got me more excited by promising to take me to my first playoff game since the 1986 tilt. That pledge, however, rested on one condition.

Bookshelves lined the walls in my room; when I turned to my left while lying on my bed, I could see the navy blue *World Book of Encyclopedias* set atop one shelf and several fancy-looking, leather-bound books resting next to each other on another. Perhaps my parents were trying to encourage me; alas they failed. (In between these books were many kids' sports books, from biographies to nearly every issue of the *The Baseball Hall of Shame* series.)

One night my father reached for a book on the shelf with the leather-bound books. *Treasure Island*. It was thick. If my father had not grabbed it and handed it to me, there was no chance I would have even looked at it. "If you want to go to a game," he said, "you have to read this book. The whole book. And don't try to pull a fast one on me either. I'm going to quiz you when you're done."

I knew he would follow through on this threat. He had once quizzed me on the contents of a *Sports Illustrated* issue when he thought I wasn't reading the magazine that he had ordered for me at age eight, to nourish my love of sports and encourage me to read more.

I was in, willing to do just about anything to go to a Caps playoff game—even if it meant reading a book I would not have touched if it were assigned to me for a book report. (Which it was not, because I was a fifth-grader and it was fucking *Treasure Island*.)

I tore into the book, making my nightly bedtime reading a tale of . . . wait, what was that book about again? I made great progress over the first few nights, clearing about a hundred pages. I calculated that if I kept up my pace, I could finish the book around the time the second round of the playoffs started.

But the Caps, of course, had to make it to the second round for me to go to a game. That meant they had to win their first-round series against the Philadelphia Flyers.

Eschewing the lessons of seasons past in favor of an eleven-year-old's optimism, I thought this was a forgone conclusion. The Flyers were on their way to a massive rebuild that would see them miss the postseason the next five years. They had finished fourth in the six-team division, the second straight year they finished around .500. (But, how quickly I forgot: They had advanced to the Finals in 1985 and 1987 and still had many of their experienced stars, including mercurial goalie Ron Hextall.) The Caps, meanwhile, had defeated Philadelphia in the 1988 playoffs and had added gritty playoff performers Ciccarelli, Dale Hunter, and Kelly Miller at forward to the nucleus that produced that outstanding 1986 season.

The Caps won the first game at home 3–2 and took a 2–0 lead in Game Two. The second goal, early in the third period, had me thinking the Flyers were done for the night.

So it shook me to see what happened next, as I sat on the edge of my parents' bed watching with them: The Flyers scored three goals in the final thirteen minutes, including the game-winner with less than a minute to play. I went to bed upset, trying to come to grips with another playoff meltdown by listening to the postgame show before I eventually drifted off to sleep.

Also that night, the Orioles beat the Red Sox again, 6–4, knocking Mike Boddicker out of the game in the third to improve to 2–0. The Orioles lost at Minnesota the next night. The following day, Saturday, April 8, they fell 6–5. Schmidt had started again but could not get out of the third. Baltimore was now 2–2 on the season.

At the same time the O's were losing the latter game to the Twins, the Caps and Flyers squared off on a Saturday night in Game Three in Philadelphia. The game had just entered overtime (sudden death) when I came home from a friend's house. I heard the TV broadcast coming from upstairs, so I ran into my parents' room and saw my father stretched out on his bed alone. The voice of Caps play-by-play man Mike Fornes echoed across the room. Just as I walked in, I heard Fornes raise that voice: "A shot . . . and a goal!"

My father yelped. Then he saw me and quickly motioned with his hand for me to come sit next to him. Together we watched replays as Miller's backhand deflected off the stick of a Flyers' defenseman and over the right shoulder of Hextall into the net. The Caps were up 2–1 in the series. Surely, I thought, they would win. There was no pressure to finish reading the book—certainly not the next day, a Sunday, my only day off from scheduled activities.

The O's hammered the Twins and ace Frank Viola that afternoon, 8–1. Ballard made his first start of the season and pitched a complete game, holding Minnesota to seven hits and not walking anybody.

Later that day the Flyers jumped out to a 4–0 lead after two periods and evened the series with a 5–2 win. Washington was now just two losses away from elimination and was guaranteed only one more home playoff game.

Still, I did not panic. There was no reason to rush through *Treasure Island* now. Mom would never let my father take me to Game Five on a weeknight and I had faith the Caps would still win the series and we would go to a game in the second round. I read another twenty or so pages of the book the next day.

The following night, I went to bed in the middle of a tense Game Five. The Caps blew leads of 3–2, 4–3, and 5–4. Just as they had in Game Two, the Flyers then scored three times successively, taking a commanding 7–5 lead late. They added an empty-net goal to win 8–5.

I arrived at school the next day to much chatter about the Caps. The general consensus among my friends and me: "They're done." While I talked a good game, I secretly held out hope—if for no other reason than I really, really wanted to go to a playoff game. That night I read more of *Treasure Island*, convinced that maybe my inability to read this book at a faster pace and my taking an NHL playoff series for granted was behind the Caps' sudden collapse.

I watched the Orioles that night, going to bed as they held the lead in Kansas City. I awoke the next morning to find no result in the *Post*, only a note that the game had ended too late for that edition. I later found out they had won, 5–4, in fifteen innings. The winning run came when Orsulak singled, stole second, and then advanced two bases on consecutive sacrifice flies. Olson pitched shutout ball over the final two innings to earn his second Major League win, stopping a two-game losing streak and moving Baltimore to 4–4.

After school, Michael and I cruised around the neighborhood on our dirt bikes delivering the weekly *Potomac Almanac* newspaper. (Yes, Mom made her third-grade son get a job.). My mind wondered as I finished my half of the route and motored up a road toward our intersecting street, pedaling hard and lifting my butt off the seat, the wind blowing my T-shirt up my back and my bushy hair flying everywhere: *What if the Caps lose again?* I felt a pit in my stomach, like it was preordained.

Perhaps it was. As in 1986, at least I was spared from having to see the ending, going to bed after the second period. Again it was a taut affair. Again the Flyers prevailed, 4–3. It was over. There would be no Caps playoff game in-person for me that spring. I was deflated. I put *Treasure Island* back where it belonged: on the shelf, never to be opened by me again.

Far more tragically, a fifth-grader and his father missed out on going to watch their favorite hockey team in a playoff game live. My father was too focused on pushing me and I was overconfident, optimistic, and undisciplined. And the 1980s Caps were chokers. So we missed a rare opportunity to bond before I really started breaking away.

And for the first time that I can recall, I felt serious despair over one of my favorite teams losing in the postseason. The Caps' loss really bothered me the next day, maybe for longer.

The O's lost three of their next four, falling to 5–7.

About a week after the O's opened their season, my rec league team finally started ours. We didn't get Joan Jett on opening day. Instead, as dozens of young players stood on the field in our full uniforms at Dogwood Park on a Saturday morning, the Rockville city mayor spoke. A year earlier he had lamented the Orioles' horrendous start, which briefly confused me because I thought he was referring to the Orioles team of our league. But in 1989, I do not recall him mentioning anything about Orioles at all.

The ceremony and preseason practices over, at last we could begin playing ball for real. My team's first game began later on that cold and windy day. I was overexcited and popped up in my first at bat, but we were the more talented team and won easily.

A couple of weeks later we faced Kiwanis. Along with the Lions, who featured the other Ritchie Park kids our age, Kiwanis was our rival. Unlike the Lions, whom we mutually respected and often hung out with, we hated Kiwanis. They were a bunch of private school kids who lived in larger houses in Potomac, with many getting individual skills training we did not receive.

What's more: Their coach had once cut Brett from a select soccer team, and he and his son kicked a few of us off a field one Friday afternoon when we were taking batting practice on our own. His son strode directly toward us with his eyes fixed on us, the brim of his ball cap yanked low over his eyes. "We have practice now; you guys need to leave," he said. Their practice did not start for another fifteen minutes, and he and his father were the only ones from their team there. I was furious, refusing to move until Steve suggested we go get SLUSH PUPPIES at the High's down the street.

Kiwanis was more talented than we were, but we usually played better together. Our frequent sniping at each other was brotherly, designed usually to wake a teammate out of a funk with the ultimate goal of winning. When they yelled at each other, it sounded like personal attacks.

This game was at Potomac Woods, on a warm and sunny late Saturday afternoon. The game was close throughout, and we were behind in the final inning by a run or two but had a man on. Jason, our worst player, was up.

I was on deck and I sized up the situation: *Come on*, I said to myself, eyeing the Kiwanis pitcher. *Walk him please!* He quickly got two strikes on Jason. I felt anxious and helpless as I stared again toward the mound. *Maybe hit him.* The pitcher threw a ball seemingly yards outside. Jason swung anyway and missed badly, ending the game.

My heart sank. I squatted and buried my head in my hands, walked back to the dugout, ripped off my helmet and sat on the bench as we prepared for our coaches' postgame chat.

I don't recall anything they said; I was too hung up on being that close to having a chance to tie or win the game. A year earlier, I had taken baseball losses in stride. Even during football and basketball season earlier that school year, I did not suffer losses too much. But this was baseball, my favorite sport, and I was creeping into adolescence. Everything mattered now. A lot. I dwelled on this loss during my entire ten-minute walk home and while I ate quietly at the dinner table by myself, as Brad (our babysitter) and Michael played Nintendo in the living room: *What if Jason had walked or been hit by a pitch?*

I could not wait for our next game.

Late in April we played Optimist, another solid team. Before the game, an older umpire had a minute with us. "Gentlemen," he said in a hoarse, direct tone, staring a hole through us from a few feet away as we stood by our bench as ordered. "Keep it clean. Make sure your shirts are tucked in. Have a good game!"

I swallowed hard, pulled on my white baseball pants, and shoved my green jersey inside them.

We were an even match in an unusually low-scoring game. In the sixth and final inning, we trailed 4–3. But with one out, Adam was on third, and a teammate lifted a fly ball to the outfield. After the Optimist outfielder caught it, Adam tagged up and sprinted home to easily beat the throw and tie the game. We rushed off the bench to greet him.

As we finished celebrating and returned our attention to the game, the Optimist coach asked his pitcher to throw the ball to his third baseman. He caught it and stepped on the bag, and that egotistical maniac of an umpire shouted loud enough for people in Bethesda and Gaithersburg to hear: "Heeeeee's oooouuuuut!" The ump ruled that Adam had left the bag before the ball was caught. It may have been close, but not close enough for him to make such a clear decision.

We were crestfallen. I stood in the dugout in shock for maybe a minute.

The Optimist coach, by contrast, was overjoyed. As we begrudgingly lined up and shook hands with the grinning Optimist players, he bellowed to our head coach, Stan, in between chuckles: "That's Little League baseball!"

Not in my mind, it wasn't.

Stan did not retort. Adam hung his head as we tried to cheer him up. I rode home in silence, mourning another lost chance. We were much improved, but losing even to good teams was starting to wear on me.

As usual, I recovered from a crushing loss within a day or two. There was always something to do and somebody to do it with. That weekend, the older Gromley boys were over when we walked up the stairs from our basement, through the hallway to the living room to play Nintendo one afternoon. The wall was covered in pictures, mostly of me and my brothers. You could essentially watch us grow up just by walking the hallway, viewing photos of my parents holding me as an infant, to me holding Tyler when he was a baby, to my fourth-grade class picture. They were all framed, with larger stand-alone pictures and collages with smaller photos. Mom had labeled all of them.

One of the collages featured several pictures of me as a newborn and toddler, including a photo of me at about a year old standing up while holding on to an exercise bike. I had on a T-shirt but nothing else, giving anyone who passed by a full view of my tiny behind.

So, to recap, there was a picture of me half-naked on our wall, even as I had turned eleven and preferred to keep my modesty to myself. The picture could get lost among the other photos because it was small, measuring maybe three by five inches.

But by now, my friends, cousins, Michael, and I were quite astute at embarrassing each other. Steve was no exception. After years of walking past it, he suddenly noticed the picture. "Ryan, look at you!" he smiled widely, his big eyes fixing directly on the photo. He and Sean chuckled. Michael covered his mouth to stifle a laugh.

Humiliation shot through my body. I stared straight at Steve and Sean. "Shut up!" I responded, my voice rising to match my embarrassment as my face wrinkled in anger.

The moment may have lasted just that long, but the humiliation lingered. Later that day, I found Mom and led her downstairs to her work of art. "Take this down!" I demanded. "We can't have pictures of me naked hanging on the walls!"

Mom turned her head toward me. "Why do you want me to take this down? You were only a year old. It's a cute picture."

"Take this down now!"

"Why should I? I love this picture."

"Because it's embarrassing! My friends can see my butt!"

For the previous eight-plus years that we had lived in that house, I had never requested that she remove the photo. So her eyes expressed wonder at what would suddenly lead me to protest so vigorously. At that moment, though, perhaps my mother harked back to her own preteen days: "Let me think about it."

"No! Take it down NOW!" I was pulling on her arm, looking her square in the eyes. My voice rose an octave, or four, as I screamed the last word, determined to unleash whatever trace amounts of masculinity I had developed very early in puberty to win this argument.

"Okay. If you are really that embarrassed, I can take it down," she promised.

Satisfied, I did not press the issue for the rest of the afternoon.

But it was far from over. The family matriarch had yet to weigh in.

Like her husband PopPop Eddie, Mom's mother Freda had grown up as a first-generation Jew in the Philadelphia slums in the 1920s and 1930s, a child of pogrom survivors. She and Eddie met as students at Temple University and married just before World War II started, relocating to the Washington area permanently after the war. She worked as a teacher for decades, giving this naturally impatient woman the right temperament to handle me and her four other grandchildren.

Known as "Flick" ("MomMom Flick" to me) because of how quickly she spoke or accomplished virtually any task, she spent hours sewing patches for the holes in the knees of my sweatpants, coddling me and her other grandchildren, and arguing with my parents about their parenting decisions. She was the most effective in the family at getting me to calm down when I (often) got worked up, suggesting I count to ten to avert a tantrum. "You get more with honey than with vinegar," she would often tell me, Michael, and Brad when we screamed at each other or argued with our parents.

That night she came over. She and Mom were organizing pictures into albums from Mom's latest motherload, straight from the twenty-four-hour photo shop at a nearby strip mall.

I walked in and reminded Mom what she had promised.

Mom had completed one step: she had taken the collage off the wall and it was now resting on a circular table. She and MomMom Flick were sitting around the table with the fresh photos resting in small paper packets next to the collage.

"Get rid of it," I insisted, pointing to the butt pic and turning toward Mom, ignoring my grandmother for the moment.

"Ah ah ah!" MomMom Flick responded, pushing my finger away.

Mom was now caught in the middle. I wanted—no, NEEDED—the picture to be removed. But my grandmother encouraged Mom to leave it in the collage and place it back on the wall. I was incredulous. Here was a picture of me half-naked, hanging on the wall for all to see. It was humiliating. And now my own mother was not going to take it down? Just because her mother protested? In her house? Where I also lived?

"Shelly, I love this picture," MomMom Flick said to Mom. They both ignored me for a moment.

"Mom, you promised!" I raised my voice again, leaning in to look her in the eyes and grabbing her wrist and squeezing for emphasis.

I must have underestimated my growing strength. "Ryan let go!" she bellowed, shaking free and returning her attention to the pictures. She then shooed me out of the room. "I will take care of this!"

I grunted, then walked downstairs to watch some game in the basement. *How would she take care of this? What is so hard about removing this picture?! Why isn't she keeping her promise?!*

Mom and MomMom Flick eventually compromised, without my input. Their idea did not sound like a solution to me, seeing as how the only palatable answer featured taking that picture down, burning it, and acting as if it never had existed.

But the compromise would stand. Mom found an old picture of Freddy that was small enough to cover up my bottom half without blocking the whole picture. So for the next few decades, the picture remained on the wall. But the bottom half was covered up by a random, tiny picture of Freddy curled up, sleeping.

And I learned more about my family. It was becoming clear to me who was really in charge in our house.

MomMom Flick and Mom may have partially held their ground and I may have failed to meet my father's condition to go to a Caps playoff game. But I always had better luck persuading him to take me and Michael to R-rated movies, especially sports-themed ones. Appropriate or not, that was also one of our things. (That, and him persuading me to watch horror movies such as *Aliens*, which gave me nightmares for two weeks after I watched it with him when I was eight or nine.)

Major League debuted the first Friday of the MLB regular season and word quickly spread among my friends and me. Brett was the first one to see it, Ross was not allowed to see it (it was rated R), and I was determined to see it at all costs.

This time we did not even have to sneak our plans past Mom. One weekend night, she allowed my father to take Michael and me, knowing I may have been ostracized at school if we did not go. The three of us first dined at a Mexican restaurant at a local mall, where I crushed an adult-sized platter of chicken fajitas and ate my father's leftovers. I mostly ate and listened as my father regaled us with tales of his own youth sports experiences.

The topic soon turned to me and Michael. "I think you can both play [baseball] in high school and college," my father said.

"What about the majors?" I replied.

"I want you to use your brain, not your body."

Michael and I stared at each other quizzically.

"What does that mean?" Michael asked him.

"It means I want you to have careers where you are using your brains," he responded.

"You have to think a lot playing baseball," I shot back.

"Maybe if you really want, you can try rookie ball after college. See how that goes."

I nodded. That seemed fair.

He looked at his watch; it was almost time for the movie to start. We finished dinner and hurried into the theater. Michael and I were probably the youngest people there; I'm not sure there were even any middle schoolers present. I can only imagine what other moviegoers thought when they heard two tween boys belly laughing at nearly every scene. We laughed especially hard at Pedro Cerrano scenes and when Ricky Vaughn modeled his new glasses. Dad loved the Harry Doyle line about the Yankees' closer throwing at his own kid during a father-son game.

Maybe it was "*juuuuust* a bit outside" for my father to take us to that movie at our ages. But it was, and remains, one of my favorite flicks and childhood memories. At a time when I was slowly breaking away from my father, watching a raunchy sports comedy with him reinforced our bond for a little while longer.

So did the play of a real baseball team that played its home games nearby.

A few weeks into the season, the O's were doing their best to mimic the miracle Indians team in *Major League* that (spoiler alert) captures the AL East division title. Albeit very early in the season, the O's were in first place, sitting at .500 as the favorites in the division— Toronto, Boston, Milwaukee, and the Yankees—all failed to get off to a solid start.

Even off the field, news was good. In mid-April, MLB owners approved the Orioles' sale to a group led by New York investor Eli Jacobs, who purchased the club from the estate of Edward Bennett Williams for $70 million. The purchase figured to stabilize a club that had been driven into the ground over the last few years of Williams' ownership. Thus began the years that many O's fans recall fondly, the short era in between the Williams and Angelos family ownerships.

On the penultimate Sunday morning of April, my father, brothers, and I went out to breakfast and then to the Super Giant on Rockville Pike. My father looked the other way when I bought a couple of 1989 Topps rack packs and filled a heaping plastic bag full of candy. When we got home, I retired to the family room to flip between the O's game and the NFL draft.

The Orioles were hosting Minnesota, winners of three of their last four games. The Twins, who had won the World Series two seasons earlier over the Cardinals, were off to a 9–6 start. But Milacki and the defense dominated as the O's won 3–0, giving Milacki his first win of the season. "He needed just one hundred pitches to finish off one of the best-hitting teams in the game, and thanks to four double plays and a runner thrown out stealing, he faced the minimum twenty-seven hitters," according to the *Post*.

Milacki worked well with his defense, Cal Ripken said after the game: "He's always around the plate, and, when the catcher calls for a fastball inside, Bob's going to throw a fastball inside. That helps a defense."

The O's prepared to leave for a West Coast swing, including seven games in seven days in three cities. After blanking the Twins, they stood at 9–8. Their .988 fielding percentage was tops in the league; they also led the AL in sacrifices and had grounded into the fewest double plays.

"We know we're not good enough to win if we make a bunch of mistakes," Robinson said. "We're not powerful enough to overcome them. But we're learning how to win. . . . I'm not saying I'm shocked by any of this, but we're all pleasantly surprised."

While Milacki was emerging, before the trip west, the club sent the struggling Harnisch back to AAA Rochester and welcomed Finley back from injury. "He remains one of their brightest prospects," the *Post* wrote of Harnisch. "He has been a disappointment, not because his pitches are less than expected, but because he seems to have lost some of the aggressiveness he showed last September. It's important to remember he's only twenty-two."

We also knew that, like Harnisch, the season was still very young. We figured to see more of the rookie at some point in the season.

Olson was also still very young.

But Gregg Olson (with two g's) was one of the few anomalies among the 1989 Baltimore Orioles. Unlike many teammates who had been discarded by other teams or picked late in the draft by the O's, Olson was the team's top pick in 1988 and the fourth overall selection. So Olson was quickly tabbed as a building block, part of a staff full of potential. Unlike Schilling, Harnisch, and others, however, Olson was ready for the majors when the 1989 season started. Actually, the rookie right-hander with the baby face and menacing glare was already set to dominate.

Olson had enjoyed a strong college career at Auburn, after playing for his father in high school in Omaha. Nicknamed "Otter" because of the way he walked, he had pitched well as a September call-up in 1988 and during the spring. So Olson started 1989 pitching out of the bullpen for the O's, but he was not Baltimore's primary closer when the season started.

That essentially changed one weeknight in Oakland in late April. One night after blasting the Angels 8–1 to split a two-game series in Anaheim, the O's led Oakland 2–1 after seven-and-a-half innings. Olson relieved Bautista to start the eighth and promptly retired Walt Weiss, Mike Gallego, and Luis Polonia in order. They represented predominantly the bottom of Oakland's order.

Due up in the ninth were Dave Parker, Dave Henderson, and Mark McGwire. By 1989 Henderson had made his mark as a clutch hitter, McGwire was the best power-hitting first baseman in the majors and Parker was a surefire future Hall of Famer. Even at thirty-eight, he would sock twenty-two homers and drive in nearly one hundred runs that year.

Still leading only 2–1 as the frame began, Olson fanned them all. First he got Parker and Henderson swinging. The game then ended when Olson dropped a breaking ball into the strike zone on a 2–2 count, the baffled McGwire buckling his knees as he helplessly watched the pitch.

Olson hardly reacted to his dominating performance, as if he had expected it. "He may already have the best curveball in the big leagues, and his fastball is better than anyone expects," beat reporter Richard Justice said of Olson in the *Post* a few days later, in his one-month club assessment.

The performance marked Olson's second career save. With only seventeen thousand fans in attendance and most O's fans likely fast asleep (the weeknight game ended past midnight local time), it's hard to call his dominance memorable. But it marked a turning point for the Orioles and the entire 1989 Baseball season: The Otter had arrived. Teams trailing the O's late would be in trouble.

Another arrival later that week further demonstrated that maybe, just maybe, my father was right: These O's would not be so bad.

After that win in Oakland, the O's lost three straight. They sat at 11–12, yet they still were tied for first in the division.

The next evening Ballard held Seattle to seven hits and one walk over seven innings, but the O's trailed 3–2. They were on the verge of finishing the road trip 2–5, falling out of first place. With one out in the top of the eighth, Cal Ripken doubled off Seattle reliever Michael Jackson. Steve Trout replaced Jackson and retired Sheets on a pop-up to short.

Up stepped Tettleton.

Mickey Tettleton has the same first name as a couple of all-time greats (Mantle, Lolich), was once famous enough to appear as himself in a movie (*Little Big League*, in 1994) and crushed 245 homers while driving in 732 runs in a Major League career that lasted until 1997.

But when the 1988 season started, he was a mid-career player without a job when Oakland—the team that had drafted him—cut him in favor of Ron Hassey and Terry Steinbach at catcher. Oakland also eschewed keeping him around as a switch-hitting bat off the bench, opting for veterans Don Baylor and Parker instead.

Tettleton had been selected in the fifth round of the 1981 draft at twenty, platooning for the A's and making frequent trips back to the minors between 1984 and 1987. Those A's teams rarely contended, so the franchise had little to lose giving him opportunities to stick in Oakland. But with Tettleton at age twenty-seven entering the 1988 season and Oakland loading up (the A's would reach the World Series that season), he was deemed expendable. The A's were out of patience and roster spots, so they let him go for nothing.

Tettleton soon accepted Baltimore's offer to sign, earning a mere $160,000 that season and platooning with Terry Kennedy. His salary was bumped up to $290,000 for 1989, when he began platooning with Melvin.

As Tettleton stepped up to bat in Seattle that inning, he was barely batting .200 on the season and was hitless in his previous ten at bats. He had hit just .194 in 1987 and .204 in 1986. His power was always evident, if only he could hit for average consistently enough to play every day. Now, despite Melvin's presence, he had the chance to earn that opportunity. Every Oriole had a shot in 1989. But he appeared to be squandering his early on.

Making his ninth straight start after Melvin was knocked out for a couple of weeks in a game against Minnesota, this at bat was crucial for Tettleton. He was facing a veteran lefthander in Trout and worked the count full. With two out, Ripken took off with the pitch. Tettleton swung and crushed a line drive to right-center. It kept carrying, carrying, carrying . . . and easily cleared the wall, giving the O's a 4–3 lead.

In retrospect, Tettleton's blast was important (to this O's season and his career), but not too shocking. It was already his fifth homer on the season.

"What was surprising is that the Mariners allowed Trout, a lefty, to pitch to Tettleton, a switch-hitter who is hitting .300 against lefties and .173 against righties. First base was open, and Manager

Jim Lefebvre had right-hander Julio Solano ready in the bullpen," the *Post* noted after the game.

"I was surprised, too," Tettleton said. "I know he had the right-hander out there."

Fortunately for Tettleton and the O's, Lefebvre opted for Trout. Tettleton soon began earning regular starts. Starting in mid-May, when Melvin returned, Robinson would pencil him in at designated hitter when Melvin caught. His average would rise to .249 by early June, never dipping that low again, and he would soon become a national phenomenon.

The latter was still a few weeks away from that day in Seattle, when Williamson came on and retired six of the next seven Mariners—getting Jim Presley to fly out to center to end the game.

"Other than opening day, this was probably our biggest game of the year," Robinson said afterward. "This was the first time we had what you'd call a down situation. We had a chance to lose four in a row, then go home, and have an off day to think about it."

But instead they won and happily jumped on a plane back east. Baltimore was back to .500, remaining in a tie atop the AL East. The O's had salvaged a tough trip and avoided a collapse. But they were still relatively untested and unknown.

"What they do know is that the AL East is mediocre," Justice wrote in the *Post*, "and that, if shortstop Cal Ripken Jr. gets hot and if the pitching and defense can keep them in games, they could stay in the race a while. By August, all their many holes will have been exposed, but, no matter what happens then, they've had a fun ride in April. . . .

"A defense led by third baseman Craig Worthington and four outstanding outfielders has been terrific, has caught dozens of balls that would have been hits in 1988, and helped keep a team without much hitting in a lot of games."

By the end of the month, the O's were generating respect around the majors. "They're different," Boston's Dwight Evans told the *Post*. "You used to go play them and you could count on winning three out of four. Now, they play you."

With the Caps done, March Madness long over, and the O's in first place as the season's first month ended, we were now paying more attention to the regional baseball team. Not quite buying into the O's as contenders—that was still impossible, even to fifth-graders. But we were a bit more interested in how their season would turn out.

For one month at least, they were not so shitty.

With my grandmother MomMom Flick, Brad, and Mom in happier, healthier times at my aunt and uncle's house, circa 1988 or 1989.

Chapter 4

MAY: MAY FLOWER(ING), WITH HEAVY SHOWERS

As May began, unbeknownst to me, my adolescence had as well. I had been slowly growing apart from my father for a couple of years already, getting fed up with his inconsistent pushing and irrational decisions despite his often taking us to games and rated-R movies. But many boys in my generation outgrew their dads early in life.

What was more significant: I was starting to drift away from Mom too. I no longer told her every last detail of my life, no longer was even honest with her all the time. None of this was intentional. It just happened, over the course of that school year.

When I had been issued detention for the first time the previous fall, I tried to hide it from her. My strategy was simple: I would avoid eye contact with her upon returning home, head straight for my room, stay there until we had to leave for Hebrew school, then go back to my room after we got home. It was the exact opposite of what I usually did, but I hoped she would not suspect a thing.

So that afternoon I walked in the door with Michael, avoided eye contact with Mom as planned, and walked toward the corner of the kitchen. I never made it up to my room. Instead I began playing with something on the wall, staring at it, thinking intently about how I was never going to be able to hide this news from my father, and what he was going to do to me. Mom quietly walked over and got me to talk—on the condition that she promised not to tell my father. (I don't know if she ever did.) I still felt a bit upset and worried, but now I was relaxed enough to pay attention for roughly five whole minutes of Hebrew school later that afternoon.

For years this was one of her greatest skills: getting me to open up when I was embarrassed to share something, then keeping our relationship tight by playing down whatever I was up to. Take the time earlier in 1988, when I had worn the same pair of underwear for about a week after reading about a Major Leaguer on a hot streak doing so in one of my *Baseball Hall of Shame* books. She got me to admit it, pretended not to be disgusted, then bought me several new pairs and left them on top of my bed as a hint.

Throughout most of fifth grade, she remained my closest confidant. I could barely get anything by her—not that I tried too often.

But things were bound to change, and maybe that started even before 1988 ended. One Friday afternoon a couple of months after the detention, Steve and I were walking home from school when we made a detour to hang out at the creek coursing through the park next to our neighborhood. I was tightroping a log when I began to lose my balance. I felt panic grip my body as my balance completely disappeared and I plunged sideways into the creek. I quickly popped up, unhurt. But I was cold and slimy and my clothes were soaking wet.

"Yo! You okay?!" Steve called over from dry land.

I picked myself up and wiped the gunk off my body, still standing in the water. "Yeah," I replied, "but let's go."

Steve agreed to come to my place so I could quickly change. But first I had to get by Mom, who I knew was home. I also knew that if she saw I was soaked, she would probably send Steve home and start asking questions. And not necessarily in that order.

We concocted a plan. Steve would go in first and distract her. I would dart upstairs to my room and change before she could notice my plight. Fortunately I was wearing black sweatpants which, by the time we rolled up to the house, were no longer obviously water-logged. My shirt, a replica Scott Stevens Capitals red-white-and-blue cotton jersey-T shirt, was no longer visibility wet either.

We entered the door leading right into the kitchen, where Mom had strategically placed her satellite home office. Steve entered first. Mom was indeed sitting at her desk and spun around in her office chair to greet us.

"Hi Shelley!" Steve called out.

"Hi Stephen," she replied, smiling widely at him.

This bought me the time I needed. I shot Mom a quick nod and then sprinted through the kitchen and up the stairs and into the safety of my bedroom. I shut the door, took off the wet clothes and tossed them into the hamper. Never mind that Mom would undoubtedly discover these clothes within a matter of days while doing the laundry, or that she would probably notice within a matter of seconds that I had changed clothes after school for no good reason. We were going through with this plan.

I heard a knock at the door; it was Steve. I put on dry, gray sweatpants over clean, dry underwear and opened the door.

"I don't think your mom noticed," Steve said in a hushed tone.

I was shocked. We went about our Friday afternoon without Mom bugging us. We never talked about my quick change.

The precedent had been set. And as spring arrived, the advent of my adolescence and our corresponding separation revealed itself in other moments, too.

One morning in early May, I woke up groggy. Somebody was sitting on my bed facing me, rubbing my chest lightly. My bedroom lights were on. I wiped my eyes, looked up, and noticed it was Mom. She was looking at me with mournful eyes, smirking a bit. "You slept in honey. It's time to get up for school."

"Whuh . . . What?" I whispered, stretching.

Pretty soon, I would be sleeping in every chance I could, until eleven or twelve on Sunday mornings the very next school year. I would relish every minute of sleep I could get.

But on this morning, sleeping in felt very odd. When I was a toddler, I would sometimes scream bloody murder when my parents tried to put me to bed. When I was seven, I would rise just before 7 a.m. on Saturdays to catch *Woody Woodpecker* reruns and make toast for me and Michael. Throughout the rest of elementary school, I never set an alarm, waking up with enough time to shower and eat breakfast before heading to school.

Mom must have been surprised too, because she had almost let me snooze right through breakfast before realizing I was not in the shower yet. Now, sitting on my bed and staring intently at her first child who was just weeks away from finishing elementary school, I detected a hint of sorrow in her vexing look.

That morning was only a mild harbinger. It would be a difficult month for my family, especially for her. By the time it was over, we would all be on a much different course than the one I knew from my previous eleven years. I had no idea what was about to hit me. Worse, I was completely unprepared.

But I would find solace in following a miraculous Major League club's sudden emergence.

May started inauspiciously for the O's as well. After finishing April tied for first in the AL East, the O's lost five straight during the first week of May at home—including a three-game sweep by the middling Mariners. A loss the next day at home to Oakland dropped them to 13–17, three games out of first. Much of their struggle was due to lack of offense. By that week, for the season Larry Sheets was hitting .204, Jim Traber .206, Craig Worthington .191, and Mickey Tettleton .198.

The next day, Baltimore trailed Oakland 3–0 midway through the fifth. The clubs only needed to play the bottom of the inning for the game to become official. But before the frame started, umpire Don Denkinger halted play because of rain. Despite protests from

A's manager Tony LaRussa, Denkinger called for a delay (I imagine the scene looking like the famous Norman Rockwell painting "Tough Call"). The rain kept coming and the game's result was nullified when the umpiring crew later called it an official rainout.

Two days later the clubs resumed their series. The struggling O's offense tattooed Oakland ace Dave Stewart for twelve hits in six and two-thirds innings—the most hits he had permitted in a game in his nine-year career. Ballard scattered nine hits and held Oakland to a single run in seven innings, as the O's snapped their losing streak with a 6–2 win. What looked to be a possible sixth straight loss before the rain delay turned into a win against baseball's best team.

But the victory and a few others over the first three weeks of May were mere reprieves for a team that, despite overachieving, was still sitting where most had expected them to: below .500.

What's more, warts were showing. Offensively, the O's were held to two runs or fewer in six of fourteen games dating from May 3 to mid-May. Regarding the pitching staff, O's brass grew concerned with Bautista, now twenty-four and in his second full season in the majors. His velocity was low and he appeared tentative; Robinson couldn't decipher his forkball from his fastball. He was removed from the rotation in late May and only made one more start all season. Meanwhile Ballard had to miss a start with a groin pull.

Brian Holton and Jay Tibbs slid into the rotation to replace them. The O's had to temporarily scrap their plan to use Holton as a reliever, where he had had been effective in 1987 and 1988 with the Dodgers, and took another flier on Tibbs, now on his third team in the sixth season of his career: the same Jay Tibbs who posted a 5.39 ERA while making twenty-four starts for Baltimore in 1988 and had only pitched twice—out of the bullpen—thus far in 1989.

It all added up to this: The O's were seemingly on their way to a fourth straight losing season. They lost ten of fourteen bridging late April and May, bottoming out at 15–19 with an 8–5 loss at home to the White Sox on Sunday, May 14. The O's couldn't hold a 5–4 lead after six, with Ron Kittle smashing a two-run homer off Williamson in the seventh to give Chicago the advantage for good.

Baltimore went 3–2 over the next week, punctuated by a 2–0 loss at home to Cleveland on Sunday, May 21. They were 18–21—yet somehow only one game out of first. At roughly the one-quarter mark of the season, no team in the AL East stood above .500.

But it was just a matter of time, we thought, until a more talented team got hot and left the O's in the dust. One of those teams had to get hot at some point. But surely not the Orioles. The team that had not enjoyed even a mild hot streak in two years? Unlikely.

I can scarcely recall those O's games over the first half of May, with most of their action a blip in my world. They had not yet corralled my imagination despite being better than expected. It was still the school year so most of their games ended after my bedtime, and they had to compete for my attention with my numerous after-school activities and the NBA and NHL playoffs.

Then something besides sports and activities hijacked my attention, something that upended my whole family's world. This, while I confronted other changes that were starting to frustrate and confuse me.

It hit seemingly out of the blue, but I guess many of life's curves do. One Sunday night, I was sitting in the kitchen eating a snack and watching a game after dinner. Sitting behind me at her desk, Mom was planning the week when she answered the phone. Within minutes, she was sobbing. She was on the phone with her sister. The news was grim: MomMom Flick, seventy-three, had been diagnosed with terminal lung cancer.

My parents soon told me and Michael of her diagnosis, but they would keep her terminal prognosis from us for the duration of her battle with the disease.

I knew what cancer was and what it usually did; I also knew nobody had lived past their seventies in recent family history. But while at first I only casually worried about losing my beloved grandmother, it was Mom's sudden spontaneous outbursts that concerned me much more.

My parents had always put up a strong front for us. I only saw my father cry when his father died, about three years earlier. The first time

I can remember seeing Mom cry, it shocked me. I was about five or six, had pushed her too far, and she started tearing up. I could not understand why she was crying; she had always seemed so strong and strong people never cried, I thought. Crying was only for little kids, and track and swimming stars who had just won Olympic gold medals.

By the time we were tweens, when one of my brothers or I started sniffling about something, my father would often respond, "You'd better knock that off or I'll give you something to cry about!" That meant hitting us with his belt. Along with my brothers, cousins, and friends, we learned from family and our culture that the only appropriate times to cry were at a funeral, or after failing or succeeding in an important sporting event. Sick family member? Keep those tears in! Crushing strikeout in a baseball playoff game? Let 'em roll down your cheeks.

This familial and cultural norm made it difficult for me to understand and abide Mom's outbursts. Unlike when my hug and apology had smoothed things over a few years earlier, there was nothing I thought I could do to soothe her on the night she learned of our matriarch's diagnosis—or for many nights thereafter. I must have sensed that immediately: I just sat there, continuing to eat my snack while she raced upstairs to talk with my father.

One night later that year I came home and ran upstairs to her bedroom to greet her, only to find her sobbing as she lay on her bed watching the last scene in the movie *Big*. Watching young Josh Baskin and his mother greet each other reminded her of coming home to her mother when she was a kid, she told me.

But I could not understand why this made her so upset. *Wasn't that almost thirty years ago? How could she even remember that? Didn't she know* Big *was just a movie?*

She reached for me, but I recoiled, uncomfortable seeing her cry. Perhaps I was too green and sensitive to face reality, too. Or afraid that if I tried to comprehend her feelings, I would melt down and break the rules of the crying game as unwritten—but well understood—for preteen Gen X boys.

I moved through my busy life as if MomMom were not even sick. She kept coming to family events and calling our house, so she must be doing well, I thought. That she did not attend my elementary school graduation about a month later or come to the beach with us in August (as she and PopPop Eddie usually did) should have been clear signs, but I was too caught up in boogie boarding, walking the boardwalk, and playing hotbox (a baseball-themed game) on the sand to notice.

Over the next two-plus years, as she fought the cancer and the adults in my family continued to hide her prognosis from me, I would encourage Mom to remain optimistic—even after her father was also stricken with terminal cancer. One night in September 1990, we were driving home as I sat next to Mom up front. "If you just believe he will be all right," I said of PopPop Eddie, as lung cancer was quickly killing him, "then he will be. I believed MomMom would be okay and she has been."

(Let it be known that I was hardly hoping for miracles by mid-1990; my denial about my beloved grandparents was simply that powerful. When a school administrator came to my class later that month to tell me, "You need to go see your grandfather right now" in the hospital, because he had slipped into a coma, I still refused to believe he was dying—until I walked into his room and saw him lying there.)

Mom kept driving, not responding or even glancing at me. MomMom Flick had been given only six months to live at the time of her diagnosis. By this night she had already outlived that, but her health was gradually declining. (PopPop Eddie had only recently been diagnosed and his health was rapidly declining.)

Emotionally, I kept my grandmother's illness at arm's length. I cannot remember how I eventually figured out that she was not going to get better and was actually dying—or if I ever accepted that. My denial was strong. Until the morning she died while in hospice care in October 1991, part of me believed she would never actually go. She was just too important to our family. This was merely a case of a woman battling cancer, and people beat cancer all the time. Or so I thought.

Despite my denial, her diagnosis, ensuing illness, and death irrevocably changed our family.

Perhaps it was fitting. As I needed Mom less and less, with a very sick mother of her own to care for, she could no longer be there for me as much anyways. The paradox: sometimes, no matter the front I put up to the outside world, I still needed my mommy. For the first time in my life, I was facing real, adult-level adversity. This was only the beginning in a month that started shifting my life. There would be no going back.

Compounding MomMom Flick's diagnosis, I was worried about Freddy, and living with him presented daily reminders of his own decline. He was approaching nineteen and showing obvious signs of slowing down. The once plump cat who dove into your ice cream if you left it unattended for a second and shared peanut butter off spoons with me? He was now ignoring those treats and looking much thinner.

Nearly every night he used to leap to the counter in our hallway bathroom on his own, where I would fill the sink for him to drink from before I went to bed. By May 1989, however, I had seen him miss his jump too many times and was resigned to using every ounce of strength I had to pick up this large cat and place him on the counter.

The first couple of times this happened, my heart sank. I felt for Freddy and was upset for myself; he had only recently begun to bond with me (once I advanced out of the stage when I tried to drape my underwear over his face or tail).

I must have known it was just a matter of time until he was gone, but I refused to think about that. I was simply woefully unprepared emotionally to lose my pet or my grandmother. The only real loss I had experienced came when my paternal grandfather died in early 1986. But I was only seven then and scarcely mourned. At his funeral, a family friend gave me a game to keep me busy, and I was largely content.

Mom was also dreading Freddy's inevitable demise and understood well just how precarious her mother's health was. She had been much closer to both of them for longer than I, having adopted Freddy with my father when he was a kitten right after they married.

She continued to put on the same face, volunteering at our school and hugging me, my brothers, and my friends when we walked into the house just as she always had. She also buried herself in my and Michael's activities, especially our baseball games. But inside she was breaking down as she handled an aging, beloved pet and very sick mother, on top of the usual chaos of raising three boys, all while trying to maintain a career and a marriage.

She tried to help herself and her children the only way she knew how, by plowing ahead, acting on the outside as if nothing were wrong. "The whole world is a stage," her father had always told her, and she was really embracing that mantra now. Only close adult family and friends knew how she was truly feeling.

She became so laser-focused on the tasks in front of her, so intent on outwardly denying her feelings, that part of her closed off and froze. In the process, she unconsciously ignored some of the seemingly minor problems in her orbit—including burgeoning anxiety disorders that I was suddenly experiencing and trying desperately to ignore and hide.

Mom missed the seemingly minor problems in part because plowing ahead meant finding a middle school for me—not just any school, the best school.

The school board's switcheroo placed another burden on Mom, who had been expecting me and my brothers to matriculate through the highly esteemed Frost and Wootton public schools after completing sixth grade at Ritchie Park. Both Julius West and Richard Montgomery (RM) had much worse reputations, while my cousins attended Frost and Wootton and I had long assumed I would go there too—even pushing Mom to let me play football once I got to Wootton.

Mom, like many parents of Ritchie Park students, had fought the school change. They bought homes in our neighborhoods in large part because of the schools. But the board and advocates who bought in the Julius West-RM district (including my first-ever youth sports coach, of all people) simply did not care about how important education was to our families.

A lot of us had similar stories. Most of our Jewish or Asian grandparents had clawed their way from being low-class immigrants and first-generation Americans as children to the middle class when our parents were growing up, and our parents worked hard to achieve the upper middle-class lives they were providing us. Many parents attributed our families' rises in part to the solid public educations they had received. Both of my parents, for example, went to public high schools and the University of Maryland; my maternal grandparents, of course, met as Temple University students.

When the school board issued its final decision one night early in 1988, Mom and several other Ritchie Park parents attended the meeting. I went to bed before she got home and she woke me up the next morning. She sat on the edge of my bed and stared directly into my eyes as I rubbed them and sat up. "We tried our best, honey," she said, "but they still changed your schools."

I shrugged. This change would still not affect me for over a year, which felt like a very long time seeing as how I was nine and rarely thought beyond any given day.

About a year later, my parents made up their mind. Rather than allow me to attend Julius West or move our family into a different school district, they planned to send me to private school. Only they did not explicitly tell me that for a while.

Landon, Bullis, and Georgetown Day had the best academic reputations in the metro area. I was admitted to all of them, but I was in complete denial about ever attending any of them. Somehow, I convinced myself that I would be matriculating to Julius West with the majority of my friends. I loathed the idea of going to these other schools because I feared being pulled away from the friends that I had become so close to, and I hated the thought of attending any private school. Wasn't that where the Kiwanis kids went?

But my parents decided to follow the many parents who had acted more swiftly a year earlier, when a few of my friends were enrolled at Bullis to start fifth grade. By May I did not know of this decision yet, with MomMom Flick's diagnosis pushing out my parents' talk with me. They explained away my taking school admittance tests as a way for them to gauge where I stood academically. I bought the lie, probably because I wanted to—and because I wholly trusted them.

One night I saw a brochure for Landon, an all-boys private school in Bethesda, lying on the kitchen island. I brushed it off, figuring if I simply ignored its existence maybe I would never have to go there. But I felt a lump in my throat. I had an eerie feeling when I visited the campus, and the cover photo told me all I needed to know. It featured a mostly white group of kids clad in dress shirts and neck ties, and kids playing lacrosse. It was not for me. At eleven, I may not have known much about the world, but I knew what I did not like—Jams, the Dallas Cowboys, and private schools that forced kids to dress up.

I still thought I was staying in public school as late as the final few weeks of the school year. One morning, my fifth-grade class loaded onto buses and toured Julius West. As we sat in the dimly lit gym bleachers listening to an administrator talk, I took in the scene; scoreboard sat high against the wall, meant both for the basketball teams and for competitive gym classes. I felt excited about the prospect of middle school.

The charade continued as we practiced singing graduation songs in music class. "Next year we will all be at Julius West, but Ritchie Park will still be the best," one of my classmates suggested adding to our school song.

"But not everyone will be at Julius West next year," our music teacher responded.

Who is not coming with us? I wondered, with a few classmates voicing the same sentiment out loud. After most of us had been together for six years, it seemed implausible that I would be separated from them—even after we had already lost a few classmates.

Then one evening at home, according to Mom, my parents asked me to come to their room. (I have no recollection of this whatsoever.) I sat on their bed facing them. "Ry, we need to talk with you," Mom said. They both looked me straight in the eyes as Mom continued, her tone direct. "We had to make a tough choice, but as you know, Julius West is not a good school. We want the best school for you.

I know you're going to be disappointed, but we are sending you to Landon next year."

My heart must have dropped, because my head immediately sank and I stared at the floor as they continued talking.

"We really think this is best for you," my father chimed in. "Landon has great sports and they practice every day. You'll get better than your friends at Julius West. Plus they have a lot more days off."

I did not respond.

"You can keep playing on the same basketball and baseball teams as your friends," Mom said, referring to our rec clubs. "And you know they are always welcome here."

That provided little solace to me. After six years—more than half my life—of seeing so many of the same kids every weekday, feeling safe and knowing my place, I now knew that life soon was going to abruptly end. Even if I still saw many of my closest friends a couple of times a week at practices and games in the winter and spring, there would be no more goofing off in the hallways and outside the school with them, no more crowds gathering around me gawking as I meticulously performed my unique pizza-eating at lunch every Friday, no more ultracompetitive recess games together.

Then also there was the matter of attending a new school with new classmates. I knew exactly one student at Landon—Neal, the stud baseball player whom I had played with for two seasons earlier in elementary school.

I argued with my parents about a lot growing up, but I knew I had no choice where I attended school. That was too important to them and they had the final say, even if I felt it in my bones that they were wrong. But I buried my thoughts. As their decision sank in and we all sat in their bedroom, I did not utter so much as a word.

Maybe a few days later, Ross, a couple other students, and I were called out of homeroom to join other fifth graders in another room down the hall. Several mothers of current Julius West sixth-graders greeted us, standing by tables with big smiles, bigger books, and packets stapled together. "You all have been selected for a unique program at Julius West," one of the moms said, raising her voice.

"Here are some reading materials for you for the summer, to get you ready."

The moms started handing out the materials. Ross was almost glowing from having been chosen for this program. I don't think he had figured out that he had just been assigned summer reading for the first time.

My heart sank. I wanted this to end so I could go back to homeroom, back to denying that I was going to be pulled away from my friends and sent to a new school where I knew exactly one kid and would have to wear nice clothes every day and. . . . Help!!!! It was way too overwhelming to even think about.

One of the moms approached me with a packet and I saw my name clearly printed on it. "I, I, uh . . ." I put my head down, unable to look this woman in the eyes, or even the midsection. "I won't be going to Julius West next year," I finally stammered softly, still looking at the ground.

"That's okay love," she responded. "Thanks for letting me know." She walked away, setting that packet on a table. It was a packet meant for a gifted public-school student entering sixth grade in the fall at Julius West, along with many current classmates.

I would never pick it up.

It was a shame I would be going to an all-boys private school for a lot of reasons, one being that this switch would occur just as something else was changing inside of me.

It was around this time, the end of the school year, that I saw Natasha's butt. Not only saw it, but could not help but stare at it. We were in music class one afternoon. Our teacher ordered us all to sit "Indian style" on the carpet in a large circle for some exercise, per usual. I was sitting near Natasha, a bubbly brunette who was one of the popular girls in our class. Somebody tossed a small pink rubber eraser, which flew toward the carpet in front of Natasha. She leaned forward to try to catch it.

Perhaps driven by our recent sex ed classes, my eyes did not fix on the eraser or Natasha's lunging arm, as they would have in the past, to satiate my competitive instincts. Instead I peeked to my left at her backside as she lunged. And there it was: Her butt! I only got a quick glimpse, but it was enough. I quietly told a few friends in the class. "You saw her butt? You sure?" they asked, eyes bulging as they covered their mouths with their hands.

I was (and I still am).

Pretty soon word leaked out in the classroom. The girls found out. Uh-oh. Natasha was becoming embarrassed, blushing. They were not pleased. A few of them confronted me immediately after class: "You did NOT see Natasha's butt!" they said.

"Yes I did!"

"NO, you DID NOT! You LIAR!" They stormed off.

So that was the end of that conversation.

But I took it home with me. My classmates had called me a liar, and I was not lying. I had indeed seen her butt. *Why didn't they believe me?* I wondered. When I got home, I was still too upset to talk to anyone about my frustration—or about the weird feelings I had when I saw Natasha's tush.

Life was really getting confusing.

But I kept going as if nothing were changing, barely acknowledging the storms brewing inside of me, the declining health of my pet and my grandmother, and the impending school switch. This was likely because I still had sports to follow and the school year was ending. Those were always a magical few weeks in elementary school. We got many extra recesses, and the weather was good enough for us to be outside every day.

Alas, this time of year also meant important events, important to the adults in my world, at least.

On top of my other scheduled activities, I also had those piano lessons. By fifth grade I had not improved my skills much since Mom signed me up as a second-grader. That was mostly due to a complete lack of effort. I had weekly one-hour lessons taught by a very sweet, pear-shaped man named Rick, whom I hope was compensated generously by my parents and several neighbors who forced their squirrely kids to sit and consistently butcher his favorite instrument. Rick had patience, even for kids like me who made no secret that we did not want to be there and put minimal practice into our craft. I had musical interests; I loved singing and pounding away on Brad's old drum set. Yet I was enrolled in piano lessons.

Late that school year, Rick organized a recital for his students, renting out a school auditorium nearby. I agreed to play "Money Can't Buy Everything" because it was the easiest song he had taught me. There would be no need to practice before the recital, I thought. I had played the song a few times with Rick sitting next to me and felt like I could handle it without that crutch.

Mom thought differently. For the week leading up to the recital, she begged, cajoled, and attempted to coerce and bribe me to practice. By the night before the recital, she was getting desperate. "Just play it one time, sweetie," she urged, squeezing my shoulder as she tried to subtly move my body from the couch situated by the TV to the piano about ten feet away.

"No!" I responded. "I don't need to. I've got this covered, Ma."

Eventually she gave up.

The recital day came, parents arriving en masse for a couple hours of torture and—if they were lucky—a few minutes of charm watching their child bang out Beethoven's symphonies. Or at least "Money Can't Buy Everything."

I spaced out for the first half-hour or so. Then, "Next up," Rick called out, "Ryan Basen will play 'Money Can't Buy Everything.' " I walked briskly to the piano in front of the crowd, already uncomfortable from having to wear a button-down shirt, sport coat, and dress shoes. But I knew that if I could handle that Hebrew school speech, I could handle this. I sat down and noticed the book was not there. Although I had surely been told it would not be, I must not have been listening. For a second or two I froze.

It was long enough for a thought to creep into Mom's head, as she sat in the crowd facing me. *It would not be the worst thing if he fucks this up*, she thought. She believed I needed to learn the value of practice and repetition, that I could not just rely on my natural talents to excel in life.

But what she had failed to recognize was that I had sports to teach me that lesson. In two years I had transformed myself from a good rec soccer goalie and pickup street hockey player inexperienced in every other sport, into a blossoming multi-sport athlete—in three other sports. In addition to team practices, I spent hours on our driveway basketball hoop honing my jump shot, watching tapes of football games to learn different receiving routes, and developing a consistent baseball swing and throw in yards and parks with Michael, Brad, my father, and friends.

I did not need a lesson in the value of practice and repetition. What I needed was to not play the piano, attend Hebrew school, or have a weekly paper route. I was barely eleven, suddenly facing multiple challenges that demanded serious attention. But I was giving them hardly any attention, in part because I was so overscheduled.

That did not matter in this moment as I sat facing the cursed instrument, the right side of my body opposing the crowd. For a second I almost panicked. Then it hit me: the first note. Followed by the second. And I was off, my natural talents carrying me to victory over the cult of piano lessons. I crushed the song, playing the last note and rising almost simultaneously. I quickly returned to my seat oblivious to any applause and went back to daydreaming.

Perhaps I thought of the O's. In late May, as we had predicted, an AL East team did go on a tear. It just was not a club anyone expected.

Instead, it was a team that had endured three straight losing seasons, posting a .356 winning percentage (135 wins and 244 losses) from early August 1986 through the end of a 1988 campaign that featured a record-setting losing streak, a team that merely flirted with .500 for forty games in 1989 while playing mostly rookies and castoffs.

That team suddenly won thirteen of their next fourteen ball games and seized firm control of the division. The run happened so fast, it started just before Memorial Day weekend and ended two weeks before the school year did. Incredibly, all but three of those fourteen games were on the road.

In a span of two weeks, Baltimore vaulted from one game out of first in a muddled division to five games clear of any other club. By early June, the Orioles were the clear frontrunner in the AL East for the first time since I had begun watching baseball seemingly so many (three) years earlier.

More than three decades later, it is still hard to explain how the O's suddenly caught fire and became a contender.

The run started with a six-game road trip to Chicago and Cleveland, with the O's 18–21 and one game behind Cleveland following that 2–0 loss to the Tribe. Baltimore took the first game against the White Sox 5–1 on May 22 behind Schmidt, never trailing before fewer than ten thousand fans at the old Comiskey Park. Schmidt held Chicago to two hits and walked nobody over seven innings; the O's staff held .340 hitter Harold Baines hitless in four at bats. Devereaux had three hits and scored the winning run in the third on Bill Ripken's sacrifice fly.

The next two games in Chicago were also laughers. Milacki was solid as the O's won the middle game 9–3, and Tibbs and Williamson combined to shut out Chicago 8–0 to complete the sweep. Baltimore was back to .500.

After a day off, the O's traveled to Cleveland and beat the Indians 5–2. Ballard and Olson combined on a seven-hitter as Baltimore moved into sole possession of first place for the first time since May 2. The O's won again the next night, 5–1. Only a walk-off 1–0 loss the next day prevented another sweep (and ruined another great Milacki start), but Baltimore stayed one game up in the standings and one game above .500.

Reporting from Cleveland, the *Post* credited the young cast-offs for a start to the season that now bordered on miraculous. On Milligan, Justice wrote: "For a couple of Class A players, the Orioles got the guy who appears to be Murray's replacement. He has not only shown power, but runs well, has performed defensively and has a personality that is a ray of sunshine in a clubhouse that resembled a morgue at times in 1988."

On Devereaux: "The Orioles love Devereaux, a young outfield flier with a quick bat who'll play more and more."

Tettleton, the *Post* noted, led all MLB catchers with ten homers and twenty-one RBIs. "You have to have some luck in this game," Robinson said of the O's acquiring Tettleton when he was outright released. "But some of that goes with giving a guy a chance. Mickey has been a steal."

All of the sudden, the surging O's joined the Mets and the NBA and NHL playoffs among regular conversations in my world. "Can you believe the Orioles are in first place?!" one of my baseball coaches asked us before one of our own games. The O's surge that week shocked and started to energize their Washington area fan base.

Nobody thought it would last.

The O's then traveled home for a good test to see if this was all real—a post–Memorial Day weekend showdown with a contending Rangers team. They promptly swept the three-game set. Finally the O's won four straight at Detroit and the first of a two-game series in New York against the Yankees. Thirteen of fourteen, just like that. The rebuilding Baltimore Orioles.

In the midst of that torrid streak, Ballard (8–1) started May 31 against the Rangers. The O's led the division by two games over second-place Boston and two and a half over third-place Cleveland as he took the mound at 7:35 to face one of the best lineups in baseball. It would be another barometer for the emerging young southpaw.

Baltimore had taken Jeff Ballard in the seventh round of the 1985 draft out of Stanford. He was the fourth player selected by the O's, who inexplicably lacked a pick until the fourth round. He was so lightly regarded that—despite being a left-handed pitcher who was only twenty-one with a few years of experience pitching in a top college conference—he was the 177th player taken overall. Guys named Tinkle (David, a high school shortstop) and another Olsson (Dan, a college pitcher) were chosen before him.

Ballard had already been drafted twice. The Brewers took him in the sixteenth round in 1981 out of Billings West High School (Montana) and the Orioles chose him in the twenty-seventh round in 1984. Both times he opted not to sign and reported to Stanford.

The six foot three Ballard did sign a pro contract after the O's drafted him again a year later and quickly rose through the Baltimore ranks. In Low-A ball he immediately won ten games with a 1.41 ERA while making thirteen starts in 1985. Ballard then made twenty-nine starts across A, AA and AAA in 1986, winning fourteen and posting a 2.53 ERA.

After posting similar stats in AAA in 1987, Ballard earned two call-ups to the O's that season. He started seven games between May 9 and June 8, but was demoted after lasting just two innings and giving up five hits against the Red Sox on June 8. Ballard returned to the O's when rosters were expanded in September, making seven more starts. But he was charged with five losses and did not earn a win during that span, finishing the 1987 season with a 2–8 record and 6.59 ERA in the majors. The control pitcher walked more batters (thirty-five) than he fanned (twenty-seven) and gave up one hundred hits in 69.2 innings.

The next season, Ballard failed to earn a rotation spot when camp broke for one of the worst teams in Major League history. While he pitched well in Triple-A, he struggled again in the majors upon being called up May 21. His ERA sat at 5.45 after his thirteenth start with the O's that season, a 9–4 loss to the Royals July 29 when he was pulled in the fourth inning after giving up five earned runs. When he lost his sixth game in seven starts against Milwaukee August 7, his ERA still sitting over 5, his confidence hit its nadir and he feared being demoted to the minors again.

The O's could have sent him down, could even have given up on him. He was a mere seventh-round pick already a few years into a pro career. He seemed ready to give up on himself, having hit a wall after his quick ascent through the minors.

But Robinson and Hemond stood by him. Robinson told a reporter that Ballard, about to turn twenty-five, "isn't going anywhere."

Ballard promptly earned complete game victories in his next two starts, holding the powerful Brewers and Athletics to a combined seven hits and one run. The first win especially, on his birthday, "really helped set the stage for me in 1989," he told Snyder for the book on the 1988 team. Ballard seized on that momentum, shocking baseball by winning his first five starts to post a perfect April (5–0, with a 1.46 ERA).

The day after he earned his fifth win in that April 30 comeback at Seattle, one of my friends clipped the "League Leaders" section from the *Post* and brought it in to school. Several of us gawked at it as we sat at our lunch table. "Jeff Ballard leads the AL in wins??" It did not seem real. We laughed, figuring it would never last. Even fifth-graders knew many April surprises soon fade. Quietly, though, I hoped this miracle would endure.

It did. After dropping his next start, he held the A's to one run over seven innings to win again May 11, then lasted at least seven innings in both of his next two starts, beating Cleveland each time. He was 8–1 with a 2.24 ERA, having issued only twelve walks over 60.1 innings. He had emerged as the unquestioned ace of a first-place team just hitting its stride.

In hindsight, it was no surprise that Ballard's performance dove-tailed with the O's hot streak. "He got on a roll like no other pitcher in baseball that season," Joe Orsulak recalled to Snyder. "It just gave the whole team confidence."

But his roll—and likely the O's season—was almost untracked before the end of May.

On May 31, Ballard shut out the Rangers for the first four innings. But in the top of the fifth, with the O's leading 3–0, Texas slugger Pete Incaviglia smashed a line drive that glanced off the left side of Ballard's neck and collarbone, knocking him down. For a split second, it seemed as if Ballard's magical season and perhaps career could be over. With him gone, there would be no way the O's could continue competing for the division title. A serious injury would also derail the rise of Baltimore's most promising young starter since Mike Boddicker's breakthrough in 1983.

But Ballard quickly rose, retrieved the ball, and threw Incaviglia out. Medical staff checked him out, but he stayed in the game, getting two more Rangers to retire the side. The O's only removed him after the inning.

The middle relief promptly gave up five runs. But, because this was the 1989 Orioles, Tettleton—Baltimore's hitting equivalent to Ballard—smashed a three-run homer in the sixth to break a 5–5 tie. Fans demanded a curtain call, with teammates pushing the reluctant, shocked Tettleton out of the dugout. Fans also tossed boxes of Fruit Loops onto the field, honoring a new tradition after Tettleton's wife had revealed during a TV broadcast earlier that week that he ate the cereal every morning. Soon Baltimore area grocery stores were selling out of it.

"The game was tied, and I'm just trying to get a base hit and put us ahead. I just can't explain how the ball keeps going out of the park," Tettleton said after the game.

Williamson and Olson combined to shut out the Rangers over the last three innings, retiring ten straight to close the game and an 8–5 victory.

After the game Ballard walked around the clubhouse with an icepack strapped around his neck. "It's amazing he wasn't hurt worse," Robinson said. "That could have been very serious."

Said Ballard: "It's not scary when it's happening, but later, when you're thinking about it, you tell yourself, 'That could have been my face.'"

A year earlier, it probably would have been. But this year, it wasn't. Ballard did not miss a start because of the Incaviglia shot, contrary to what some fans may recall. He, like his unfazed teammates, was still standing. They were quickly becoming an inspiration to the Baltimore and Washington regions.

After the game Boswell took stock: "Last year, 0–21. This year, first place, for 25 days already, in the bumbling American League East," he wrote. "Nobody associated with this team wants to get visibly excited. This is balm for old wounds, they seem to say, but not substantial, not hard-earned and surely not a thing to trust.

"Still, any fan who isn't rooting irrationally for the Orioles to stay in the hunt has a heart of stone. This is too rich to miss."

My heart was still pure, so I was now pulling hard for them.

Since division play had begun in 1969, Boswell noted, only five teams had improved their regular season win total by at least twenty-five over the previous season. The most: the 1980 Oakland A's, who won twenty-nine more games than 1979. The O's would only need to barely break .500 to set a new modern record.

That still seemed like a lofty goal, most experts posited. But already the O's were showing glimpses of a team built to contend sooner than the targeted 1992 opening of the Camden Yards stadium.

"A great deal of the radical improvement has a durable foundation. For the first time in five seasons, the Orioles are once again playing like a smart, interlocking, hustling team," Boswell wrote. Defense had become their hallmark. "Nobody has a better outfield defense. . . . Nobody has a better double-play combo than the Ripken brothers, who've become a joy. And third baseman Craig Worthington can pick it."

Offensively? "Orioles hitters aren't much good, but they know it; that's their saving grace. They'll bunt, hit and run, steal, go to the opposite field, and take extra bases. Also, they are on a pace to draw 120 more walks than in '88."

"By no means can we get caught up in this," Cal Ripken Jr. said. "We have the potential to get better and no one is smart enough to see where potential might go. But this is no time to get big-headed and think we belong here."

But by all means sportswriters and fifth-graders could get caught up in what the O's were doing.

"What if the AL East is just bad enough and the Orioles just good enough to stay in contention with this cast of kids and castoffs?" Boswell wondered.

It was almost unthinkable. It was not yet June. One of the more talented teams in the division would surely start playing better and lap the O's. But their recent strong play had some thinking that the O's may actually be legitimately good, at least good enough to win one of the four divisions in the majors—including optimistic dreamers like myself, who was now unwittingly desperate for such an enthralling distraction.

Of course I should have known better. I had already consumed massive amounts of media about the 1951 Brooklyn Dodgers, 1964 Phillies, and 1978 Red Sox—to name just a few teams that blew leads far greater and later than a few games in late May. I had also watched much of the last weekend of the 1987 regular season series between Toronto and Detroit, when the Blue Jays finished blowing a three-and-a-half-game lead with seven games to play by dropping the last three in Detroit. (Virtually the same Blue Jays team had also blown a 3–1 series lead in the 1985 ALCS to the Royals.)

Yet these Orioles would be different, I thought. They had come out of nowhere, sure, but they were good. They did play hard. They did play great defense. They were getting great seasons from unproven players, but maybe those guys just needed to play every day to enjoy success. Tettleton had been buried primarily behind Terry Steinbach in Oakland, Milligan behind Keith Hernandez and Dave Magadan with the Mets, Devereaux behind several veterans in Los Angeles.

They just kept winning as the month closed with the final game of the Texas series. They had started that series by homering three times off future Hall of Famer Nolan Ryan in a 6–1 win, then closed it by surviving the Ballard scare. As May ended, they were four games over .500 and two games ahead in the division.

As the month ended, did I still believe in miracles? Yes. Did I believe in this potential miracle? I think I needed to. Nearly four months still remained in the season. That was a lot of time for the O's to fall apart, as most people expected them to. Too late. I was now strapped in for the ride.

Throughout a month when so much in my world was coming apart, too quickly for an eleven-year-old to even try to grasp it all, baseball provided me with some solace.

That was true not just in Baltimore, but in the Washington suburbs as well. While the O's were making their shocking move to the top of the AL East standings, my youth team was playing good ball too. Like the O's, we were probably better than the sum of our parts, especially after losing our two top players from a year earlier and not adding any talent.

Those losses forced some of us to step up. Rather than filling out the bottom of the lineup and moving around between the outfield, third, and second base—as I had for most of the previous year, when I was not on the bench—this season I suddenly found myself usually hitting in the middle of the order and stationed firmly at third for every competitive inning.

It was a quick ascent. My coaches' implicit confidence in me, manifested by playing me consistently, settled me down and I enjoyed a breakthrough season, gaining confidence seemingly with every game. Just as many of the young O's started succeeding when they were given a chance to play more and were maturing as professionals, I flourished in the same fashion.

At first, my success surprised me and, for much of the season, I had trouble accepting it. One night early in the season we were playing at Dogwood Park. The lights were on and it was cool out; I loved playing in night games and was laser-focused. I was stationed at third. Two or three times in the early innings I snared sharp ground balls with my backhand, making the throw accurately to first.

Stan noticed. As we walked off the field after the third out of one of those innings, he greeted us at the dugout. "All right Ryan Basen!" he exclaimed, clapping his hands.

But I was embarrassed by the positive attention. I looked down, away, anywhere but directly at him.

A year earlier I had beamed when he awarded me game balls after a couple contests, singling me and a couple of teammates out. A few months earlier I felt overjoyed during a basketball game when I launched a "heat check" jumper that bounced in and my coach pulled back a sub, sending only four new players in. "Everyone but Ryan," he called out loud enough for the entire gym to hear.

Now, Stan's praise on this cool spring night on the diamond did not make me beam or fill me with joy. It made me uncomfortable.

I had no idea why I suddenly felt this way about public praise. And I told nobody how I felt.

This discomfort soon became a trend. A week or so after that night game, we played on another weeknight against the Lions—the other team full of Ritchie Park kids. They were 7–0. We were above

.500 and, despite our losses, knew we could hang with anyone. We relished the thought of ruining the Lions' undefeated season. There was legitimate hype for this game. We talked about it all week in school, building until the Thursday game. That day Gary, the sketchy history teacher, said aloud to a room full of us: "I understand there's a big game tonight." We worried he might attend.

After all my practice and rapid improvement, I was ready, thinking endlessly about the game right after school. My excitement built so much that I forgot to put on my hat as I dressed (though I did remember to tuck in my green jersey into my white baseball pants). Even when I saw my reflection in Mom's station wagon window as we prepared to head to Dogwood, I failed to make anything out of seeing my full head of unkempt, dark brown hair staring back at me.

Fortunately one of our backups lent me his hat and I sprinted out to third as the game started. The leadoff man for the Lions, a right-hander, fouled off the first pitch. As I ran in a couple steps to pursue the ball before pulling up, I watched it crash off the lights down the right-field line. I smirked. It seemed like an omen, and I now had an even better feeling about the game.

I was right. Everyone clicked. Our offense built a big lead and the Lions could not score. I reached base my first three times up.

In the middle innings James was up for the Lions. Our classmate and friend, he was also the fastest kid in our grade. He hit the ball hard on the ground and down the third-base line toward my right.

Since I had started following baseball, I absorbed any content I could find about the sport. That included thirty-minute highlight reels about each World Series going back a few decades airing on ESPN. So I had seen O's third baseman Brooks Robinson make dazzling play after dazzling play during the 1970 Series, including a couple incredible backhand plays. I dreamt that one day I would make plays like that.

James's smash presented such an opportunity. When I saw it veering toward third base and away from me, I reflexively dove onto the ground, extended fully and opened my glove to the ball.

It flew smack into my mitt and, without hesitating, I popped up on my knees and put everything my thin upper body had into a throw toward first. My friend Aaron scooped my one-hop toss just before James crossed the bag. "He's out!" the umpire called.

I rose to my feet as our crowd of team parents and siblings sitting behind first base erupted. Ignoring their applause, I immediately reset myself back at third to prepare for the next batter.

The Lions scored a couple of runs in the sixth and final inning, but we held on to win easily. After the game Mom let me grab something from the snack bar. As we were walking from there to her car, we passed Brett and his brother Kevin. Three years older than us, Kevin was a great athlete and somebody I looked up to. I often played on his team in vicious two-on-two basketball games at their house against Brett and Kevin's friend Mike. (Those games almost always ended with Brett and Kevin arguing and sometimes physically fighting.)

"Nice game, Basen!" Kevin called out.

I did not respond verbally. Instead I nodded softly and put my head down as we kept walking toward the car.

"Honey," Mom said, looking at me as we approached her car. "I have told you this before. When somebody gives you a compliment, you look them in the eye and say thank you."

I knew she was right. But, despite the win, despite how well I had played, despite who the compliment came from, I had a hard time accepting it. After years of often craving being the center of attention (including a few summers at theater camps), I suddenly no longer wanted to be publicly recognized.

I still did not know why. Yet I still refused to tell anyone about how I felt—not even Mom.

I looked away from her and climbed into the front seat, flipping on Q107 in silence.

Despite the brutal seeds planted in May, thanks to baseball the month ended for me on an upswing, just as it had for the O's.

By the end of our rec team's regular season, I was a confident everyday starter on a good club. Still, I had never hit a legitimate home run. At this stage that usually meant hitting the ball over everyone's heads and racing around the bases for an inside-the-park homer.

One weekday afternoon we were playing Rockville Mailing Service at Monument Park. In the middle innings I took a pitch on the outside part of the plate and crushed it into right-center. I could see the center fielder with his back turned racing after the ball as I rounded first. Sensing my opportunity, I began sprinting around the bases. Our third-base coach waived me around and I crossed the plate standing up as the throw came in late to their catcher, sealing my first legit homer.

Our bench erupted and embraced me, just as Mom and Tyler walked up to the bleachers. ("I heard lots of yelling and I saw your body running around the bases," she told me later. "I knew something good had happened.")

We built a large lead. Toward the end of the game, the coaches pulled me and a few other starters for the last inning. At first I was upset. I did the math in my head: I had played in nearly sixty straight innings at third. Now I was watching somebody else play my position for my team. For a few moments I felt some resentment, even though I recognized the only reason I was pulled was because it was a blowout.

Aaron and a few other usual starters were on the bench with me. No longer worried about the outcome of the game, we were not concerned with boosting teammates and were too hyper to ever sit anywhere quietly together. As each Rockville Mailing Service player walked past us into the on-deck circle, we asked him: "Who's up?" Each time, the foolish kid responded with an honest answer. After giggling with delight that these kids would volunteer such information so easily, we took to riding their batters. We were savvy enough not to directly insult them, so instead we showered them with support. Kind of.

"Come on Brady, be a hitter!" Aaron yelled to one kid, eliciting a fresh round of laughs from our bench mob.

"Let's go Bobby, let's go," we sang in unison, as another Mailing Service hitter walked up to the plate.

Bobby was thrown, turning and looking toward us in surprise.

It was not the classiest half-inning of our season, but one I relished anyway. I felt like I had made it. After two-plus years of chasing my friends to get to their level athletically, especially in baseball, I was there. I was not the best player on our team, but that was never my goal. I had wanted merely to earn their respect and contribute on a winning team. So I was perfectly content smashing a legit homer and goofing off with my teammates while we let a win sink in.

In those minutes with the blowout bench mob, I thought nothing of Freddy, MomMom Flick, the impending new school, or the odd way I was suddenly feeling about receiving public attention. I certainly did not recall the Hebrew school panic attack.

I was in my safe place, around baseball. As my life continued down strange new paths, I needed it. But how long could it carry me?

With Michael and Brad on the blacktop behind Ritchie Park Elementary School in Rockville, Md., after my graduation ceremony. That tie was unloosened the second the ceremony ended.

Chapter 5

JUNE: "IT'S ONLY JUNE"

hile Baltimore's late-spring surge was captivating the region and keeping alive my belief in sports miracles, as June began I was simultaneously forced to stop believing in another miracle: the power of Grayskull.

In early June, Mom hosted a garage sale one weekend. She sold off furniture, as well as old toys belonging to Michael and me. Every He-Man and Transformers action figure disappeared from bins in the basement and ended up on tables on our driveway, as other parents descended like hungry hawks hunting bargains.

I had not played with these toys in a few years, since I had dumped them for sports cards and video games, so I felt little sentimental value toward them. Like most of my clothes by the end of every summer, I had outgrown them, so I barely cared to see them discarded.

But there was one exception: Castle Grayskull. He-Man's power source had once been among my most treasured possessions. Now Mom just wanted to dump it on some child who could not possibly appreciate such an impressive structure from a show that had been off-air for a couple of years.

"Mmmmmaaaaahhhhhhhm!" I pressed her upon seeing the great, though chafed, castle sitting on a table with the price tag: $10. "You cannot sell Castle Grayskull!"

"Honey, you haven't played with this in a few years."

Mom had quickly and skillfully put me in a bind: Either I could raise a fuss and reveal that I wanted to keep a toy that I last played with when I still wore Underoos, or I could bite my lip and pretend I was mature enough to let my favorite childhood toy go.

Mom had already unwittingly steered me toward a choice by patronizing me earlier that morning. As Steve and I attempted to dash through the kitchen past her to enjoy a sunny June Saturday, she pulled out our class picture from kindergarten and showed it to us. "Humor me for a second Stephen," she said. My heart sank. "I was just going through old stuff getting ready for our garage sale and I found this. I forgot how cute you guys were!" She held up the eight-by-eleven-inch photo for him to see.

I shot back the moment I heard the word cute: "Mom!"

Steve chuckled and smiled uncomfortably.

Now, as I faced losing Castle Grayskull, the goofy, sweet child still very much alive in me caved to the nascent adolescent who hated being called cute. I gave up the argument. Castle Grayskull sold that day, as did all my He-Man and Transformer action figures.

The whole experience went from bad to worse when Mom gave me a share of the revenue she had generated from slinging our stuff. Michael had helped her for much of the weekend, ever the dutiful son. I skipped town—or at least the sale—most of the weekend to hang out with friends and play in my baseball game. She had promised us each a portion of the sales, hoping to encourage us to help. The tactic worked on Michael, but not on me. Most of the toys she sold were mine, but when she handed me an envelope full of bills, I noticed there was only $23 in there. Michael got $24.

I was furious. "How come Michael got more than me?!" I loudly complained, standing on the steps of the basement and looking up a couple of steps at Mom.

"Because he actually helped out. You didn't help at all. You should consider yourself lucky you're getting anything."

I did not. Instead I felt intense jealousy and anger. I forgot all about Castle Grayskull.

My baseball season continued and about a week later, we won another game. It was a Saturday afternoon at Monument Park. The win kept us right in the middle of the postseason standings (only sixteen of the twenty or so teams in the league qualified).

After the game, my teammates and I sat on the bench for the usual post-game talk. I could see that Stan was holding a small piece of loose-leaf paper in his hand. On it he had written a few names in black Sharpie. Because the ink had bled through the papper, I could read the names backwards (my Hebrew school training was good for something, it seemed).

I figured out four names and recognized what this list was. It featured the names of our three clear top players: Brett, Ross, and Pete. It also featured the name of another top player—but not mine. My heart and my head sank as I pretended that I had not deciphered the notebook paper and continued listening to Stan.

"All-stars for this season," Stan raised his voice, as if I did not know. He read off the names one by one. I was too upset to notice anyone's reaction, too focused on controlling the storm that had suddenly started brewing inside me. I felt like I had earned a spot, even if it was razor thin between me and the fourth player named to the team. Missing out was proving too much for me to handle emotionally, even if being selected for the game was not within my wildest imagination when the season started. I bit hard on my lip, squeezing my glove and looking down as I waited for Stan to finish.

After he read off the last name, our coaches congratulated the all-stars. Our parents then slowly converged on us as we walked up the hill toward them, their cars parked in rows behind them on this warm sunny afternoon. I said goodbye to nobody, turning and walking briskly toward Mom. She greeted me with a big smile, expecting me to be in a good mood after a win.

"Just go!" I barked at her, motioning toward the car. "Walk!"

Her expression quickly turned to one of concern and surprise—the large, oval, hazel eyes she had passed down to me now fixed on me. Her smile flattened. "What? What's wrong?" she wondered.

"Just get in the car!" I growled under my breath, trying not to draw attention to us while holding in an emotional hurricane that was swirling toward some swift conclusion.

Finally I made it inside the station wagon, climbing into the passenger seat as Mom hopped into the driver's seat. As we shut our doors, a cascade of tears started flowing out of me.

Mom was really concerned now. While spontaneous crying had been routine for much of my childhood (in private at least), by fifth grade it was very uncommon and never happened in public. I had learned the crying game rules and was doing my best to follow them. One of them: Crying in sports was only permitted in response to team results.

Mom kept looking at me, speechless as I stuttered while trying to explain why I was bawling after winning a baseball game on a team full of my friends on a Saturday afternoon in June.

"F-f-f-ffucking all . . . all-stars . . ." was all I could get out at first.

In between sobs I tried to explain the rest as I put my head down, too ashamed by my emotional display to even look at my own mother as I kept sniffling and tears continued streaming down my cheeks.

Eventually she figured out what was wrong, turned on the ignition, and drove us home. "Honey, you've had a great season," she said at one point. "You can't let one decision take away from that."

She was right. But for the duration of that ten-minute drive home, our team's success was of little solace to me. Plus this was sports, and my main confidant was there sitting right next to me. While I knew I could not cry in front of my friends that afternoon, I dealt with the massive disappointment with Mom literally at my side. We may have been gradually growing apart, but that afternoon at least, we were still very much attached.

Then, one weeknight as the school year wound down, I was sitting on the floor of my bedroom doing homework. Freddy sat next to me curled up on a sheet of composition paper I had ripped out for him, as Q107 blared from my clock radio. I sang along as I raced through a worksheet.

The door was wide open as Mom walked in. "I have some good news and some bad news," she said. "The bad news is that Peter is injured and is going to miss the rest of the baseball season. The good news is that they picked you to replace him in the all-star game."

Any concern I had for Pete's health or our team's chances in the postseason without him quickly dissipated when I heard her say I was on the all-star team. At this point I hardly cared about playing in the game itself; the recognition from our coaches had me beaming inside.

I must have been beaming on the outside too. "I figured you would be excited about that," Mom said, smiling.

A week or so later, Dogwood Park hosted our all-star game on a warm, sunny weeknight. We would be playing under the lights again, the sun setting early in the game. I made sure Mom got me there early, dropping me off just as the first bunch of kids arrived.

The highlight of my night came at the plate. I stepped up in my first at bat with runners on second and third. The pitcher was way off on the first three pitches, giving me nothing to even ponder swinging at. With a 3–0 count, I was content taking a walk and getting on base. The next pitch came in low and tailing away, landing in the dirt off the plate.

"Steeeriiike" yelled the umpire.

It was a brutal call. There was no way I could have hit the pitch. I was pissed, but I had little time to bristle. Instead I stepped out of the batter's box, took a practice swing, and stepped back in.

The next pitch was in the actual strike zone. I swung and hit a sharp ground ball up the middle, took off for first and immediately heard cheering. As I approached first I looked up and saw a teammate rounding third. Excited, I slowed my pace and watched to see if he would score.

"Come on!" our first base coach yelled. "Get two!"

Snapping out of my trance, I returned to a sprint and rounded first. By then the center fielder had fielded the ball and thrown to his cutoff man, who was holding on to it. The first base coach barked at me to get back to the bag, and quick. "If you had been paying attention, you could have made it to second," the coach yelled.

I tried to ignore him and savor my hit. Single? Double? I could not have cared less. I had just notched a hit in the all-star game and driven in two runs. I was plenty satisfied. Baseball's role as my solace was only growing.

The ensuing week was it: our final one of elementary school. After six years at the same school, my classmates and I had our last days together. I was too excited about the impending end of a school year to relish what I knew would be my last days attending school with my close friends—at least through middle school. (Mom had left open the chance to return to public school in high school.)

On Saturday, I prepared for a graduation party organized by several parents. Mom had volunteered to help and was charged with getting prizes for some contests. She figured a local radio station might donate to our cause. "Which station should I call?" she asked me one day.

"Q107!"

"What should I ask for."

"New Kids. Bobby Brown. Tone Loc. Um . . ." I stammered to think of anything else. Music was still a couple years off from becoming one of my things.

The party fittingly was at Corner Kick, an indoor soccer complex about a ten-minute drive north near Gaithersburg. This event would serve as the capstone to one era of our lives, even if many of us still thought of "ERA" only as "earned run average." I had attended countless birthday parties at Corner Kick, and Mom had even hosted my father's surprise fortieth birthday party there a year earlier, renting out the facility on a Saturday night and dividing guests into four teams to play pickup games.

I dressed in my nicest T-shirt—an aqua Ocean Pacific variety—clean, unripped dark gray mesh shorts, and white Nike sneakers with black trim and a black swoosh. As I was getting ready, I saw my father putting on his shoes too in the kitchen. "What are you doing?" I asked.

"What do you mean? I'm coming."

My heart sank a bit. A party with my entire grade was right up Mom's alley; she had spent hours over the past six years volunteering in our library and on field trips, sitting through dozens of games with other parents. While my father was often a fixture at my games, he was safely in the stands and implicitly discouraged from interacting with any of my teammates. That was good because most of my friends were afraid of him and I worried that he might embarrass me.

But he did not on this night. I forgot my father was even around as soon as I got there. I ran around like a sugared-up maniac and danced up against a net while standing on top of the boards. We ate pizza and got royal blue T-shirts with our signatures ironed over a big, bold '89 in white lettering. Ross' Mom handed out buttons that read "I survived Ritchie Park," which my Mom did not find amusing.

We also played elimination Newcomb ball, with me and most of my friends on one team. It came down to me on our side and a classmate on the other. When I released a throw with a high arc and eliminated her, I raised my arms in unfiltered joy and let out a high-pitched primal scream. My friends also rejoiced, sprinting from the sideline to mob me and briefly hoisting me on their shoulders to celebrate.

Could I really move on without them?

It was almost summer. I was so excited that night, I completely forgot that I would not be going with most of them to Julius West. When the next school year started, one friend told me years later, "It was like you just suddenly were not there."

The O's kicked off June by winning a game on each of the first five days of the month, capping off their thirteen-of-fourteen stretch to improve to 31–22. They started the month with four games in Detroit, against a Tigers team a few games under .500 but just one full season removed from their second division title in four years. Worthington was out with a pulled hamstring, while Milligan sat with a sore right hand after being struck by a pitch. Gonzales replaced Worthington at third, Traber Milligan at first. Not much was expected of the offense.

But Traber promptly blasted a three-run homer and the light-hitting Gonzales a solo shot, as the O's won 8–3 in the opener. Milacki held the Tigers to two hits over eight and one-third innings the next night as the O's won 4–1. The O's won again the next day 4–2, with Traber driving in the winning run in the eighth, then completed the sweep when Milligan returned to the lineup and bashed a three-run homer to key a 7–4 win.

The final O's win during this torrid stretch was the next day at Yankee Stadium on June 5. That Monday night Ballard faced a Yankee team that had fallen from just one-half game out of first on May 21 to six games behind the Orioles.

Ballard faced a lineup including all-stars in outfielder Rickey Henderson, second baseman Steve Sax, and first baseman Don Mattingly. Andy Hawkins started for New York. The O's scored three in the first and added eight in the third, taking an 11–0 lead. Baltimore cruised 16–3, with Ballard improving to 9–1 despite issuing an uncharacteristic six walks and giving up nine hits over seven innings. "Moons and stars continue to align for the Baby Birds, who've made some breaks and gotten some breaks to win eight games in a row and sixteen of nineteen," the *Post* wrote.

The O's owned the best road mark in the majors (17–11) and were already just three wins shy of their road win total for all of 1988.

"It was never their intention to put together a division champion in 1989," Justice wrote in the *Post* the next day. "Their goal in 1989 was to be respectable, to throw a dozen or so youngsters out and hope they could find two or three who would stick around. . . . They wanted a team built around defense and pitching, because as Hemond said, 'That's the fastest way to improve. None of us ever guessed we'd get these results.' "

"I thought all along the talent was here, Robinson said. "The only thing they were lacking was Major League experience and a track record. What I couldn't imagine is how quickly it would come together."

Things were indeed changing fast. This team that had only become a regional fascination a week or so earlier was now a national story. *Sports Illustrated* dispatched veteran writer Steve Wulf to catch up with them that week, as the O's stretched their division lead a full one-third into the season. Tettleton was leading the AL in homers (sixteen) and Ballard almost had ten wins already. Even as the NBA Finals kicked off, a fierce four-team battle raged for the AL West crown and the nationally beloved Cubs were a surprise leader in the NL East, the surging O's were a story too rich for the country's preeminent sports magazine to ignore.

I felt excitement and pride as I read the table of contents and spotted Wulf's article in the issue that arrived in our mailbox the following Thursday. Despite an uneven week (losing three of four after the June 5 bloodbath in New York), the O's were still four games up in the AL East and preparing to host the Yankees on the final Thursday of the school year as I tore through all 2,083 words.

The piece was titled "O You Beautiful Birds," with the headline in bold white lettering superimposed over a picture of Finley running down a drive at the fence in Memorial Stadium. With sections on "The Surprises" (including Olson and Tettleton), "The Ripkens," and "The Brain Trust" of hitting coach Tom McCraw, Robinson, and pitching coach Al Jackson, the piece was interrupted only by full-page ads for Guinness, the new Subaru Legacy, and Vantage Ultra Lights cigarettes.

"The shocking, sensational and unbelievable success of a team that lost 107 games last year is attributable in part to the fact that this season the American League Least is, well, the reason birdcages are lined with newspapers. Baltimore went 2–4 last week and lost only one game to its pursuers. However, the O's would be in the hunt in every other division, too," Wulf wrote.

The piece shared details explaining how the O's were orchestrating their turnaround. They had mined the Mets' deep reservoir of coaches to hire both McCraw and Jackson. Jackson persuaded Ballard to shift more to finesses pitching, helping him develop a sinking fastball, and taught him to position his right leg slightly closer to third base to throw more strikes with his fastball.

Jackson and McCraw were Black coaches, Wulf noted, and Robinson was a Black manager. This likely gave the O's an edge. A decade after he became baseball's first Black manager, Robinson was still managing during an era when most other teams eschewed Black coaches and managers regardless of merit. "The Orioles have almost as many Black managers and coaches in their minor league system," Wulf wrote, "as some teams have had in their entire histories." Robinson was also one of the first managers to leverage the fax machine, securing updated reports from the team's advance scouts.

Then there was the fact that many of these O's were, like my friends and I, still kids going through life with limited concern. Security was called to the hotel room in New York where Olson was rooming with Traber one night in early June "to investigate a disturbance," Wulf wrote. They found Olson and Traber shouting as they played the video game *Gauntlet*.

"Good mental training for the pennant race," Olson had quipped to Wulf.

Wulf also spoke to Cal Ripken, who had signed an extension with the club during the awful 1988 campaign. "I re-signed because I love this organization, and I felt that eventually we would be back, though not this soon, certainly," Ripken said. "Remember, though, it's only June."

Only June?

That meant the season was almost halfway over. I was used to baseball being my prime obsession in June, but usually it was the Mets we were all following closely because the O's were already out of contention. This year, that the O's were also in a division race when it was "only June" seemed incredible.

But throughout a childhood where so much had gone well, it also seemed fitting. June was also my favorite month—when school let out and we spent hours unsupervised at the creek and on the basketball and tennis courts at our nearby swim club before we started attending organized camps. I typically spent the rest of this downtime studying the *Post* sports section and *SI*, and watching full episodes of *SportsCenter*. It was bliss.

This annual June experience combined with Baltimore's sudden contention probably made it easy for me to reflexively ignore my burgeoning problems swirling beneath the surface. But there they remained, with no hint of disappearing: My grandmother's illness, my impending school change, Freddy's health problems, and my nascent anxiety disorders. Not to mention the advent of my adolescence and all that comes with that.

How long could baseball prevent me from having to confront these issues?

Perhaps, for the rest of the 1989 season, at least. Even as they flew to the top of the standings and stayed there for a while, the O's still seemed shy of peaking. As much as any other team, they were primed for late-season reinforcements who figured to contribute.

The same day that Ballard shut down the Yankees in the Bronx, the O's made their most anticipated off-field move in years. With the top pick in the amateur draft, they selected right-handed pitcher Ben McDonald, "one of the most highly regarded pitching prospects in history," the *Post* wrote, "who at twenty-one has been compared to Dwight Gooden and Roger Clemens because of his ninety-five-mph fastball, knee-buckling curveball and major league poise."

Clemens and Gooden had established themselves as the top power pitchers of their generation. Skip Bertman, McDonald's coach at LSU, noted he had seen Clemens, Frank Viola, and fellow All-Star Greg Swindell pitch in college. "At this point Ben is ahead of all of them," he said.

Most draft picks, even top college players, spent at least July and August in the minor leagues, maybe enjoying a September call-up. So they rarely helped their teams that season. But McDonald, according to reports, was different. "It's a near-certainty he will pitch in the major leagues at some point this summer," the *Post* noted.

How hyped was McDonald? The buzz around him regarding pitchers would perhaps only be rivaled twenty years later, when the Washington Nationals selected Stephen Strasburg out of San Diego State with the first pick.

McDonald provided yet another young arm to add to the O's developing arsenal. And it seemed that—like Harnisch, Schilling, and Milacki—he would be ready to help the O's in September, after rosters expanded to forty players. Maybe they would still be battling for the AL East title then.

Drafting McDonald only added to the excitement around the O's. Adding the most hyped pitching prospect in years figured to only help a rebuilding cause that was starting to look like a one-year project. They were now getting the attention of baseball fans and others in Washington. While the O's were a nice sports story, they were becoming a cultural phenomenon in the area as well.

For the second half of the 1980s at least, the O's had been everyone's second favorite team—the team we rooted for, but not that hard, then stopped paying attention to when they were out of the race. They were the team whose games we attended to watch Cal Ripken and Eddie Murray play, and because they were the only Major League team within a short drive of the metro area.

Not in 1989. Over the first twenty-five home games, attendance was up 11 percent over 1988, for example. The *Post* ran an account of their rise on the front of the metro section June 10: "This spirit has carried over to the Washington area as well," *The Post* reported. Sales at the Orioles-branded team store in Farragut Square downtown were up 35 percent. " 'We've had lines out the door in the last few days,' " the store's manager told a reporter.

The team that had been aggressively marketed to the Washington area by former owner Edward Bennett Williams throughout the 1980s had finally captured the region. It seemed like everyone was flipping; now the O's were our favorite team, with the Mets and Cubs and Red Sox relegated to second-favorite status.

For many of us, glued to every Ballard start and Tettleton plate appearance, it was now too late to turn back. Baseball fever had gripped the area for the first time since I had started following the sport. The O's became a frequent conversation topic at my baseball practices, school, and the pool; Fruit Loops boxes and "Comeback Kids" banners were visible at packed home games, and one local TV station even cut a bit of Tettleton singing the hook to an old song about Yankees Hall of Famer Mickey Mantle ("I Love Mickey").

It was intoxicating.

But it was still "only June."

While the O's had captured hearts, especially the young ones, all over the Washington and Baltimore regions, the team still had plenty of doubters elsewhere. The middle of the month thus presented a litmus test, with four games in Baltimore against the powerful Athletics. Oakland entered this weekend series leading the AL West with the best record in baseball. The O's were five games up on second-place New York, at 34–27, after walking off the Yankees 3–2 at home Thursday night on a Gonzales single in the tenth. (Tettleton scored the winning run after doubling to lead off the inning.) They had not lost any ground in the standings since June 5 despite a 3–5 stretch.

The clubs opened the series splitting a doubleheader on Friday, June 16. Baltimore took the second game 5–1, and over the course of the day won over Tony LaRussa, who had guided the A's and White Sox to division titles already in the 1980s. "The Orioles are a legitimate team. They will be in the division race [for the long haul]," LaRussa said after the game.

The next day, they played an afternoon tilt before a national audience on NBC. It was the first "Game of the Week" broadcast from Baltimore in three years; in the final year before ESPN regularly gave viewers more than one or two national broadcasts a week, that meant something. The "Boys of Wonder" were getting more national exposure.

(The 1989 season served not only as the unofficial end of a baseball media era, but also the last season before the money in the game really exploded. As a *Post* staff writer named Malcolm Gladwell put it in a business section feature published July 17: "This year, the team [Baltimore] is making about $9 million as its share of a national television deal between major league baseball and the ABC and NBC networks. But a new blockbuster contract with CBS and cable sports channel ESPN that goes into effect next year will increase the Orioles' share of network TV revenue to $14 million a year—enough by itself to more than cover the team's major league payroll.")

The game did not disappoint. Bautista, Williamson and Olson combined to shut out the A's over the last eight innings. Bradley drove in three runs with doubles in the third and fourth, and Baltimore won 4–2.

It was not quite the midway point, but this miracle season was starting to seem very real.

Everything I had consumed about baseball told me that a four-game lead in mid-June meant very little.

But history would not ruin this moment for me. I was not thinking about collapses. I still had dreams, big ones, and not just for this baseball team. If I could be anything I wanted to be when I grew up, as I was frequently told by many adults in my orbit, why couldn't the Baltimore Orioles go from losing more than one hundred games with proven veterans, to winning a seven-team division the very next year with a bunch of rookies and castoffs? After all, while I knew all about the 1951 Dodgers, 1978 Red Sox, and 1987 Blue Jays, I also was well-versed in the stories of the "Impossible Dream" 1967 Red Sox, the "Miracle Mets" of 1969, and the "Miracle on Ice" (the 1980 US men's Olympic hockey team). In short, I believed. Each win only reinforced that belief.

The O's and A's were due to meet again the next day to close the series. At some point that spring my parents had promised to take us to a regular season game. We picked the game as a family: Sunday, June 18. It checked all the boxes—Father's Day, a day game so we would not have to rush home early (unless my father wanted to beat the traffic), and the opponents were the mighty Oakland A's.

I circled the date in my head for weeks, again promised that we would go early so I could hover over the Oakland dugout; flash my dimple, shiny new braces, and doe eyes; and beg Oakland's star-laden lineup for autographs.

Maybe a month before the game, one of the shul's rabbis came to our Hebrew school class one afternoon and handed out fliers advertising a synagogue get-together. I looked at the flyer: "An outing at the ballpark," it read, replete with Orioles' game tickets, a chartered bus to Baltimore directly from the synagogue and brunch at the synagogue banquet hall before the game. It was as if somebody (our rabbi) really wanted to go to an O's game and concocted a plan to get approval from his wife. What congregants could resist this?

The date: "Father's Day."

"Oh!" I shouted roughly one-tenth of a second after processing the flyer, and probably a full second before raising my hand. "My family is already going to this game."

"Well maybe you could join us," the rabbi retorted.

I scowled. Upon returning home, I tossed the flyer into the trash—the typical destination for any handout I received in Hebrew school. I thought nothing of it.

Until Michael pulled the flyer out of his bookbag to show Mom.

"But we are already going to this game," I asserted, standing in the kitchen with them hovering over the flyer, which Michael had placed on a table.

"Well I think it could be fun to go with the synagogue," Mom responded. "Plus then Dad won't have to drive."

(My father not driving us to an O's game meant the family being spared roughly two hours of cussing and shouting, round-trip. That only seemed to affect Mom, who helped him navigate and calmed him down after somebody would suddenly yank their Volvo station wagon in front of his car on Charles Street. Michael and I sat in the back, listening to our Walkmans and reading, mostly oblivious to his ranting, or so we thought. It was only when we got older that we recognized the road rage he passed down to us.)

I was aghast. "I don't want to go with the synagogue! That sounds really lame! Plus you promised we could get there early for autographs. and they have a stupid brunch before the game!"

The flyer stated the brunch would start at ten. I did the math. No way my family alone could eat brunch and get inside that stadium for a little autograph time before the one-thirty start. Throw in a large group of congregants and buses, as opposed to my father's aggressive driving and knowledge of shortcuts through inner-city Baltimore . . .

"Let me talk to Dad," Mom responded. It was a deflection, her way of quickly punting on a confrontation and buying time. She knew I would not forget this unresolved argument.

But a little while later she informed me we would indeed be taking the synagogue trip, with Brad and his parents. Forget about Michael and me or Brad. This was what my parents and my aunt and uncle wanted: to engage with the synagogue community while spending time with their children and nephews, all under the guise of taking us to an O's game.

I was pissed, but I eventually came to terms with the notion that I would not be getting any autographs that day either. At least I would be attending a marquee game between the AL's two division leaders, the first time I would see these surprising Orioles during the regular season live.

I awoke on game day, the day after my graduation party, packing my Walkman and a few cassettes into my backpack, and donned my new black Orioles hat with the team's new logo that I had received as an early graduation gift.

Brunch was brutal. Sitting with my family at a table inside the auditorium, I ate quickly and then squirmed as I watched the time tick by while my congregation did what it did best: kibbitzed and dawdled. "We are going to be late," I said loudly, to nobody in partic-ular. "Why can't we take this food to go?"

The outing's organizers eventually called for attention, standing by a microphone at the front of the room. I assumed we would be getting dismissed to jump onto the buses and head to the game, stat. I felt unquenchable impatience, tapping the table with my fingers furiously. Then an organizer had the gall to launch into a speech. He thanked every-body for coming, discussing the virtue of communitas and promoting other upcoming synagogue events. This was clearly going to take a while.

I audibly groaned, placed my chin on the table, and stared a hole through my mother. After a few minutes, I was losing it. "Let's go already," I said loud enough for several tables to hear.

Finally, after what seemed like hours, the self-minted emcee began dismissing us by table to ascend two large buses parked in front. I looked at my watch: 12:15. Forget the O's winning the division; it was going to take a miracle just for our congregation in the Washington suburbs to get to the stadium and walk to our seats by game time.

We made good time until we could see the stadium ahead. But then, as always happened when we arrived at any contest around gametime, we hit traffic. For a while we did not move at all. I saw people walking to the stadium pass us by, strolling up the sidewalks of Thirty-Third Street in the city's Waverly district as we sat, the ballpark now taunting me in faint view a few blocks ahead.

I stared out the window as people briskly kept walking past us. "Can we just get out and walk," I asked Mom loudly, speaking over the song playing on my Walkman.

"Just try to be patient," she responded, looking away from me, her own patience starting to wear thin.

Finally we arrived at the stadium and got to our upper-level seats along the right-field line in time to see the Orioles hit in the bottom of the first. They loaded the bases without notching a hit, with two out against Oakland starter Curt Young. Melvin stepped up, launching a deep fly ball into right-center field. We rose and watched as the ball arced toward the gap, with Oakland outfielders Stan Javier and Steinbach turning their backs to pursue it. The ball dropped over their heads, clearing the bases. The O's led 3–0.

That lead stood up as Schmidt and reliever Mickey Weston combined to hold Oakland to four hits over the first eight innings. Late in the game I heard fans sitting behind us kvetch that they had arrived after the first, missing the game's only real drama.

(In the eighth, Weston retired a pinch-hitter on a groundout to Worthington at third for the second out. The pinch-hitter, a utility player who usually caught, stayed in the game and played third in the bottom of the inning. His name: Jamie Quirk. Remember that name.)

The O's still had to get through the top of the ninth and Olson had already made four appearances that week, including the day before. So we stood, clapped and prodded as Weston took the mound again to start the ninth, with Baltimore ahead 4–2. The journeyman had just been called up from Triple-A Rochester.

He needed only seven pitches to retire Javier, Dave Parker, and Mark McGwire. Billy Ripken was the star of the inning. First he made the play on Javier, then "Ripken sprinted behind the mound for Dave Parker's grounder, and, in one motion, bare-handed the ball and threw toward first as he was falling away," the *Post* reported. Milligan squeezed his throw for the out. When Devereaux then caught McGwire's fly ball in dead center, the crowd of more than forty-six thousand roared.

The O's had taken three of four games from the mighty Oakland A's. Just as they had swept the contending Rangers at the end of May, they had again proved they could hang with the AL's contenders.

I was so thrilled, I forgot all about missing out on autographs again.

The win stretched Baltimore's division lead back to five games after the Yankees simultaneously lost to Texas. The O's took flight to Seattle for seven games in seven days against the Mariners and Angels.

The next day marked the end of a major chapter in my childhood, a true ridge point in my life. That day we officially graduated from Ritchie Park. I wore a light dress shirt, dark brown sports coat, matching pants, and a dark tie. When Mom dropped me off, getting there early to jostle with other parents for prime seating, I walked to the blacktop behind the school and quickly found my friends.

It did not occur to me that this would be the last time we would all be together, after most of us had hardly been separated for six years. We studied each other's clothing. We had rarely seen one another dressed in any tier above sweatpants or shorts; Ross was the only one who even regularly wore jeans. Brett looked at me and said, "Basen, you and I must be the most uncomfortable right now."

I nodded. "I can't wait to change later."

After the ceremony in the gym, we walked back outside to the blacktop where I had played in hundreds of recess football and basketball games over the years, posing for pictures with family. I smiled some; Mom smiled wider.

The next day we had to return for the last official day of the school year. At the end of the day we raced down the stairs, our backpacks popping up and down on our shoulders as we made the mad dash out of the school building as Ritchie Park students one final time. Kevin was at the bottom of the staircase, I assumed to fetch Brett.

"Basen! No more Ritchie Park!" he yelled, high-fiving me as I ran down the final few stairs.

I ran outside and jumped on my dirt bike, which was resting on the rack in front of the school, did not wait for my usual crew, and pedaled as fast as I could home. I timed myself on a portable speedometer/timer fastened to the handlebar. As I pulled into the garage, I found Mom tidying up and looked up at her. "Mom!" I said, my voice rising with excitement. "I made it back in only three minutes!"

If I had known how much and how quickly my life was going to change, I would have pedaled much more slowly.

Bittersweet endings continued that week. A few days after graduating, our baseball team got a rematch against Optimist in the playoffs. We both had 9–5 records after playing to that near tie. Nobody on our team complained that, had we beaten them earlier, we would have finished 10–4 and drawn an easier first-round opponent. We wanted Optimist.

This time we were missing Pete, our cleanup hitter and a sure-handed fielder who could play multiple positions. But I was confident nonetheless. The game was at Potomac Woods. It was another Saturday afternoon at my home ballpark, potentially my final game there after three years if we lost.

Again the game was oddly low-scoring. No margin for error. In the middle innings Optimist had a runner or two on base. I was anchored at third, crouching with the pitch. The Optimist batter hit a hard shot on the ground to my right. It would be a tough play, but after making so many back-handed snares during the season, I thought I would make it.

I instinctively dove to my right, keeping the ball in my sights as I watched it career toward the bag. I dipped my left knee into the ground, extended my left hand toward the ball and placed my glove on the ground just as the ball arrived.

I really thought I had it.

To this day I am not sure how that ball eluded me, but it did, skipping into the outfield. My heart sank as I heard the crowd behind the Optimist bench erupt, hollering for their players to circle the bases. I quickly rose to my feet and covered the bag. There would be time to mourn missing the grounder later (plenty, it turns out), but not at that moment.

Optimist scored at least one run on that play. We scored the same number of runs as we did the first time we played them. Again, it would not be enough, as we lost 5–3.

After the game our coaches and parents said all the politically correct things: what a great season we had had, nearly doubling our win total from a season ago (and after losing our top two players); how hard we had worked; how enjoyable we had been to coach. To a boy, we pretended we were not too upset with the loss.

But this enjoyable season had come to a rather sudden end, one victory shy of our goal of winning at least one playoff game. I did not feel like crying this time, possibly because I was in shock. As I walked home—and several more times over the next thirty years—I replayed that hit in my head: How did that ball get under my glove? If I had made the play, would we have won? ("Mr. Destiny" has not visited me, so I never have found out.)

I would need to learn to let things go someday, but it would not happen on this afternoon.

I scarcely had time to process this loss because about a week later, everything froze—it was as if Zack Morris called a timeout on my life. One Sunday morning, I boarded a bus and headed to a place where we would have no access to game broadcasts or *Sportscenter* highlights, *Sports Illustrated*, or any media beyond scrambled AM radio stations. I would be separated from most of my friends and family in a location where I had never been.

During previous summers, Michael and I, our friends, and Brad had spent hours following the baseball season, watching games every night after day camp or unscheduled weekend days. Not so for much of this summer. Instead we left for sleepaway camp—the first time Michael and I would be going, the first time I would be away from Mom, my friends, Freddy, and Tyler for more than a couple of days. Our destination: Capital Camp, a Jewish camp a few hours away by bus.

I was not at all looking forward to it, so much so that my denial about attending this camp was almost as powerful as it was about starting a new school in the fall. Before we left for camp, Mom implored me to help pack for myself. I chose two or three pairs of sneakers, including my favorite: a pair of white Nikes with red trim and a bright red swoosh. I also packed a couple of baseball caps, including my new O's cap, my Walkman, and a few tapes. Finally I grabbed the most recent issue of *Sports Illustrated*. (Mom promised to mail every new *SI* as it arrived and often sent Sunday *Post* sports sections too.) Otherwise I put little thought into packing, confident Mom could handle the rest.

She was more than up to the task. Parents were encouraged to label their kids' clothing, so other kids did not take them. Most parents took black Sharpies and wrote their child's last name or initials on the white tags fastened to shirts, shorts, and underwear. Mom went further. On every item of clothing I took to camp, save for socks, she fastened a paper label. And "Ryan N. Basen" was printed in dark red font all over my clothing tags. Her efforts accomplished their desired effect.

Most of the time, at least. One kid, Zvi, must have swiped a pair of my underwear when our bunk's laundry was returned one week. He was busted when we were playing cards one night, lying on our stomachs in the all-purpose room and facing each other in a circle. I noticed his underwear sticking out over his shorts. He had folded the elastic waistband to fit his even scrawnier body, revealing the label.

"Dude, why are you wearing my underwear?" I called out.

"I'm not."

"Yes you are! I can see my name right on them!"

Witnessing a bunkmate wearing my underwear was far from my only uncomfortable moment in my first summer at sleepaway camp. In fact, I set a great tone right away. On the day we left I sat next to Jon on the bus, as my Ritchie Park chum was the only kid besides Michael that I knew attending that session.

Maybe an hour into the trip another kid sitting behind me noticed I was wearing a Mets hat. "Are you a Mets fan?" the kid asked.

"Yup. You?" I turned around to face this kid.

Yes, the kid said, and soon proved to possess deep knowledge of the club. We talked about the Mets and the rest of the baseball season for maybe fifteen minutes. The kid had bushy, curly hair that covered most of the kid's head and a high-pitch voice. The kid was definitely a little older than us, that much I could tell.

Jon and I were not sure of something else, however. "Is that kid a boy or girl?" Jon whispered into my ear. It was a legit question. Boys our age simply did not have longer hair and few spoke with a pitch as high as his (Ross excluded).

"I don't know," I responded.

"Ask him."

"Why don't you ask him?"

"I'm not asking that."

But now I needed to know. I summoned the courage, turned back toward the kid and shot my mouth off: "So, um, I uh, we, want to know . . . uh, are you a guy or a girl?"

He frowned. "I'm a guy. What did you think . . .? Really?" he replied.

I don't think I spoke to that kid again all session.

I was placed in a room of bunk beds for ten boys, all eleven years old or soon turning eleven. There was another bunk nearby of boys our age, including Jon, and I became much better friends with them. Michael was in yet another bunk nearby.

I never tried hard to fit in with my bunkmates, outright disliking some of them, and my bunk's counselors quickly tired of my act. This performance included freezing out unathletic bunkmates during basketball games ("Don't pass to Eugene!") and dumping most of a bottle of shampoo on the bowl-cut Mikey as he showered. ("I'm bliiind," he had shrieked, roughly twenty-five years before *Anchorman 2*, as the shampoo oozed over his face and into his eyes. His yelling scared the living shit out of me for a few seconds. I really thought I had actually blinded him until he emerged from the shower and declared that he could magically once again see).

I soon was getting lectured about behavior nearly every day. I missed my friends, Tyler, Brad, Freddy, and my parents, and I was often bored and frustrated because activities rarely included competitive sports. I sometimes took my feelings out on other kids. Besides messing with Mikey, I mocked another bunkmate for sleeping with a teddy bear. Jason, our teenaged counselor, tried to explain how I was hurting his feelings and therefore should stop.

But as a newly minted elementary school graduate, I was starting to think that feelings were for the weak. And so were teddy bears of course. How could I stop acting out?

It is hard to explain to young baseball fans who did not attend sleep-away camp in the late twentiethth century what it was like, but here goes: We. Had. No. Idea. What. Was. Going. On. Major League games were played every day, injuries sustained, positions in the standings swapped. And we knew of none of it. It was mild torture.

But the season rolled on without us nonetheless. After taking the last three of their series against Oakland, the O's swept three from the Mariners in Seattle, capping a six-game win streak that stretched their record to 40–28 and their division lead to seven games. Were they starting to run away with this division? The rebuilding Baltimore Orioles? It may have been "only June," but it was already late June and nobody else in the AL East was even above .500.

The O's won the final game of the Seattle series 8–6, then flew later that night to Southern California to take on the Angels. California was only a few games behind Oakland in the AL West, so this series would be another barometer for the O's: Beat good teams at home? Check. But on the road, how would they fare?

Less than twenty-four hours after finishing off the Mariners, the O's jumped out to a 5–0 lead over the Angels in the series opener before another national audience, on ABC's *Thursday Night Baseball*. They chased Angels starter Jim Abbott after four innings, but Brian Holton and the relief corps could not hold the lead. In the bottom of the seventh, Brian Downing doubled off Williamson to score Devon White and tie the game 5–5.

But in the next inning the O's promptly took the lead right back. The left-handed Traber pinch-hit for Milligan with one out against Angels right-hander Willie Fraser, homering to right for a 6–5 advantage. It was one of only four homers Traber hit all year.

In the bottom of the eighth Baltimore still led 6–5 when Olson came on with two outs and a runner on third. He retired Johnny Ray on a groundout, then worked through the heart of the Angels order in the ninth, getting Chili Davis to ground out with Downing on second to end the game.

The O's had their seventh straight win, improving to 23–7 since May 21. Yes, that's right, a team everyone picked to lose one hundred games on the season enjoyed a thirty-game stretch with a winning percentage of .767. That matched the best thirty-game span the Mets enjoyed during their famous 1986 season.

California promptly took the final three games of the series, but Baltimore still led the division by five and one-half games over the Yankees by the end of the weekend. Four other teams were within seven and one-half games of the lead, but this was hardly a worry. Even Oakland and the Giants, who sported the game's best records, had yet to put much distance between themselves and middle-of-the-pack teams. In fact the O's enjoyed the biggest advantage of any division leader, by nearly three games, and faced the weakest competition on paper. The deeper into the season they moved, the more likely this miracle seemed possible.

After the Angels series, the O's returned home and welcomed the surging Blue Jays for a three-game series at the tail end of June. Toronto had recovered from a 12–24 start. The Jays had gone 16–7 in June after replacing Jimmy Williams—their manager for their late-season collapse in 1987 and a coach during the 1985 ALCS meltdown—with former coach Cito Gaston in mid-May. On the eve of this series, they stood six games behind Baltimore. But they were beginning to play like the division favorites they had been pegged as at the start of the season, after they had finished a disappointing third in 1988 with eighty-seven wins.

The series opener was historic. On a Tuesday night, June 27, Gaston and Robinson became the first Black managers to face each other in an MLB game. The O's promptly destroyed Toronto 16–6. The next day, after Michael and I left for sleepaway camp in the morning, we missed the O's winning 2–1 over Toronto. Ripken broke a 1-1 tie by homering in the eighth and Olson struck out the side after yielding a leadoff single in the ninth, as the O's stretched their division lead to a season-high seven and one-half games. Although they dropped the series finale 11–1, they had stood up to the soaring, more talented Jays and had taken a series from them. For the second time in June, they had won a series against a contender at home.

"When the Angels beat us the last three games in California, it was good for us. We just got drubbed. We had a long flight home to think about it," Billy Ripken told Boswell, for a column published the day after the Toronto series ended.

Heading into a four-game series in Baltimore against Detroit as June concluded, the O's were seven up on Toronto and led the division by six and one-half games over the second-place Yankees. These were the same Yankees who had just traded Henderson back to Oakland, for a package including pitchers Greg Cadaret and Erik Plunk, and outfielder Luis Polonia. Henderson would finish the season ninth in AL MVP voting, while the players the Yankees received were barely regulars.

But injuries were starting to pile up for Baltimore, including Williamson, who headed to the disabled list with a sore hip. That depleted an already thin bullpen. So even as they concluded the season's third month with a sizeable division lead, few in the media or around baseball still believed the O's would hold on.

But it was possible, Boswell noted, especially if division rivals kept dealing with their own problems. "The Orioles need tons of help. The Yankees have to keep finding ways to subtract great players," Boswell wrote. "The Blue Jays need to keep on playing thirty-six holes of golf on ninety-five-degree days before a night game on the road. The Red Sox need to keep [beleaguered star third baseman] Wade Boggs aboard. And the Brewers have to keep getting hurt.

"Also, the Orioles will probably need pitching help from Pete Harnisch and Curt Schilling, now at Rochester, and maybe six foot seven Ben McDonald."

That help was coming, but not until after a brutal stretch that threatened to kill the Orioles' dream season before I even returned from camp. Straddling the end of July and early August, Baltimore would play fourteen straight on the road, including four at Oakland, three at Kansas City, and four at Boston. If they could survive this gauntlet with the division lead still intact, they would firmly be entrenched as contenders.

They almost did not.

With Michael and Mom just before Michael and I boarded a bus to head to sleepaway camp for the first time, at the parking lot outside Potomac Woods Swim Club. I'm all set for the ride with the Post sports section and a small cereal box.

Chapter 6

JULY: THE BOYS—AND GROWING PAINS—OF SUMMER

On the first day of July, a Saturday night, before forty thousand fans at Memorial Stadium, Ballard held the Tigers to five hits and one walk over seven and one-third innings, earning his tenth win on the season as Baltimore cruised 8–1. Six different O's drove in runs to pace the offense as they took a 4–1 lead after seven and added four runs in the eighth to cement their forty-fourth victory of the season and maintain a five-and-a-half-game lead over second-place New York.

Despite the O's injuries and two straight losses to close out June, they remained THE story in MLB as July began and the season approached its midway point. The baseball world was shocked, but beginning to catch up with my childlike optimism.

"It has become the club for whom every day is April the first," Boswell wrote in *Washington Post Magazine*. "No club has ever improved by more than thirty-three wins in a single year; conceivably, the Birds could. No team has ever gone from being the worst in the game to finishing in first place the next. The O's could."

This was a year that *Time* magazine would later dub "The Year that Changed the World." June featured former President Reagan's speech asking Soviet leader Mikhail Gorbachev to "tear down that [Berlin] Wall" and the Tiananmen Square massacre, and the fall was filled with notable world events.

But July was fairly tranquil, a good time to relax and watch baseball. So even as Don Henley's new single "The End of the Innocence" climbed into the top fifty of the Billboard charts, the O's were dragging many grown fans down to my guileless level, cynical sportswriters included.

"For adults, the ability to make even a small emotional commitment to the Orioles—to answer the question 'Are they for real?' with a firm 'Yes, I think so'—is almost a litmus test of the ability to show irrational faith in something that ought not be possible," Boswell continued. "The Orioles have become an excuse to reclaim some of what is left of our innocence—the part of our nature that is enthusiastic, pliable, even gullible. As long as the worst team in baseball (last year) is in or near first place, the laws of diminished wonder have been revoked."

"Hemond, Robinson, and [assistant general manager Doug] Melvin knew that they would have a hustling, hungry team because they had players who'd be crazy not to hustle or act hungry. What they did not know—and are still afraid to believe completely—is how well these disparate, flawed parts seem to blend together into a pretty dangerous team."

By the midpoint of the season, Boswell noted, the O's were giving up one fewer run per game and scoring one more run per game than in 1988. These were not fluky statistics; they were derived from the club's much-improved defense, control on the mound, and an emphasis on speed and hitting for average (over power). It was a much different Orioles team from the previous few years.

But, Boswell posited, could they keep it up over the season's second half?

"Yes, barring lots of injuries to pitchers, there's no reason the Birds won't continue to play in the style to which they've become accustomed. Defense and speed don't suddenly disappear. Morale should not disappear quickly," he wrote. "For every overachiever like Tettleton and Ballard, who have been ridiculously hot, there are several players, statistically long overdue, who could pick up the slack when they cool off."

"The Orioles have already reached a point where all that stands between them and the impossible—finishing in first place—is an entirely plausible amount of good fortune. If other American League East teams continue to play poorly . . . If the Orioles stay healthy . . . If a few key Baltimore players perform fairly well . . ."

The club's success had altered its strategy for the season, Robinson told a *BusinessWeek* reporter. "We were building for the future," Robinson noted. "But I said [to the brain trust]: 'What's wrong with trying to win now?' "

"But will this glorious season's bright beginning last?" the *BusinessWeek* reporter pondered rhetorically. He quoted Hank Peters, Baltimore's former general manager who held the same job in Cleveland then. "Peters is one of many skeptical baseball men. 'Not to take anything away from the players, but right now they are probably what we call overachievers,' " he said.

Countered Boswell: "If the summer heat melts the Orioles' wings, it would be a shame to see the moral of their tale as some baseball equivalent of the myth of Icarus. The Orioles have not flown too close to the sun. Rather, they have shown us how close, and even reachable, a star can be."

Off somewhere about an hour or two from Baltimore, I knew of the myth of Icarus (from the Nintendo game *Kid Icarus*), but I was unaware if the O's were still flying high or melting down. I was not happy about that, nor about being at this particular camp. With so little sports competition and so many annoying bunkmates, I was developing a bad attitude and continuing to draw the wrath of counselors.

This was all new. I had always been a popular camper in prior summers, including with counselors, but I had never attended a camp against my will before. And my will was growing stronger.

On July 4, my counselor Jason shouted at me when I had the audacity to place an uncooked hot dog in my pants, telling everyone at the table that I had the biggest wiener. Another afternoon I got in trouble again for something else. A lecture from my counselor Mike ended thusly: "I know you are in a bad mood Ryan. But Color War starts tomorrow. Orange vs. White. I think this is something you will like."

I picked my head up, sensing Mike was right. The idea that the whole camp would be keeping score, that I could sign up for several events and help my team compete in a long-lasting tournament, that got my attention.

Alas, even Color Wars was not a salve. One event featured basketball free throw shooting. As we began, about a dozen of us gathered to hear a counselor read the rules one morning. I spaced out for a bit as I kneeled on the blacktop, staring off into the bright blue sky. Then I heard: ". . . and sportsmanship gives you the chance to earn up to five more points for your team."

Sportsmanship?! I thought. *'What?! Why would that count? This is a competition. The ability to knock down free throws should be the only thing that counts.*

I kept my thoughts to myself as the competition started. One of my opponents was up first. I stood in line a few kids behind him, crossing my arms over the thin cotton T-shirt adorning my thinner chest, pressing my white Nike sneakers hard into the concrete and watching closely. I said nothing, rooting hard in my head for him to miss.

Around me, a few kids were clapping and cheering. "Come on guys! I can't hear you all. Let Josh hear your support," the counselor bellowed.

I was not having it. Nor was David, a kid a year older than me whose attitude was often worse than mine. The two of us, on the same team, were doomed to harm our sportsmanship score.

"Come on Ryan," the counselor said as Josh bricked the free throw, the ball bouncing high in the air toward the sky and beaming sun. "Come on David. Sportsmanship counts."

The competition ensued as both of us refused to cheer for our opponents. We took turns hoisting free throws, sometimes cheering on our own teammates, sometimes just watching quietly and intently. The outcome of this event simply mattered to me—but only the free throw shooting itself. I could not bring myself to cheer for my opponents.

So as a bunch of preteen and early teenaged Jewish boys mostly bricked free throw after free throw, David and I knocked our sportsmanship score down. After the event closed, the counselor took some joy in announcing our poor mark, addressing the whole group as he extolled the virtue of sportsmanship in a condescending tone I knew so well from many adults in my life. He kept lecturing us for what seemed like an hour as we knelt in a group on the blacktop.

It was probably only ten or fifteen minutes. But that was enough time for me to lose not only my focus, but my wits. I needed to DO SOMETHING, to move, to scream, to tackle somebody. I had enough self-control to stay put, but not enough to listen and certainly not enough to sit still. I racked my brain for anything to do, finally reaching into a pocket of my black mesh shorts and finding a half-pack of Certs breath mints in the bottom. I pulled it out and stuck one in my mouth.

But sucking on a Cert was not going to be enough to survive a lecture on sportsmanship, not when there were basketballs and unused baskets in sight. Plus, I had other Certs in my pocket. So I pulled out another one. Without thinking for a second about potential consequences, I began writing on the blacktop with the Cert. When that one ran out, I removed another one from my pocket and began writing with it.

Around this time the counselor was wrapping up his lecture. He looked down at me and my work of art. "What is that?!" he asked, looking straight at me, his voice rising. "Did you draw on the blacktop? . . . With Certs?!"

I smirked and lowered my head a bit, refusing to meet his stare.

"What does that say?!" he called out. "Let's . . . go . . . Orange?!" He kept staring as he continued moving closer.

I smirked more, trying hard to suppress a smile and laughter as I kept looking down. I was very proud of myself.

He shook his head. "Ryan before you go anywhere, you need to clean that off. Then when you are done, go to the pool and cheer for the water polo teams. Debbie will be keeping track of sportsmanship points there."

My point made, my freedom to move granted, I did not protest. I quickly rose and bolted for the pool.

About halfway through the session, I got a reprieve when the rest of my immediate family joined me and Michael. My father had volunteered to be the camp doctor for a week while Mom got to enjoy a week at sleepaway camp in her late thirties. Even better for her, she had virtually unfettered access to spy on her two oldest children.

One night I had trouble sleeping. I lay on my thin mattress on the top bunk, tossing and turning in my single bed, my legs stretching out past the edge when I lay flat. Finally I hopped off the bed and walked out of the bunk.

There was a counselors' meeting that night, so we were unsupervised inside the bunk. But a female counselor-in-training was sitting outside, keeping an eye on us and the bunk next door. I walked over to her. "I don't feel good," I said, lying as I looked her straight in the eyes.

"Come here. Let me feel your keppie, sweetie."

I leaned forward as she placed her hand against my forehead.

"You don't feel warm. Are you sure you don't feel well?"

"Yeah," I nodded. "Really. My stomach hurts."

"Oh," she grinned, "you just want to go see Dad."

She had a point. Even though my father had been the camp doctor for a few days by now, I had spent the first two weeks of camp away from him and then barely interacted with him once he arrived. His role was to care for the kids who truly needed his attention. For once we were in the same location and those kids did not include me. Yet. Now I suddenly and urgently wanted his attention, even if his version of caring for me often meant barking at me to watch the street as I chased errant balls or yelling louder about eating sugar cereals before dinner.

"Na-ah. I really don't feel good, promise," I replied, flashing the doe eyes.

"Okay," she smiled, knowingly. "Let's get you to the infirmary."

I forgot my ruse and walked quickly there. When I arrived, my father greeted me with a smile. Though he had been a practicing physician my entire life and I had often been dragged to his office when I was younger, I had never paid attention to his craft. It simply did not interest me.

Yet it did on this night. I watched closely as he examined a younger girl sent to him for a lice check. He fiddled with the girl's hair for a moment and then chuckled. I leaned in to get a closer look.

"See that," he said, pointing with a wooden popsicle stick at a tiny white object in the girl's hair. "There it is."

"Ewwww. Is that what lice look like?"

Soon any disgust I had was replaced by satisfaction. I was hanging with my father while he was doing his thing. Not getting in his way as he tried to work out in the basement, not drawing his ire by bouncing a ball in the house and breaking Mom's tchotchkes. But actually helping him—sort of. And we were alone, without my brothers, without Mom. I felt the same pride I had when he picked me first for the soccer games at his fortieth birthday, when I had been sure he would pick Michael.

Eventually I was sent back to my cabin, where I fell asleep almost immediately.

Jewish sleepaway camps have long been a place parents send their kids, not only to get a break from them for a few weeks or give them time to blow off steam in between school years. They also function as a spot where many kids have their first sexual experiences and significant others. True story: My parents met as counselors at a similar camp when they were teens (a major reason Mom pushed this camp on Michael and me).

I had left for camp with a burgeoning interest in girls, but that was mostly inactive for much of the session. Early on, I was eager to find anyone I could vibe with besides Jon. While I had quickly dismissed most of my bunkmates—none of them were good athletes, one tried to climb onto my bed in just his underwear to fart on me one night and another had a bowl cut a couple of months before starting middle school, for fuck's sake—I quickly meshed with a few kids in the other bunk with boys my age.

Our friendship started early in the session. One of the camp traditions forced upon us was to sing the *Birkat HaMazon* prayer after every meal, the entire camp packed into the mess hall chirping in unison. Like many Hebrew prayers and songs, several words sounded enough like English words and slang to easily be transformed, while phrases could often be added to the ends of stanzas as well. Other campers had already figured out a few wisecracks well before I got ahold of this prayer. So "*rachamim*" became "sow-er [sour] cream" and the commercial tagline "pass the Old El Paso" was added to the end of the line "*Uv'tuvo hagadol.*"

But my favorite twist quickly became another line. Toward the end of the prayer, the phrase "*asher* [ah-share] *asha* [ah-shah] *bara* [buh-rah]" finished one stanza. Some young genius had realized what that sounded like. And so, early in the session, I sat at a table with Andrew and Tom as we prepared to sing the prayer one afternoon after lunch. Bright sunlight shined into the mess hall as the counselor assigned to our table turned to look at them and said aloud: "Not today guys. If you say it, you're in trouble."

"What do you mean?" Tom replied, pokerfaced.

"You know what I'm talking about."

Being a new camper who had just recently met Andrew and Tom, though, I did not know. So as the prayer started, I stared them down, listening carefully. The prayer unfolded with us dropping the usual non sequiturs— "*l'olam va-ed*" became "*l'olam* DROP DEAD!" That was somehow okay.

Then came *asher asha bara*. At least it was written to be sung that way, likely by some of our very weary, diaspora-laden ancestors who had sacrificed much to persevere—so that their descendants could one day enjoy sleepaway camp and the other trappings of our upper-middle class lives in late–twentieth century America.

Tom looked straight back at me, his big, dark round eyes locking with mine. He then muttered quietly enough so that—he hoped—the counselor would not hear, but loud enough for me: "I swear I saw her bra."

There was no mention of breasts. But at an age when a girl unwittingly flashing the waistband of her underwear (or her butt, as I had found out a couple of months earlier) got our attention, I had to work hard to stifle a giggle.

My poker face must not have been as steadfast as Tom's. When the prayer ended moments later, the counselor went off, looking straight at Tom and Andrew: "I told you not to say that!" he said from the head of the table, raising his voice and looking over the heads of several other campers.

"I did not," they protested in unison.

Well, maybe Andrew did not.

Andrew, Tom, and I looked at each other and giggled, becoming instant friends. The counselor dropped it. Others did not fight us. So, for meals every day for the next few weeks, the lyrics of this prayer at our table forever changed.

Pretty soon, at least one of us would not have to pretend we saw a bra.

One evening later in the session, our bunk teamed up with a girls' bunk for an activity. The girls were a year older than us, and some of them had been through a year of middle school; I sensed they were much more mature than me.

We were sitting outside the girls' bunk on picnic tables, and I soon found myself split from the other boys, hanging with a few girls. One of them offered me a piece of Hubba Bubba, which I began chewing loudly, showing off the large pink bubbles I had mastered blowing through endless hours of practice during Hebrew school. Sometimes the bubbles popped and stuck on my face, which made a few girls laugh (perhaps with me, perhaps at me). They did not seem to mind that, my other crude manners, or whatever brilliant things I had to say.

I wanted them to like me, to validate me. They were older and they were girls. Plenty of boys thought I was cool, but virtually no girls that I knew of did. They also projected a certain poise in a large social group that the girls and boys my age did not.

I was sitting between Kate and Beth. "Hey Ryan," Kate said, "come with me for a second. I need to get something. Beth, you too." The three of us got up and walked toward their bunk. "I left something in here," Kate said, pointing to it.

I had no expectations for what may happen next. Not for a moment did it cross my mind that I was breaking a camp rule. Nor did I recall that Mom was sitting just outside the bunk, helping other campers with their projects. I was completely in the moment. It was like walking into an enchanted forest. I could see a few panties and bras scattered on the floor. *Are girls messy too?* I wondered.

"This is our bunk," Kate said, playing tour guide as she pointed out her bed.

The three of us sat down on it. I had no idea where this was going.

"Do you want to see something?" she asked.

"Sure."

She lifted her shirt up.

Bras were also being displayed all over Memorial Stadium in July, as fans enjoyed an intoxicating baseball summer while the O's captivated two cities. On July 4 the O's got their formal star turn, leading the AL East by six and one-half games as they prepared to play at Toronto that night. In the morning Robinson was interviewed on *Good Morning America*, and he then joined Tettleton and Olson on the *Today Show*.

The attention did not seem to distract them, as the O's won that night 8–0 and the next night 5–4. Despite losing the third game, they had taken another series from their more talented division rivals.

Although they then lost two of three in Milwaukee, Baltimore started the All-Star break with a five-and-a-half-game lead over the second-place Yankees. At 48–37, they remained the only AL East team over .500, leading the majors in fewest errors committed and fewest earned runs allowed.

Could this new version of "Orioles Magic" last?

For a little while, yes. The O's lost their first game after the All-Star break, at home to the Angels. But they rebounded by winning their next five, including back-to-back walk-off victories at home against the Angels on July 15 and 16.

Both victories showcased the resilience and charm that had become this team's hallmark. On July 15, they fell behind 7–3, but pulled within 9–7 as the bottom of the ninth started. With one out, Tettleton and Milligan walked, then advanced to second and third, respectively, on a wild pitch. Sheets pinch hit for Melvin and promptly hit a line drive into right-center, scoring both runners to tie the game.

Up stepped Devereaux. On a 1–1 pitch he lifted a high fly ball down the left-field line. It landed in the stands just behind the foul pole. The crowd of more than forty-seven thousand erupted as umpire Jim Joyce ruled it a game-winning home run—even if replays still appear inconclusive regarding whether the ball was fair. One angle seems to show the ball striking the foul pole, while another looks like it just misses the pole and flies foul.

The next night Olson, who had earned his fifteenth consecutive save since the start of the season on July 14, allowed Brian Downing to score the tying run in the top of the ninth when Jack Howell blooped a single into left field with two out. He was furious, "yammering a blue streak," Boswell later wrote, but he promptly struck out Dick Schofield on a called strike to retire the side. Kevin Hickey and Mike Smith then held the Angels scoreless for two innings, with Smith retiring Max Venable on a groundout with the bases loaded and two out in the top of the eleventh.

Cal Ripken led off Baltimore's half of the eleventh by drawing a walk from Willie Fraser, and then Tettleton pulled a hard ground ball over the first base line. The ball skipped into the outfield, caroming into foul territory and off the right-field stands. Ripken raced around the bases. Was it a fair ball? Who knows. But umpires again ruled fair, and Ripken raced all the way home, scoring easily to secure another walk-off win.

Two wins over the next two days against Seattle moved Baltimore to 53–38, seven and one-half games up on second-place New York. The second game, a 4–3 triumph, was almost as dramatic as the two against the Angels. With two outs in the eighth and Baltimore nursing a one-run lead, Olson faced Dave Valle with the bases loaded. The Seattle catcher hit a grounder that bounced off Worthington's glove. The third baseman recovered, though, and fired a strike to Milligan just ahead of Valle. "Another laugher," Tettleton joked afterward.

The next morning a Boswell column ran in the *Post* about Olson, who earned another save in this win over Randy Johnson and Seattle. Olson had scattered two hits, intentionally walked one, and fanned three while recording the last five outs. He was emerging as a favorite for AL Rookie of the Year, seizing the O's closer job full time.

" 'He's got great stuff, good control, and an arm that bounces back. He wants the ball—he's not timid,' " O's coach Johnny Oates told Boswell. " 'And he's conveniently wild.' "

"When hitters get two strikes, the mischievous Orioles infielders—especially the Ripken brothers and Jim Traber—begin doing little knee bends, to amuse each other and remind rivals of what might be coming," Boswell wrote. " 'When you see Mark McGwire start to squat down,' " Traber said, laughing, 'nobody's safe.' "

Said Olson of his temperament: "I feel like I have so much aggression that if I didn't get it out playing baseball, I'd explode."

The O's seemed to be peaking. Since sitting at 18–21 nearly two months earlier, they had gone 35–17 over nearly a full third of the season—winning two of every three games. But there were still seventy games to play, and teams had blown leads far more secure than seven and one-half games in mid-July throughout baseball history.

One of those teams was the 1987 Toronto Blue Jays. They just happened to resemble the 1989 Toronto Blue Jays quite a bit—but with more experience and a new, calmer manager. After Olson's close against the Mariners, Toronto sat third in the division, eight and one-half games out and still below .500. While many experts predicted the Jays would eventually wake up and catch both the Yankees and O's, they were running out of time. Since their early surge when Gaston replaced Williams as manager, they had cooled, going just 10–12 since late June. These perennial laissez-faire talent-wasters needed another jolt.

They soon got one.

Meanwhile, back in the Pennsylvania woods, I was finishing up my first session of sleepaway camp. My magical mystery tour to a girls' bunk over, my thoughts soon returned to the baseball season: How were the Orioles doing? Who made the All-Star team and how did that game go? These were among several questions I carried around in my head as I survived my first summer of sleepaway camp in the pre-internet era.

Midway through the session, we were creating a camp newspaper and I had volunteered to write a sports column. Somebody on the campus had come across a *Post* sports section and we learned of the All-Star team selections. I was irate. While Cal Ripken and Tettleton made the AL team, Ballard and Olson were left off—along with a few other Major League players I felt were deserving. I resolved to write my column about the All-Star game selections, highlighting the snubs in particular. I turned in a column measuring close to a thousand words—much longer than anything I had written in school.

I handed my column to the editor, a camp counselor. A few days later the newspaper was published on eight-and-a-half-by-eleven light-yellow construction paper. I quickly grabbed a copy and looked for my column, finding a headline mentioning baseball with my name printed just below. It was my first printed byline.

It pissed me off: As I finished reading the column, I realized at least a couple hundred words—my arguments for the snubbed players—had been cut. "We only had so much space," the editor replied when I confronted her soon thereafter. "We could not let everyone write for as long as they wanted."

"Why not?!" I countered, raising my voice and looking her directly in the eye.

"Because we simply did not have enough space."

It was my first argument with an editor about story length; it would not be my last.

My frustration passed and my attention diverted to the second half of the season. The O's had enjoyed a great first ninety games, but as it approached mid-July, even baseball fans as young as I knew their lead was far from a sure thing. One evening late in the session, an older camper came to us with news, like an ancient oracle greeting our forefathers in the Holy Land. The camper had read a local sports section on a field trip that day and regaled us as we gathered around him outside the mess hall. The Mets were still a few games out of first, he told us, but the O's were still seven games up in the AL East.

I was relieved. The O's had not collapsed while I was gone.

I thought they never would.

Over the course of a 162-game season, even the 1986 Mets and 1998 Yankees endured losing stretches. The 1989 Baltimore Orioles were far less talented and would be no different. Their slump began innocently enough, the third and final game of that mid-July series against Seattle. It was an early Wednesday afternoon start, but more than thirty-five thousand still packed Memorial Stadium to see if this impossible juggernaut could sweep a series from the .500 Mariners.

In the press box sat Tony Kornheiser, Boswell's colleague with the *Post*. Kornheiser had grown up in New York and closely followed the 1969 Miracle Mets. He compared them to these Orioles in a column filed that day: "The overriding thing that links these teams is the pervasive sense that they're in the midst of doing something extraordinary, something mythical. As the Mets did then, the Orioles go onto the field every game thinking they can win," he wrote. "The essence and the spirit of the turnarounds are the same. It's the American Dream, the romantic preoccupation with long shots."

"California left here and said, 'Their [Baltimore's] pitching won't hold up. It won't last through September,' " Robinson told Kornheiser. " 'Maybe so. But I'm glad they're taking that attitude.' " Robinson referred to all the arm talent that would likely join Baltimore after the September 1 minor league call-ups, when Major League rosters expanded from twenty-five to forty. "His eyes half-closed, a serene smile on his lips, Robinson said: 'Look up in September and we may not need that pitching.' "

They needed such pitching that day, alas. Brian Holman shut out the O's over seven innings, while Brian Holton gave up five runs in two innings as Baltimore lost 7–0.

"They will leave town with a seven-and-a-half-game lead in the American League East and they likely will begin to think all this is for real if, when they return home August 4 [after the fourteen-game road trip], the lead is similar," the *Post* reported the next day.

Regardless, the O's had already captured the hearts of two major markets—including jaded DC, a political town always ready to embrace the distracting fairy dust of a winning sports team.

"Yesterday the lunchtime lines were five deep at the store in downtown Washington where Orioles tickets are sold," according to an op-ed published in the *Post* the next day titled "Sunny Days at the Stadium."

"But this team, with its combination of youthful enthusiasm and old-fashioned attention to the fundamentals, has an appeal that extends beyond its immediate geographical area, and even perhaps a bit beyond baseball. In this overcast season of Pete Rose [the superstar-turned manager suspended that month for gambling], the Orioles are, so far at least, brightening days in many places."

The O's hoped to keep the bright days going as they flew to Oakland for a four-game tilt to face the A's, who were locked in a dogfight in the AL West. Four teams were within five games of the lead, shared by the A's and Angels. Oakland, which had loaded up to make sure they made up for blowing the World Series a year earlier to the underdog Dodgers, were facing the very real prospect of missing the playoffs altogether. Only a few weeks had passed since Baltimore had taken three of four at home from them.

The A's promptly swept this series, including a pair of 3–2 triumphs. The O's staff held the A's to fourteen combined runs, yet the O's scored only seven. Essentially, Oakland did to Baltimore what the O's had been doing to opponents all year: grinding out narrow victories cemented by a tough bullpen. Oakland closer Dennis Eckersley was one of the game's best and earned three saves in the series.

After a day off, the O's started a three-game series in Minnesota against the .500 Twins. Minnesota was essentially out of the playoff race by now, but still featured several players who had won the World Series just two years earlier.

Minnesota promptly swept this series too. The middle game was especially brutal; Baltimore took an early 4–0 lead and slowly frittered that away. Milacki allowed two runs in the sixth and one in the seventh before being pulled after 116 pitches. On his last pitch, Doug Baker tripled with two outs to score Randy Bush from first, tying the game 4–4. In the bottom of the ninth, Williamson gave up two hits to put runners on the corners with one out. Baker then singled to right field to score the winning run. (These marked two of twenty-two MLB RBI Baker would amass total in a professional career spanning 1984–1990, while playing mostly in the minors.)

After falling 10–6 the next day, the O's losing streak had stretched to eight games. They now stood 53–46, only four games up on both Cleveland and Toronto—with Boston four and one-half games back, and both Milwaukee and New York within seven games. Just like that, every team except Detroit was back in the AL East race.

It was still "only" July, but this potential miracle had taken a real shot. As the road trip continued, more than half a season of solid baseball was in danger of being undone before the month even ended.

As the O's were in the midst of this losing streak, the last day of sleepaway camp finally came. After four weeks away from home, not seeing the friends and family I had grown accustomed to seeing nearly every day, I was thrilled to return. My stuff miraculously got packed up without Mom's help; I said goodbye to Tom and Andrew and boarded the bus with Michael, Jon, and other kids bound for Montgomery County.

I arrived to find the O's had suddenly blown most of their lead, but I was too excited being home to care too much at first. The first night I was back, I marveled at how comfortable and large my regular twin bed was.

That soon changed. One night shortly after Michael and I returned, my parents went out and Brad babysat us. Around ten, Brad and I retired to my parents' room so he could keep an ear on my brothers sleeping in their rooms, as we watched the Orioles play in Kansas City. It was the first contest of their three-game series against a Royals team that was still in the AL West race, sitting six and one-half games behind division-leading California.

Baltimore had not won since the 4–3 triumph over Seattle on July 18, around the time I had assured myself that they would never be caught for the division title. Their lead had felt secure despite what I knew about baseball history, with my long-established will (need?) to believe in miracles still exceeded my growing need to rationalize the world. I must have sensed it: there would be no trade-backs.

Speaking of needs, the O's needed to start winning again, and right then. Ballard started and pitched brilliantly, holding a potent Royals lineup to one run over eight innings, and Baltimore led 3–1 going into the bottom of the ninth.

But then Brad and I watched in horror as another game seemed on the verge of slipping away. After the Royals' Pat Tabler singled with one out, Robinson lifted Ballard for Olson. But Olson promptly gave up two runs to tie the game, then loaded the bases with two outs. Veteran Willie Wilson hit a flare targeted for left-center. We held our breath for a split-second as the TV camera quickly cut away from the tight shot of Olson pitching to Wilson and panned to follow Wilson's shot.

Fortunately the next frame showed Cal Ripken leaping to snare the ball, ending the threat. In a season full of extraordinary defense, Ripken's catch was one of the best and most important plays.

The game lasted deep into extra innings. It was already well past my bedtime, so I closed my eyes, stretched out and stiffened my body, pretending that I was asleep so Brad would not whisk me off to bed. My cousin either bought the act or did not care. I listened intently as the game continued.

Finally in the top of the thirteenth, the game still tied 3–3, Orsulak was at second and Traber at first with two out when Royals reliever Jeff Montgomery uncorked a wild pitch. Catcher Bob Boone quickly chased it down near the backstop and threw the ball toward second to try to get the slower Traber. But his throw escaped and skidded along the Astroturf into center field. Orsulak, who had already advanced to third on the wild pitch, dashed home. Traber was gunned down trying to advance to third, but Baltimore now led 4–3.

In the bottom of the inning, the Royals put runners on first and second with one out against Williamson. But he retired Gary Thurman on a flyout and got Wilson to pop up to Tettleton.

The O's losing streak was finally over.

"Some four hours thirty-six minutes later—as well as a blown Gregg Olson save, two wild arguments with umpires, an unearned winning run on Bob Boone's throwing error," according to the *Post*, "they could retire to their hotel across the street to savor a surreal thirteen-inning, 4–3 victory."

The losing streak had been ugly. Baltimore as a team hit just .217 with a .269 on-base percentage, drawing just fifteen walks and whiffing fifty-two times while hitting only three homers. They scored in just eight of seventy-six innings.

But they had finally found a way to win a game, even if it took thirteen innings. I felt relief and bliss. I was home. I still had more than a month of summer vacation left. The O's were still in first place, now up by three and one-half games over Cleveland and four over Toronto. It felt like the beginning of summer all over again.

But this summer was different than previous ones, more a capstone in my life than the usual break I had grown accustomed to. My first venture to sleepaway camp had already killed a month, for starters. And when this summer ended there would be no more morning walks to school with the Gromleys and Michael, no more huddling in front of the Ritchie Park building hanging with friends while we hoped the bell would never ring.

It had not yet hit me that those days were over, that when the summer ended, I would start an entirely different school-year experience and there would never be any going back to the comfortable old one. Instead, my mind was fixed mostly on the baseball season.

But it did not matter that I wanted life to stay the same as it had been for as long as I could remember, that I wanted the AL East standings to remain as they had for weeks, things were changing—for me and for the O's. What once was a seven-and-a-half-game lead and a seemingly unflappable, carefree team was starting to come unglued. The gutsy thirteen-inning triumph proved to be a mere small break from all the losing. Baltimore dropped the last two games of the series in Kansas City, the opener of the Boston series on July 31 and both ends of a doubleheader at Boston the next day, the first of August.

By the end of August 1, they stood at 54–51, just one game up on the Red Sox. Four other teams were within five games of the division lead. The O's had lost thirteen of fourteen games, including a 1–12 mark thus far on this four-city road trip that took them across three different time zones.

"It hasn't happened overnight, but it's very hard to believe we're playing the way we're playing," Robinson told the *Post*.

The younger players were pressing to force their way out of the slump, according to Robinson and a few veterans. "When you've got young players and they go bad, they turn into themselves," Bradley said. "They wonder if they belong here. I'm sure they think they do, but when you start going bad, there's some doubt that creeps into your mind."

"Everyone made a big deal out of this trip," Traber said. "We went out to Oakland and lost a couple of well-pitched and well-played games and some guys started to believe it. I think there's a tightness now that wasn't there before."

To make matters worse, the doubleheader sweep in Boston came just after the trade deadline, July 31. That was the last good chance for teams to add talent from outside their organizations. (Clubs could still make trades in August—but only if players cleared waivers, so good players were rarely moved then.) After the deadline, the O's would be essentially locked into what they had, plus the largely untested—if not gifted—young players they would call up in September.

Before the deadline, Oakland added Rickey Henderson; the Rangers nabbed the All-Star Harold Baines (for a package including a young outfielder named Sammy Sosa); the Brewers signed veteran starter Jerry Reuss; the Yankees acquired veteran starter Walt Terrell.

The O's did not make a splashy move, but did not totally sit pat either. On July 20, they acquired outfield depth by trading for Stan Jefferson, sending pitcher John Habyan to the Yankees. Both were in Triple-A at the time. Then on July 28, Baltimore sent a prospect to Detroit for veteran Keith Moreland. Moreland, thirty-five, had helped the Cubs win the division in 1984 while playing four different positions and had driven in eighty-eight runs as recently as 1987. He would add another bat to the lineup, likely as a designated hitter much of the time, and another experienced presence to guide the kids as they chased a division title.

On deadline day, the Jays also made a couple of moves, though. For one, they claimed veteran outfielder Lee Mazzilli off waivers from the Mets.

Teammate Mookie Wilson was unhappy and struggling. So a mere six weeks after dealing their other popular center fielder, Lenny Dykstra, New York flipped Wilson to Toronto for a lefty bullpen specialist and a minor league pitcher. The switch-hitting Wilson had famously helped the Mets win the World Series in 1986 and another NL East title in 1988. He had lost some speed and was hitting only .205, but was thirty-three, healthy, and still capable. If he even approached the form he had displayed consistently since breaking in with the Mets full-time in 1981, he would improve Toronto's lineup.

That he did. Wilson would earn AL MVP votes for the way he played for Toronto the rest of the season, just one-third of the year.

He joined a team that was three games out of first and still under .500 as July closed, even after a decent month (15–12). They would stay around .500 for a bit longer—until they didn't.

The O's would play much better in August than they had in late July, but their division lead would be seriously threatened. It was later than anyone expected, but here came the Big Bad Blow Jays.

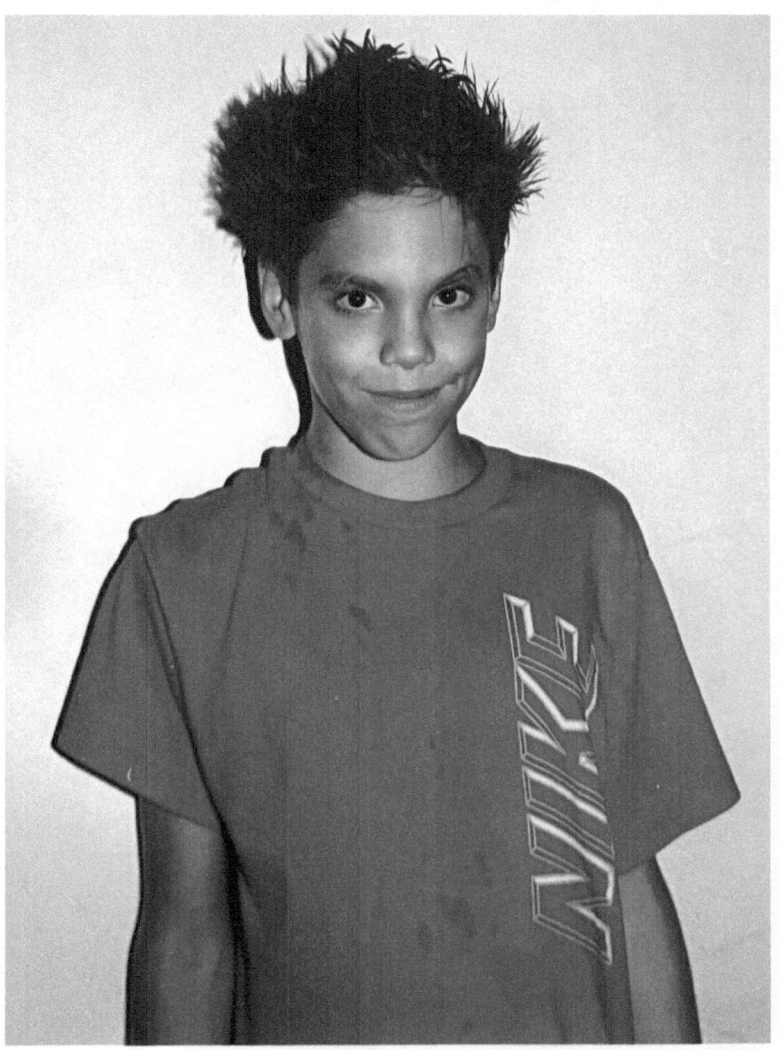

Trying out a new hairstyle at home one night in August. Unscheduled time, especially in the summer, always brought out my creative side.

Chapter 7

AUGUST: HANGIN' TOUGH

After Baltimore lost both games in the doubleheader at Boston on the first day of August, the O's and Red Sox were tied in the loss column as the clubs prepared to finish their series the next day. A Red Sox victory would mean the O's would no longer be alone in first in the AL East for the first time in two months; in fact they would technically be second based on winning percentage.

The Red Sox promptly jumped out to a 6–0 lead after five, knocking Ballard out of the game in the third. This Baltimore team that had been kicked around for two weeks seemed destined for their fourteenth loss in fifteen games, the miracle-to-be now looking like a classic fade by a team short on talent and experience.

Perhaps they deserved that fate. They certainly had the prospects to trade for Harold Baines or Mookie Wilson—even Cy Young winner Frank Viola, who the Mets acquired in a blockbuster trade with Minnesota. But the O's refused to part with any of their top-tier young talent, trying to simultaneously win the division in 1989 while building for the future. Now it looked like they would fall off that tightrope and blow the division, destroy dreams, and crush young fans everywhere.

Baltimore promptly rallied for three in the sixth, cutting the deficit to 6–3. In the seventh, Cal Ripken singled and Tettleton walked. With one out, Milligan blasted a high fly ball to right-center. The ball carried, carried, carried . . . well past the wall, suddenly tying the game. The O's bullpen and dugout erupted in unison.

In the bottom of the seventh, Red Sox star Jim Rice came up with two on and two out, the game still tied. But Williamson induced him to ground out to Cal Ripken.

The O's kept the momentum going the very next frame. With Bradley at first and one out, Cal Ripken doubled to right-center, scoring Bradley to put the O's up for the first time that night. Baltimore tacked on two more that inning to stretch their lead to 9–6, capping a third straight three-run inning.

Williamson gave up a two-run homer with two out in the ninth, but Mark Thurmond replaced him and retired Boston's Randy Kutcher on a groundout to Cal Ripken, securing the victory. It was only Baltimore's second win in fifeen games, but it prevented a sweep, pushing their division lead back to two games. After trailing 6–0 amid a torrential slump, the O's had improbably held their ground.

Maybe they did not need other teams' stars to secure this division title after all.

Meanwhile, back home, I quickly readjusted to my life of recent summers past: sports camp during the day, then the pool or playing video games (*Tecmo Bowl* or *Blades of Steel* on Nintendo especially) and massive pickup games with kids in our neighborhood and the one connected to ours by a short, narrow concrete path. In high school, we would use that path to do some other things in the dark; that summer we used it as a conduit to hours-long games of manhunt, street hockey, football, and baseball.

Michael and I also started another new camp, a sports day camp for four weeks through the Rockville Jewish Community Center called Maccabiah. Brad had been going for a few summers and had taken a job as a CIT with the JCC camps for the summer. I expected him to be one of our CITs at Maccabiah. I was genuinely excited about that, and about the prospect of a competitive sports camp.

For a few years I had been alternating between another pure sports camp and a hybrid sports-computer camp Mom signed us up for primarily to help us build computer skills. (Because learning LOGO has really helped me as an adult.) If they called it "computers" and slid in sports and the pool, perhaps we would not notice we were also sitting still indoors and learning every weekday for a month during the summer. The trick worked on me. I loved both camps and grew accustomed to the caring approach of their counselors and friendly campers.

But the days of being a junior camper (age ten or younger at most camps) were over. I was placed in Maccabiah's senior camp with kids ranging from eleven to fourteen to put me—a scrawny, immature eleven-year-old—at the bottom of the food chain for the first time in years.

I had some fun competing, but what I mostly remember from the one summer I spent at Maccabiah is how so many teenagers went out of their way to put down me and the other young senior campers. In retrospect it was probably not a great idea to have so many moody Jewish teens in charge of and around unassuming, sweet-natured preteens who were much closer in age and maturity level to the junior campers.

I was still largely unassuming and sweet-natured, but I was apparently no longer cute enough to get away with my act—at least around male counselors. That was established at Capital Camps and reinforced the very first day at Maccabiah, when my lead counselor, a college student named Avi, reacted to my climbing on his back in the pool by yelling loudly ("Get off me!") and tossing me away.

I was shocked. This had been standard pool protocol for years. Older kids and adults gave younger kids piggyback rides and sometimes threw them around the pool; even I often gave Tyler rides in the shallow end (and one time in the deep end, when I almost drowned us both). But Avi was having none of it.

I was dealt another blow when I found out Brad was not working that session. So it was up to me alone to keep an eye out for myself.

And I had to be vigilant. The older kids provided a preview of what middle school would be like, with their love of employing the word "faggot" among other cutdowns, angry stares, and overall douchey dispositions.

But they were older and better at nearly every sport than me, so at first I sought their affirmation. I quickly found I could not earn their respect off the field, however, because my interests were still limited to sports and pop music. In the mornings before we split into our assigned teams, we would shoot around in the gym or hang out in the bleachers as other campers arrived. The mostly male CITs and counselors, theoretically being paid to teach us sports skills and look after us, instead lounged while listening to the New Kids and DJ Jazzy Jeff & The Fresh Prince at volumes so loud that when it echoed through the gym, you had to walk right up to them and shout to get their attention. I gave up after a few days of them mocking anything I said.

Some of the campers were not much better. One morning I approached David, twelve, also a big Mets fan, but one who had a possible psychopath for an older brother.

"Mets won last night, only three and a half games behind now," I told him, hoping to get his attention.

"I know, you faggot!" he replied, walking away.

I just stood there, hurt and shocked. Hurt because I had actually tried to connect with that brat. Shocked because essentially every other time I had approached another fan around my age to talk baseball, they had engaged me. Like any sports-obsessed preteen boy, I knew my shit and other young fans respected that.

I was also surprised because this was not a word I ever used—and not because I was some young champion of LGBTQ rights or respectful with my language. I cussed nonstop around my friends, brothers, and cousins—as did they. (Tyler first uttered the word "shit" at age two, mimicking one of Michael's friends.) But we had an unspoken ban on the word "faggot." The word "motherfucker" was thrown around more often than "hi," but "faggot" was simply off limits.

In my mind, the counselors and CITs were supposed to behave like adults. Plus they were the same age as my cousins, who rarely cussed at me and usually doted on me. But I quickly learned that profanity, derogatory terms, and cutdowns were the norm at Maccabiah. And while some older kids also threatened to kick my ass more or less for being eleven, I was still eager to show them I belonged. When we played baseball, I volunteered to crouch being home plate to warm up pitchers without a chest protector, mask, or even a simple helmet (or a protective cup). I had just my underwear, mesh shorts, a T-shirt, and a trucker's hat to protect me, even as some of these teens threw fairly hard. My mortal fear of getting hurt by one of these young Mitch Williamses served me well, enabling me to quickly move my glove to catch their missiles as they darted toward my face, a chest made of only skin and bones, and my barely developed midsection. I moved especially quickly any time one of them bounced a ball in the dirt, which was often.

If I ever earned their respect from showing them how tough and seemingly fearless I could be, though, I don't recall them showing it. Pretty soon they expected me to sacrifice for them and I went along with it. That set a dangerous precedent for middle school. About two months after graduation, I was already a long way from my Ritchie Park days.

Like Capital Camps, Maccabiah had its moments. One Monday night in early August, we took a camp field trip to Baltimore to see the O's host the Twins. With one-third of the season still to play, Baltimore's division lead, which was seven and one-half games just three weeks earlier, now held at two and one-half.

This game followed two straight O's wins, including walking off the Rangers in ten innings the afternoon before. Trailing 2–1 in the ninth against Texas ace Kevin Brown, Cal Ripken singled and later scored to tie the game on a Milligan single to center. In the tenth, Williamson worked his way out of a two-on, two-out jam to hold the Rangers scoreless. Then with one out in the bottom of the inning, Devereaux smashed another deep shot to left. This one landed well inside the foul pole for a clear game-winning homer, sending the crowd of over 28,000 into a frenzy.

The day before that, Milacki had outdueled Nolan Ryan in a 5–2 victory. Milacki lasted into the ninth, scattering seven hits for his first victory since July 5 and marking the first win by an O's starter in sixteen games. Olson, who had blown four of his last five save opportunities, retired the last two batters to earn his seventeenth save on the season.

So the O's seemed to have rebounded from their mid-summer swoon. The victories over Texas gave them three wins in four games since the doubleheader sweep by Boston on August 1.

But if they were going to take this division from the more talented and experienced competition closing in on them, they were now going to have to fight through a major injury to do so. Before beating the Rangers in the walk-off, they placed Tettleton on the disabled list for three to six weeks with torn lateral cartilage in his left knee. He would not be able to catch again all season, relegated to designated hitter whenever he returned.

The O's now needed a backup to Melvin, so they signed a veteran— none other than Jamie Quirk, most recently of Oakland until they cut him on July 24. While Quirk brought experience, including post-season success, Baltimore was forced to either play Quirk or Melvin every night for the rest of the year, even when Tettleton came back. This pulled a better, veteran bat out of the lineup—often Moreland, Sheets, or Orsulak.

Had the injury occurred only a week earlier, they could have traded for any of the catchers on the market before the regular deadline. Now, they decided signing Quirk was a better option than promoting prospect Chris Hoiles or trading for any of the catchers able to clear waivers in a postdeadline deal.

Then there was the matter of not having Tettleton at all for the next several weeks. Of all the AL East contenders, the O's were the team that could least afford to lose a top bat. They simply did not have many of them, and Tettleton was tied for fourth in the AL in home runs (twenty-two) and runs scored (sixty-seven), and third in slugging percentage (.523). "It's going to be a setback and they [his teammates] know it," Robinson told the *Post.* "You just don't replace a man who's having the year he's been having."

Quirk, thirty-four, would surely try. He had lasted nearly fifteen seasons in the majors despite never being an everyday player. He was versatile, playing nearly every position before learning to catch in 1980 to sustain his career. But he had already been cut twice in 1989, marking the third and fourth times he had been outright released since 1984. He would finish his career a .240 hitter with forty-three career homers in more than twenty-two hundred at bats. But he had played in late-summer division races before, appeared in postseason games with the Royals in 1976 and 1985, and was still considered to be steady defensively.

He would have an impact on the O's finish. A bigger one than anyone could imagine when he signed.

Quirk did not play that Monday night against Minnesota, as Melvin batted eighth and caught Ballard. We boarded buses from camp for the one-hour-plus trip to Memorial Stadium, my excitement building for my first live game since Father's Day.

This was a key start for Ballard. He had only earned a win in two of his previous eleven starts dating to June 5, his slide mirroring the Orioles' dip over much of that stretch. But he had lasted at least eight innings in two of his previous three starts. On this night before thirty-six thousand, including a bunch of happy campers, he lasted seven innings and scattered ten hits with a line you may never see in today's game: zero strikeouts and zero walks. It was so unusual even for 1989 that Bob Costas cited this stat line while calling a September O's game.

But Ballard was not the story of this contest. Cal Ripken started the game at shortstop as usual, batting third. After Devereaux and Bradley were both caught looking in the bottom of the first, punched out by home plate umpire Drew Coble, Ripken argued a strike called on him. Then suddenly Coble motioned with his right thumb over his shoulder—a gesture I could see even from our perch in the upper deck of the left-field stands.

A collective gasp rose throughout the stadium, the sound of more than thirty thousand people simultaneously reacting with anger and shock: *Did he just toss Cal?! Our Iron Man? Our milk-drinking hero?* We booed loudly as Ripken made his way into the dugout and then the clubhouse, out of sight for the rest of the night. While his consecutive games played streak was intact, Coble was denying hundreds of kids (not to mention adults, I suppose) what we wanted to see most: our hero, playing live in a division race. Ejecting Ripken "was kind of like throwing God out of Sunday school," Coble said later.

With his bat and Tettleton's removed from the game, the heart of the O's order now read: Rene Gonzales, Moreland, and Orsulak—followed by a sliding Milligan and Worthington. Minnesota won 4–2, scoring the go-ahead runs in the eighth when Ballard could no longer keep the Twins at bay. Gonzales went zero for four filling in for Ripken.

The O's remained two and one-half games up on Boston, who lost 6–4 in Kansas City that night. But Toronto beat Texas 2–1 to move back to .500, within two games of Baltimore and alone in second place. The team that had been ten games back as recently as July 5, after Milacki and the O's beat them 5–4 in Toronto, had made up eight games in only a month. And they still had nearly two full months, including seven games left against Baltimore, to seize the division. What once looked like a comfortable lead had turned into a classic division race. I was no longer sure this miracle was going to work out.

The next day—Tuesday, August 8—marked another major turning point in the O's season. As so often happened in 1989, just when the O's faced major adversity and seemed on the verge of collapsing and destroying our dream, something out of a Disney movie happened to keep them upright and keep us believing.

In fact the next chapter of the 1989 Baltimore Orioles season provided perhaps the best evidence yet that this team was enjoying a miracle season destined for a happy ending. Just as the Tettleton loss was settling in and Baltimore's once-commanding division lead was on the verge of dissipating, another unlikely hero emerged. In the year of Tettleton, Ballard, and a bunch of standout rookies, an unfamiliar man with a very familiar sounding name—especially to O's fans—came up from the minors and stabilized a needy rotation.

Dave Johnson was a twenty-nine-year-old career minor leaguer from nearby Middle River, Maryland. He sported a classic trimmed mustache, slightly portly body, and the same name as the regular second baseman on the O's clubs that won four AL pennants between 1966 and 1971 (and as Mets manager later, going by Davey Johnson).

The O's needed Johnson because they had lost the suddenly promising Jay Tibbs (5–0, 2.82 ERA in eight starts since late May) to a season-ending injury July 2, dropped the unreliable Jose Bautista (2–4, 5.03 ERA in nine starts) from the rotation in late May, and had to play ten games between July 25 and August 2.

Johnson made his first home start a week after being called up, after pitching adequately in his Major League debut during one of the losses at Boston on August 1. He promptly held the Twins to one run and eight hits in a 6–1 complete-game victory to help the O's maintain their two-game lead over Toronto.

The next day I sat on the bus on the way to camp and found this headline on the front of the *Post* sports section: "Johnson's Home, Orioles Grateful; Rookie, 29, Beats Twins, 6–1."

"He allowed a tainted first-inning run, then shut down the American League's highest-scoring team for the next eight," according to the *Post*. "When Johnson was done, he had an eight-hitter and shook a clinched fist in the air, waved toward thirty relatives and a 'couple of hundred' friends and retreated to the clubhouse. Once inside, with the cameras focused on him, he cried."

"He has command of the strike zone," Jackson, the pitching coach, said. "You have to be excited about this."

Johnson's arrival injected a needed dose of more magic into the O's season, jiving with good karma they would receive much of that week. Dropping three of the final five games of a homestand that later included four with the Red Sox did not reduce Baltimore's division lead. After beating Boston 6–1 on Sunday, August 13, to split that series, the O's still held a two-and-a-half-game lead over Toronto, Milwaukee, and Boston. They were still the only AL East team over .500.

In Sunday's victory, Johnson picked up his second consecutive win, holding Boston to six hits and one run in another complete game. He was promptly named AL Player of the Week. "He throws 85 mph, moves the ball around and has a decent breaking ball and change-up," the *Post* wrote. "He doesn't overpower anyone."

But he was succeeding anyway. He had been expected to merely fill a rotation spot and eat some innings temporarily for a thinning rotation. (Harnisch, Ballard, Schmidt, and Milacki were the only healthy, trusted arms in the rotation when Johnson was called up; Robinson and his coaches were losing confidence in Schmidt, who had lost four straight decisions in July.) But after two dominating wins in a week, Johnson earned an extended look.

He quickly became a regional story. That a rookie career minor leaguer had held down the heavy-hitting Twins and Red Sox in consecutive starts to keep the O's atop the division standings in August seemed apropos for the 1989 Baltimore Orioles, even if I had no idea then what "apropos" meant.

"So much of the Orioles' journey is based on hope, part of its appeal for the record Memorial Stadium crowds," *Post* columnist William Gildea wrote that week. "The lineup Wednesday night against Minnesota had the hint of baling wire about it: a newly acquired thirty-five-year-old DH (Keith Moreland); a rookie in right field, Stanley Jefferson, who brought a .233 batting average up from Rochester the day before; a journeyman (Rene Gonzales) at second, and the second-string catcher (Bob Melvin) forced into day-to-day service because of Mickey Tettleton's injury.

"The charm of the team is irresistible."

An August segment from the popular TV show *This Week in Baseball* further illuminated just how improbable Baltimore's continued first-place status was. Players around MLB were asked to name the O's rotation—including some who were about to face them. Most stammered over the question, despite Ballard's season-long excellence and Johnson's recent honor.

Baltimore's hold on first did not seem too surprising to me. I read all about Johnson's triumphs much as I had read of the emergence of Tettleton, Ballard, and the rookies. The O's historic worst-to-first quest still just seemed like it was meant to be.

But forty-six games remained in the season, including a four-game set with the Blue Jays in Baltimore the following week.

The O's began that week by taking two of three at Detroit, but their lead shrank to one and one-half games over both Toronto (who swept Boston) and Milwaukee (who swept the Yankees). They were promptly scheduled to play that four-game set against Toronto, then three against Milwaukee. At least these games would be at home.

My family followed most of this homestand from the beach, renting a condo in Bethany in Delaware for a week. We spent hours every day on the beach—boogie boarding and body surfing in the ocean, and playing pickup football or hot box on the sand. I also read the *Post* sports section daily while sitting on a towel or chair in the sun, drying out in between ocean excursions.

One day I was inspired to create a new game. Frustrated with the high-scoring *Strat-O-Matic*, I was determined to craft a more realistic baseball simulation. Freedom from the organized days of school and camp was always the drug I needed to unleash my creativity. So I used players' statistics from the box scores in the paper, stats on the baseball cards we had bought from the general store there, and two dice. Little by little I tried out different scenarios, eventually penning loose rules on notebook paper.

I sampled the new game with Michael, my cousins, and our neighbors who joined us at Bethany. They were not too impressed, but agreed it was at least better than *Strat-O-Matic*, which was a low bar for true seamheads. I was on to something, but sadly the game would not last past that summer. Life would get too busy too fast.

At the beach, though, we were still a couple of weeks away from the madness of a new school year's start. My parents gave Michael and me both twenty dollars for the week to spend on whatever we wanted (with Candy Kitchen fudge amounts capped nightly). Michael carefully spent his money, while I ran out with a couple of days left, dropping most of it on the fifty-cent packs of Donruss baseball cards at the store.

On our last full day of vacation, my addiction kicked into high gear. I went to the store with our neighbor David, Michael and a few other kids. The two-and-a-half-by-three-and-three-quarters-inch paper "wax" packs stacked high on the counter stared me in the face. I swear they were taunting me: "Donruss Baseball," the wax paper cover of the top pack, a 1988 variety, read in blue-and-yellow letters set against a red background featuring a baseball. I had to have it.

Like most boys we knew, Michael and I were sports card junkies. We spent untold amounts of money and time assembling, trading, and admiring our growing collections—depositing the more valuable cards into binders or hard plastic cases, while tossing the less valuable commons aside.

Topps, Fleer, and Donruss had been competing for our money, time, and attention for a couple of years by now. In 1988, Score debuted, and in 1989, Upper Deck outdid them all, introducing a glossy card that could not be damaged as easily. (This was a big deal for a kid like me, who accidentally damaged dozens of cards—including, I would discover one day to my horror, a couple of Jerry Rice rookie cards.)

Earlier in 1989, when Upper Deck emerged, Brad had fleeced me in a trade. In early spring the new *Beckett* monthly price guide had not yet been mailed out, so nobody knew the value of any Upper Deck cards. As we awaited our bible to arrive in the mail, these cards were like stocks without any defined value. We knew what cards were relatively worth, with rumors floating around that the Walt Weiss issue was worth a lot, after the A's shortstop had won the AL Rookie of the Year award in 1988. But that card ended up peaking at maybe a couple bucks.

In my two years of collecting, few, if any, cards from those years posted a value beyond a few dollars immediately after their release. For my birthday in 1989, though, one of my friends got me a box of Upper Deck cards, featuring twenty-four wax packs. I ripped through these packs with the same speed and veracity that

I often chomped my way through the surface of a Blow Pop to get to the gum inside.

I suddenly had in my possession three rookie cards for Ken Griffey Jr., the Seattle phenom. Griffey got off to a decent start in 1989, his first full season, but more importantly for the value of his cards, he was often shown on *SportsCenter* running down balls in the gap and smashing the occasional mammoth home run. He also played with flare, was hyped as a generational talent, and was only nineteen, making him an instant hit with kids my age. These factors drove up the value of his cards—unbeknownst to a precocious eleven-year-old with a penchant toward taking risks and trusting his relatives.

One Saturday in March or April, as Brad was babysitting me and my brothers, he noticed my Griffey cards. "I'll trade you for one of them," he proposed.

Intrigued as always by the prospect of a deal and knowing I had two other Griffey rookie cards in my back pocket, I asked what he would give me in exchange. I had always envied his older cards, anything he had from before I started collecting. Acquiring such cards on my own usually took convincing my father to drive us to the closest card store about twenty minutes away, and me actually having money to spend. So that was rare.

Brad knew this as he vultured in. "How about an Andy Van Slyke rookie?" he said, pointing to a 1984 Topps issue in the most recent *Beckett* magazine, now approaching thirty days old. The card was worth about four dollars. "And," he added, "I will throw in a Tony Gwynn 1984 Topps."

Van Slyke was a pretty good outfielder, and Gwynn was an All-Star and one of the best hitters in the game. These 1984 cards were a whopping five years old now—a lot to me. But this was Gwynn's second-year card, so it was worth only a few dollars. Nevertheless, a Van Slyke rookie card and any old Gwynn card were too enticing to turn down. I made the deal. The next day Brad retrieved the cards from his house and I handed him one of my Griffey cards.

A day or two later the new *Beckett* arrived in the mail. Michael and I opened it up and quickly flipped to the pages listing the 1989 cards, eagerly anticipating the values assigned to several hundred cards by some random adults miles away. There at the top of the Upper Deck list was the Griffey card, issue number 1, its value reading . . ."$60."

"Sixty dollars?!" I screamed.

Michael's eyes fixed squarely on mine, his mouth agape like the Hungry Hungry Hippo toy we had played to destruction a few years earlier.

We flipped back to the 1984 cards and saw the values of the Gwynn and Van Slyke cards had not changed. Then it dawned on me: I had traded a sixty-dollar card for two cards totaling less than ten dollars. I was furious. Michael told my father, who quickly became just as upset. "He did what?! Call him and tell him to trade that card back to you," he roared at me.

I called Brad, but he refused to trade the card back. As angry as I was, I did not push. I knew the unwritten, unspoken rules of collecting cards, and one of them stated there were no trade-backs. You did your research and made your move. You had no right to expect anyone to accommodate you just because the value of a card suddenly shot up—or in the case of the Griffey card, debuted. So despite my father's continued protests, I dropped it.

But this experience was lodged in my mind a few months later, when I found myself at that store in Bethany staring at that pack of Donruss cards. I had to have just one more pack, right then. Or more. "Michael," I turned to him. "Loan me a dollar."

"Why?" His tone suggested that he genuinely wanted to know what I was going to spend the money on and figured he may not see that dollar for some time.

"Just loan me a dollar," I replied. "I want another pack of cards."

He leaned in. "Fine," he said, "but I get to open the pack."

"But I get to keep the cards."

"Yeah, but I get to go through the cards when we open the pack."

David heard the deal, so I felt confident it would be honored. Besides, I had no other recourse—short of hoping my father would fall into a very pleasant mood later that day and suggest he needed to go to the store. But that was far from a lock. "Fine," I replied. "As long as I can keep the cards, you can open the pack."

He bought the pack and we took it back to our condo. We sat on the blue carpeted floor and he started opening it up. A few cards whizzed by, failing to draw my eye or heart.

Then I saw it. It was a beautiful, unmistakable card. In the bottom right I saw: "RATED ROOKIE" in light blue caps and big bold italicized font. A fresh-faced player stared at us smiling, wearing the red "C" on his royal blue batting helmet that we instantly identified as the logo for the Chicago Cubs.

It was a Mark Grace rookie card.

By now, Grace was having an outstanding season as the Cubs' first baseman. Playing for the lovable Cubs with their huge national following gave him even more cachet. So the card was valuable.

If Michael did not know that, I gave it away by gasping audibly and pumping my fist. Alas, not even my best poker face was going to fool my shrewd nine-year-old brother into bypassing the card. He scrolled through the rest of the pack and several other good cards popped up, firing me up even more.

It also excited Michael, who was now smiling too. "I am keeping the pack," he announced.

"What?!" I yelled. "That is my pack. You promised."

"I bought the pack."

"You said you were loaning me the money!" I was incredulous. "Give me the cards!" I yelled, my eyes bulging and fixing directly at him.

Having known us for several years, David recognized what was perilously close to happening. "Ryan, calm down," he said. His harried tone suggested he feared what he may be unable to stop, as I was almost his size.

"GIVE ME THE CARDS!" I yelled again. I could feel rage building up inside me. Not only did I stand to lose the Mark Grace rookie card, but my own brother was pulling similar nonsense over on me as Brad had. I lunged at Michael. But David tackled me and held me down for a few seconds. "Those are my cards!" I yelled, struggling to finally break free. "Stop being such a faggot!!!"

Michael dashed into his room and hid the cards. He was always good at hiding things, so I never found the pack. I remained pissed for the rest of the day, at least, but something more important than baseball cards was lost that day. (That's no small statement given how much those cards meant to us then.) I had always been very close with Brad and my brothers. Michael and I—despite having very different personalities and only being two years apart—had rarely fought. The previous summer, we spent many nights lying on the floor at the edge of our bedrooms, talking about baseball and Nintendo games until we fell asleep. I worshipped Brad, who was the best athlete I knew.

The card fiascos, on top of Mom's misreading the camps and my impending separation from my long-time school friends, only furthered an existential question building in the back of my mind, as my world was spinning out of control: *Who could I trust wholeheartedly anymore? Anyone?*

(Of course: By the time I gave most of my cards away to my nephews while writing this book in my forties, I had three copies of the Grace rookie card.)

Fortunately I had effective distractions to keep pushing down my impending problems, via the beach and the O's. At the outset of the Baltimore-Toronto series, Toronto had won seven of ten to move over .500 for the first time since opening day. Milwaukee had won twenty of twenty-nine, including six straight, crossing .500 for the first time since they were 10–9 in April. It seemed like both clubs were finally rounding into form, with plenty of time left to overtake the struggling O's.

So another litmus test awaited Baltimore. This could be the moment that everyone had been predicting since the O's had taken a firm grasp on first place nearly three months earlier, that moment when a true AL East contender emerged and the miracle season in Baltimore began its final Icarus-like descent. The Jays were deep, healthy, and surging. The O's were beat up and thin. Moreland was not even approaching the impact of Wilson, who had gone nine-for-fourteen and scored four runs in the three-game sweep of Boston.

But there was still "Orioles Magic" left in the 1989 season. The series opener Thursday was tied 1–1 midway through the fourth. With one out in the bottom of the inning, Moreland singled to center off Toronto starter John Cerutti. Milligan hit what looked like a double-play ball to short, but the normally surehanded Tony Fernandez's throw to second got away. Moreland was now on second and Milligan on first with still only one out. Suddenly the O's got hot: Worthington singled to right, Jefferson homered to left, and Melvin and Billy Ripken both singled to center.

Then the Blow Jays of 1985 and 1987 fully reemerged:

- Cerutti tossed a wild pitch.
- Cerutti hit Bradley to load the bases.
- Frank Wills replaced Cerutti and faced Devereaux, who hit a grounder to short. Fernandez threw to Manuel Lee at second to retire Bradley, but Lee's throw to first was off target. That allowed Melvin and Ripken to score, while Devereaux raced to second on the overthrow.

Just for shits and giggles, Cal Ripken then smashed a homer to left. When the barrage was over, this light-hitting lineup had dropped eight runs in one inning. Ballard, Williamson, and Olson were steady enough to keep Toronto from making it close and the O's won 11–6.

But the O's lost the next two games of the series, dwindling their division lead to just one-half game over Toronto and Milwaukee as they prepared to close the series against Toronto on Sunday afternoon, August 20. The Blue Jays started ace Dave Stieb on full rest, the O's the rookie Harnisch on just three days' rest.

No matter. Harnisch and a few sparkling defensive plays kept Toronto at bay, and he left the game with a 4–0 lead in the seventh. Toronto then struck twice against Thurmond, but the O's responded with three RBI singles in the bottom of the inning, putting the game away. They won 7–2 to keep their division lead again—just as they had stiff-armed Boston a few weeks earlier.

But, while Toronto was now one and a half games back again, Baltimore remained just a half game up on fast-charging Milwaukee.

The Brewers had won three of four from Boston over the weekend. They arrived in Baltimore for their three-game set beginning the next day. Only about six weeks remained in the season, so this would be another critical series. Like Toronto, Milwaukee boasted a deep lineup. The Brewers were led by outfielders Robin Yount and Paul Molitor, both future Hall of Famers still in their primes. Rookie Gary Sheffield, a future all-star, was only a platoon player on this club.

The newly acquired Jerry Reuss started the opener for Milwaukee against Ballard. The lefty promptly held Milwaukee to seven hits and no walks in a complete game shutout, 5–0. Moreland put the O's up for good in the first, with a two-out single scoring Bradley. Jefferson homered to make it 2–0 in the fourth and Cal Ripken smashed a three-run homer in the fifth.

The next night the O's scored four early runs off Milwaukee ace Chris Bosio and Johnson pitched a complete-game five-hitter, as the O's won 4–2.

Baltimore then finished off the sweep the following night, scoring three in the seventh to rally for a 3–1 win. Milacki held Milwaukee to six hits and that single run over eight-plus innings, with Olson setting down three straight Brewers after replacing him in the ninth.

The O's had played nearly flawless baseball, especially defensively and on the mound, in outscoring MLB's hottest team 12–3 over three games.

Milwaukee was shocked. "I can't recall a mistake they made in the series," Milwaukee outfielder Glen Braggs said afterward. "It's like these three days were a blur."

The baseball world was startled too. Had this inexperienced, banged-up team just swept the surging, veteran Brewers? While starting two rookie pitchers and missing their cleanup hitter? "They've already set the record: no last-place team has ever been first on this late a date the following year," Boswell noted in a column published during the series. "Did anybody think they were going to waltz into the playoffs without a fight? What's shocking is that this team, which should be dead, is still acting extremely alive."

Milwaukee? Not so much. After the series the Brewers were essentially done. The sweep pushed Milwaukee three and one-half games back; they would lose their next three at Toronto and never move within six games of the division lead again.

For Baltimore, the sweep gave the O's a bit more cushion in the division. Their lead now stood at two games over Toronto, who had won the first two games of their series against Detroit that week.

"Their successive August showdowns with the Red Sox, Blue Jays, and Brewers are almost concluded and, somehow, the Orioles' stock has actually risen," Boswell wrote. "This month three teams—Boston, then Toronto, and now Milwaukee—have had a chance to win a symbolic game and nose ahead of Baltimore in the AL East. Each time the Orioles won. That's eighty-eight straight days in first place and counting."

But could they maintain that lead for the rest of the season? More than a month remained and, while Milwaukee and Boston were fading, Toronto was not going away. The Blue Jays were one game under .500 on August 13, after losing at Kansas City. But they then won eight of ten. Their eighth win during that stretch, an 11–3 triumph over Detroit on August 24, pulled them within a game and a half of the idle O's.

Meanwhile, the sweep of Milwaukee was not harmless to the O's; both Billy Ripken and Worthington succumbed to injuries that would knock them out of the lineup for several games. Multiple regulars were now out as the final week of August began. It seemed to baseball insiders it was just a matter of time until Baltimore's perch atop the division ended.

The O's managed to hold off Toronto for most of the remainder of the month, going 5–2 combined against the Yankees and Cleveland. Then came the final day of August. Before fewer than ten thousand fans at Cleveland's Municipal Stadium, the sub-.500 Indians knocked Johnson out after three innings. Schmidt—cast out of the rotation in early August with a five-plus ERA and five straight losses—and the rest of the bullpen fared little better. The O's lost 11–0.

Earlier that day nearly fifty thousand people had packed into SkyDome for an afternoon tilt with the White Sox. The Jays scored three runs in the first and Stieb, Jim Acker, and closer Tom Henke held Chicago to six combined hits as Toronto won 5–1.

The next day, the Friday of Labor Day weekend, I looked at the *Post* at our Rockville home and saw what I had been dreading: Toronto's win and Baltimore's loss had evened the standings, with both teams 72–62. After three months alone atop the division, the O's were no longer the front-runners on paper. Given the way the previous six weeks had gone, they were no longer considered the front-runners by anyone outside their clubhouse.

Perhaps it was fitting that the Jays caught them just as summer— that season so synonymous with childhood innocence—was ending. Frighteningly soon, the school year would start, adults would return from vacations back to busier offices, and the weather would start to cool down a bit. Our birds of summer had entertained us and made us believe over the previous three months, especially in June and the first half of July.

But now, could they rediscover that magic and let us hold onto baseball season for just a few more weeks—even as fall unofficially started? Or would the surging Jays bury them and crush the dreams of O's fans young and old?

Baltimore's losing the division lead startled me. For the first time since summer unofficially began Memorial Day weekend they were not alone in first. So much had happened over that span: I had graduated elementary school, played in my last baseball game of the season and my last game ever at my home Potomac Woods upper field, attended two very different camps with different kids, nearly killed my brother over a baseball card, and learned boogie boarding. I was also now balancing MomMom Flick and Freddy's ill health, my nascent anxiety disorders, the impending school change, and growing apart from Mom.

Yet throughout all that, nothing had changed atop the AL East standings. The O's had been my rock. But now, for the first time since they captured my heart in late May, I seriously questioned whether this miracle of a division title would occur. It had seemed so certain to me for so long, but now it appeared unlikely—at least on the surface.

But I had mixed feelings. Even as Toronto caught up in the standings, there were still plenty of reasons to be hopeful as August closed, especially for preternaturally optimistic eleven-year-olds with the innate ability to block out logic when it came to following sports. The O's had survived a brutal stretch of injuries (by the end of August they had started ten different pitchers on the season) and tilts with division challengers. New heroes such as Johnson and second baseman Tim Hulett (who came up from Triple A after the Ripken injury to drive in five runs and help secure four straight wins over the Yankees the previous weekend) had emerged to plug holes. Melvin was even hitting .290 and had driven in nine runs in sixty-one at bats since replacing Tettleton as the everyday catcher.

"It's so much fun, and we've got a quiet confidence. People seem to catch it when they come up," Melvin explained.

Tettleton would soon be back, at least to DH, with Worthington returning at third. Finley could be back soon from injury, too, and it was approaching September 1. That meant Schilling and Anderson would be called up, with rosters expanding. Another young, highly touted pitcher would likely join them as well: On August 18, Ben McDonald and his agent Scott Boras had finally ended protracted, sometimes nasty contract negotiations with the club when he signed a three-year deal.

"If Tettleton, Steve Finley, and Mickey Weston get semi-healthy, if righty Curt Schilling and Anderson (at Rochester) can chip in, and if McDonald can help in the bullpen, Robinson would have a deep pitching staff and a wealth of pinch hitters who have already contributed this year in pressure situations," Boswell wrote. "Suddenly, even that 1–13 ordeal seems like it may have been the Orioles' fortnight in the wilderness.

"'We lost as many as we could lose without losin' 'em all,' Robinson said, laughing. "'But we played hard. We didn't make any excuses. We slowly came out of it. And we stayed together.'"

"For the Orioles, a division title is probably a dream as improbable as the '67 Red Sox pennant or the world titles of the '69 Mets and '88 Dodgers [who had shocked the heavily favored Mets and A's in the playoffs]. Will it become a reality?" Boswell posited. "On one hand, the Blue Jays have the talent and the Brewers may have the heart. On the other, remember, what we are watching is not entirely baseball. It's also Bird Trek. This team has already dared to go where no team has gone before."

Posing for Mom in our kitchen just before leaving for my first day at a new school and first day of private school. I look about as thrilled as I was. Slinging your backpack over one shoulder was still in style, no matter how heavy.

Chapter 8

SEPTEMBER: END OF THE INNOCENCE

Despite the myriad TV and newspaper ads thrown at us, pages flipped right-to-left on the thickening eight-by-eleven-inch yearly calendar that sat on Mom's desk, and our annual end-of-summer beach trip, for weeks I managed to block out the reality that I would be going back to school, and soon. I had further denied to myself that I would not actually be going back to school, the school I had attended for six years, the school my friends always attended with me. Instead I would be going to a new school where I knew exactly one student and only knew *of* one other—a school that gave me a bad vibe when I visited.

With everyone back from vacations, we had about a week to lounge, straddling the end of August and start of September before the public school year started. I easily filled that time sleeping in and playing intense pickup baseball games down the street. A neighbor's fence was the perfect backdrop for home plate, with infielders strewn out on his yard and outfielders standing across the narrow street on other neighbors' driveways and yards.

The new school year would be starting very soon. The weather hovered in the nineties with nasty humidity. My grandmother and cat were very sick. Another team had caught the Orioles in the standings.

But none of this mattered to me when we were playing ball; I got lost in the competition and the week zoomed by.

Then, on the day after Labor Day, the public school kids went back to school—without me. That night we met up to play baseball again. We were intent to soak up nearly every minute of the early September evening sun before we got called home for dinner, during those precious days early in the school year when nobody yet had too many homework assignments or after-school commitments.

As Michael and I walked up to play, Steve smiled and shouted from across the neighbor's yard at me. "Yo!" he said. "Today was our first day of school. I ran out of there as soon as the bell rang. Everyone did. Our principal just stood there trying to stop us. But nobody listened!"

I nodded. That sounded fun, I thought. I could feel a pit building in my stomach. It was not just Steve's first day of middle school. It was also my first day not attending school with him—or Ross, or Adam, or any of my friends—in years (illnesses aside). Even though I spent much of that day sleeping in, playing video games, and watching *SportsCenter*, I wished I had been in school with them.

For the first time in five years I would also be attending a different school than Michael. I could barely remember first grade or kindergarten, so the house felt oddly quiet when I awoke around noon each of those few weekdays between Labor Day and my first day at Landon the following week. I quietly poured myself bowls of cereal, ate in front of *SportsCenter*, took long showers, watched more TV, crushed the computer in *Tecmo Bowl* or *Blades of Steel*. For the first time that I could ever recall, I found nobody around the house or neighborhood to hang with for a solid couple of hours; it felt like much longer as I waited for everyone to get home from school.

At least I had those rendezvous and O's games to look forward to later in the days. But this was a perilous time to follow the team with too much downtime. A 6–5 start to September entrenched them firmly in second place, pushing them two and a half games behind Toronto after an 8–1 loss at Texas on Sunday, September 10. Schmidt, making just his third start in six weeks, could not get out of the first inning, surrendering six runs. After setting a tone for the season by matching Clemens on Opening Day, he was done in the rotation for good. Schmidt would not start another game all season, with Robinson opting to ride a four-man rotation for the duration.

Meanwhile Toronto kept winning, including a 5–4 victory in Cleveland that afternoon in ten innings. After closing August strong, the Jays also won eight of their first ten in September.

September 10 was also the day of my Landon orientation. There was definitely no going back now. Being eleven allowed me to mostly avoid dwelling on my fears of attending this mysterious new school, with its dress code, lack of girls, and campus a solid twenty-minute drive from home instead of a ten-minute walk. It may have only been in Bethesda, but it may as well have been on Pluto. This was all coming, and soon.

For the most part in early September, though, I stayed in the moment, holding on to one vestige of the spring and summer of '89: the dream of the O's completing a historic miracle season and winning the AL East. Baltimore and Toronto were due to meet for a three-game set in Toronto over the season's final weekend. If the O's could just be within three games by then, they would at least have a chance.

The Blue Jays became baseball's darlings after they finally overtook the O's over Labor Day weekend, when the O's lost to the White Sox while Toronto beat Minnesota on Friday, September 1.

"We bring you the Toronto Blue Jays, who this weekend took over first place in the American League East for the first time in four and a half months. Judging by their starting pitching, their bullpen, and their rejuvenated offense, they may stay there. Who should be surprised? Well, everyone. And no one," the *Post* wrote. General manager Pat Gillick "acquired ex-Mets Lee Mazzilli and Mookie

Wilson. Wilson is running and playing as well as he has in years (hitting .339 and stealing ten bases in ten attempts in one month since joining Toronto), and the two of them have added stability and maturity to a clubhouse that didn't often have it. . . .

"With shortstop Tony Fernandez and third baseman Kelly Gruber both healthy and George Bell on a tear, the Toronto lineup may be the best in the American League. With [Jim] Acker, the bullpen has five quality arms, and with Jimmy Key and (ex-Oriole standout) Mike Flanagan healthy and young Todd Stottlemyre getting his feet on the ground, the starting rotation probably is the American League's best."

The O's meanwhile had lost two straight over that weekend, including that blowout loss Friday that knocked them into second place for the first time since May 25. That defeat came just after they flew from Cleveland to Chicago following the 11–0 loss to the Indians the night before.

"Their day had been a terrible one, beginning early this morning with a four-hour wait on a runway in Cleveland. Dawn had broken over Lake Michigan by the time they saw their hotel," Justice wrote in the *Post*. "Daryl Boston hit a first-inning grand slam and the Chicago White Sox ripped them, 10–1, before 11,574 at Comiskey Park. It was over that quickly, and so was Baltimore's ninety-eight-day run in first place."

The offense had scored one run or fewer in three of four games and showed little sign of quickly breaking out of that slump. "Phil Bradley is hitting .135 on the road trip, Randy Milligan is at .200 and Bob Melvin is in a zero-for-ten slump. Craig Worthington is hitless in six at-bats since returning to the lineup after missing eight games with a sore left shoulder," the *Post* reported.

Robinson put on a good face. "It's no big deal," he told the *Post*. "One game out is nothing. What's important is that we get back to playing well. We haven't done that the last couple of days, and if we don't turn it around it won't matter what Toronto does."

One morning that weekend I stared at the standings in the *Post* sports section for what seemed like several minutes, trying to make them change as I struggled to accept that the O's had fallen out of first. *How had this happened? And seemingly so quickly?* One minute I was sleeping in, compulsively playing *Tecmo Bowl*, competing in my baseball league, and otherwise basking in the start of summer. I left for sleepaway camp in late June with the O's comfortably ahead in the division standings, closing in on the All-Star break.

The next minute, it seemed, the school year had essentially started and the O's had fallen behind the hot, healthier Blue Jays.

With nobody around to distract me as I read the paper while ESPN blared from the kitchen TV that first full week of September, I struggled to comprehend these seemingly sudden changes. I could feel angst building up inside me, but there was nothing I could do except wait for the next game and hope.

Some fans seemed ready to accept whatever the season's ultimate outcome would be, to savor what the O's had given us that summer and perhaps stave off any heartbreak that may come from officially losing the division after leading it for more than three months. Jonathan Yardley, a *Post* style section columnist, published a column on Labor Day, with the O's one game behind Toronto. He noted spending ninety-eight consecutive days in first was a remarkable achievement for any team, especially these O's.

"If you had said, six months ago, that the Orioles would achieve this distinction, you would have been hooted out of the house, or made to sit in the corner wearing a funny hat. The Orioles, after all, by any stretch of the imagination were the worst team in baseball; the only place they were going to spend ninety-eight games in a row was the cellar, and that was a certainty," he wrote. "Back there in late July the Orioles with their seven-and-a-half-game lead may have seemed to have a lock on the division, but it's a long season."

"Of course there may still be a miracle. The Orioles, who of late have been pitching and fielding heroically, may rediscover how to hit the ball and may hit themselves into the playoffs, but don't count on it," he added. "Instead of fretting over the Orioles' fall from grace we should be thanking them for the pleasures they've already provided, and be grateful for that. . . . Yes, a division championship would be nice, a pennant would be nicer, a world title would be nicest. But when you get right down to it, could any of that be appreciably better than what we've already had?"

Yes! I thought. *How about that division championship?!* Anything less at this point, after they had projected my hopes toward the sun for so long, would be a major disappointment. They did not need to win the pennant or world title. A simple historic division title would be enough for me, just as it was for the fictional Indians of *Major League*.

Nearly a full month still remained in the regular season. Boston and Milwaukee also were within striking distance and were more talented than the O's too. But for all intents and purposes now it was the Toronto "Blow Jays" vs. the "Why Not?" Baltimore Orioles. Fate had to be on our side, I thought. Hadn't nearly every sports movie I had ever seen—from *Major League* to *Hoosiers* to most of the (only four at that time) *Rocky* movies—ended with the underdog beating the heavy favorite?

"Toronto is playing a lot of road games while we'll be at home. It's not over yet," Milacki noted.

Plus Anderson, McDonald, Weston, Schilling, and Finley were indeed called up in early September. The O's now had their young arms in the bullpen, even if they were untested, and the return of Anderson and Finley gave them a plethora of options in the outfield.

Game on.

I viewed much of this division race from friends' and family living rooms, my basement, and my parents' room. I rarely watched alone, as the race had caught even Mom's interest. The Senators had never been competitive when my parents were growing up and—despite Mom often taping Mets games for us during the 1986 and 1988 play-offs—they did not jump on the Mets bandwagon with Michael, Brad, and me. Those teams had cruised to division titles, so this race was new to all of us.

On Labor Day night, we watched the O's fall behind Cleveland 3–0 in the top of the first. They were in the midst of a forty-four-inning streak without an extra base hit. But Devereaux led off for Baltimore by doubling and Bradley walked; both later scored in the bottom of the inning. Cal Ripken homered in the third to put the O's ahead 4–3—Baltimore's first homer in over a week—and the game was tied 4–4 going into the bottom of the ninth.

As I lay on their bed between them, I begged my parents to let me stay up and watch the conclusion. The time was approaching 10:30, but my father overruled Mom in my favor: "Let him just stay up for this inning."

I was all in on the bottom of the ninth. But Worthington and Melvin were quickly retired. I sulked, thinking that I would likely miss seeing the ending. I was resigned to listening to the radio broadcast from my bedroom for as long as I could stay awake, maybe watching the TV's reflection on my parents' bedroom window.

Hulett, still playing for the injured Billy Ripken and hitting eighth, stepped up. The O's had not had a base runner since the fourth and had just those two extra base hits earlier in the game over the last five full contests. Ripken and Devereaux were regulars, Ripken an all-star. Tim Hulett was the guy the O's signed off the street in March after he had missed the whole 1988 season and then spent most of the 1989 season in the minors.

Why not?

With two strikes he swung and blasted a fly ball to left-center. The ball carried as Indians outfielders Joe Carter and Brad Komminsk pursued it . . . to the track, the wall . . .

The ball magically disappeared out of sight, landing in the bullpen.

As Hulett circled the bases, the crowd's eruption cascaded across the room. I jumped up and down screaming. Mom smiled and gasped as she watched the replays, while my father laughed loudly at the absurdity of it all: Tim Fucking Hulett! I smiled widely and watched every replay before I was finally whisked off to bed.

"Every night it's a new hero for the Baltimore Orioles. Tonight it was Tim Hulett, who smacked a two-strike, two-out home run in the bottom of the ninth inning for a 5–4 victory over the Cleveland Indians in front 32,875 fans at Memorial Stadium," the *Post* wrote. "Cleveland reliever Rod Nichols (3–4), who had come in for starter Greg Swindell in the fourth, retired fifteen straight hitters until Hulett came up.

"He struck me out the time before on a breaking ball in the dirt," Hulett said. "I was trying to get myself to stay back and not get fooled again. He threw me a couple fast balls and then hung the breaking ball."

The O's beat Cleveland again the next night. But their minor resurgence was not enough to catch the Blue Jays. Toronto won both nights, maintaining their one-game division lead.

The following night, September 6, my father and I had tickets to see the Orioles play the Indians in the finale of their three-game series. Fewer than thirty thousand turned out as public schools in both metro areas had just opened the school year. Making his fifth career start on the mound and first of the season was the brash twenty-two-year-old right-hander the Orioles had acquired a year earlier, along with Anderson, in the Boddicker trade: Schilling, the future Hall of Famer.

The Indians had outfielder Cory Snyder. At least that was what I most cared about as I fished through my most valuable baseball cards, organized much more neatly than I organized my school papers. I easily found my 1987 Topps Snyder rookie card, with the cartoonish gold trophy in the bottom right corner as Snyder, sporting a blond mullet growing out of the back of his cap, half-crouched and looked away from the camera. I shoved the card and its plastic protective case into my pocket along with a crisp ball and a black Sharpie pen, hoping to finally get a few autographs at a game.

After my dad got back from work, he drove us from Rockville through traffic into the southern limits of Baltimore. We passed the Inner Harbor and Camden Yards, still just featuring a giant warehouse and massive construction site after state authorities had approved the new stadium for that location two years earlier. We drove deeper into the energized city on a warm weekday September evening, toward the stadium on the north side that had housed the Orioles since they had moved from St. Louis in 1954.

We briskly walked in, my white Nike sneakers sticking to the floor as we moved toward the lower-level seats that my father had sprung for. A man about my grandfather's age sat behind us, giving his friend the scouting report on Schilling. I eavesdropped, eager to soak up any details. The O's were in a bind because of injuries and the schedule, he said, so they had to start Schilling. It was the first big game for a man who would become known as a big-game pitcher, who would one day match Clemens in Game Seven of the World Series.

This night, he went up against journeyman Bud Black and the going-nowhere Indians. It would be no contest. Schilling gave up four runs on six hits over two and one-third innings, and the Orioles quickly fell behind. "That wasn't me," he said. "I just couldn't get my fastball down, and that hasn't happened too much all year. I'm really disappointed. I worked hard last winter and did the things I thought I had to do. Then to have this happen."

Black held the Orioles in check and, by the bottom of the third, Baltimore trailed 4–0. Then the O's loaded the bases with two out. Cal Ripken stepped up. Everyone in the crowd stood, clapping and cajoling our hero to get the O's back into the game.

Alas, Ripken lifted a fly ball into foul territory in left. Carter settled under it and nabbed it, ending the threat. The O's would scarcely threaten again.

Earlier in the third, however, we saw enough to make me go home happy. After Schilling struggled, the likely future ace of the club jogged from the bullpen to the mound to replace him. I watched McDonald warm up like a young protégé watching his master, staring intently as he wound up, kicked up his left leg, and violently fired the ball into the waiting mitt of Melvin. From our vantage point and through the eyes of my small frame, I was awed by the sheer magnitude of this baby-faced fireballer. I had been to a handful of O's games by now, but this was the first time I had really come to appreciate JUST HOW BIG AND POWERFUL some Major League players were.

Others were impressed too. "McDonald got his first ovation when it was announced he was warming up in the bullpen, and another when he walked onto the field with the stadium PA system blaring 'Benny and the Jets,' " the *Post* reported.

McDonald fared well; he held Cleveland to one hit and one run, while fanning two and walking one over two and two-thirds innings. "I'm just glad to get this first one behind me. I threw pretty good. I couldn't really tell because I was a little nervous. I couldn't feel my arm," he said afterward.

"His fastball was overpowering and he had a real good curveball. He looked like he belonged, like he'd been out there all year," Robinson said.

But another Robinson comment to the *Post* that night hinted at the conundrum the O's faced, and not just with McDonald: "He's not ready to start and he may not be ready for a while. The one thing I can't do is overwork this kid. He's a big part of our future; he's not in game-shape yet. We're going to bring him along slowly, but I can see right now that he's going to be very usable down the stretch."

Translation: The O's were indeed still trying to win the division, but they would not risk sacrificing a future that they hoped would include many division races just to secure this one AL East crown.

Toronto, however, needed to win this year. Another failure, especially in a year when Boston and Milwaukee were barely hanging around and the Yankees had sunk, after the Jays had blown the division in 1987 and fallen just short of Boston in 1988? When the only serious competition they had was Cal Ripken, Phil Bradley, and a bunch of kids and cast-offs? That would likely force Pat Gillick to blow up the team, if he even kept his job.

Satisfied with McDonald's performance, we gave up any hope of the Orioles coming back as they fell behind 9–0. On any other night we would have headed home after McDonald left the game, or even sooner. But there was something magical about this evening despite the loss—McDonald's debut, a division race viewed in-person. So, with nary an argument from my father, we stuck it out until the end.

After the final pitch, I sprinted down toward the Indians dugout, making sure my Snyder rookie card was still in my pocket along with the ball and Sharpie. Then I waited. After Snyder and his teammates briefly celebrated their victory in the infield, he walked toward the dugout . . . and was immediately intercepted by a television reporter for a postgame interview. I sighed and fidgeted as I watched every second of an interview that seemed to last forever.

While I hovered over the Indians' dugout extending my body until it was almost completely flat, I clutched the card in one hand and the ball in another. Another Indian emerged from the dugout and made eye contact with me. With his clean-shaven babyface, he looked younger than a typical Major Leaguer. I had no idea who he was.

After noticing me, he quietly walked toward me. I extended the ball, reaching into my pocket for the black Sharpie. He took the pen and ball, signed his name in neat cursive, nodded and then walked away. He never uttered a word and neither did I.

Maybe thirty seconds after he disappeared into the darkness of the corner of the dugout, Snyder's interview wrapped. He also saw me, walked straight toward me, took the card and Sharpie from my hands and signed his name. He then also quickly disappeared into the clubhouse.

Wow! I thought. *I got Cory Snyder's autograph!* (That was likely the first autograph I secured in-person.)

As I put the card into my pocket for safekeeping, I removed the ball from the other pocket and examined it. It read: "Joey Belle." Joey would start going by "Albert" a couple of years later, then set the majors on fire with his combustible power hitting and temper. Belle anchored the lineup for Indians teams that won two straight AL Central titles in 1995–1996, leading the AL in RBI both seasons and finishing in the top three of MVP voting for three straight years (1994–1996).

That was still a few years away as I put the ball back in my pocket and later set it on a shelf in my bedroom, next to the game balls I had earned from my coaches.

The Orioles slid two games behind Toronto with the loss and Toronto's win in Chicago. But for this one night, the AL East race could wait. I had secured Cory Snyder's autograph. I had watched a Major League game from up close in the lower deck and seen Ben McDonald's debut. And maybe this Joey Belle guy would turn out to be somebody and that ball would be worth something one day— something more than that Griffey rookie card I had dealt away.

The race continued. The O's traveled to Texas, taking two of the first three games in a five-game set against the Rangers, who had faded in the AL West. They sat one and a half games behind Toronto, which split the first two games of a four-game set at Cleveland.

The fourth game of the Baltimore-Texas series, on Saturday, September 9, went past midnight. This, after Olson struck out Rangers shortstop Fred Manrique with runners on second and third and the score tied 2–2 with two out in the ninth. Then with two out and nobody on in the tenth, Tettleton singled to left, bringing up Milligan. The game was nearly four hours old.

A few hundred miles north, the Jays were also in extra innings. About the same time that Milligan stepped up in Texas, the Jays loaded the bases with two out in the top of the sixteenth and the score tied 5–5. Nobody had scored since the eighth inning and somebody named Jeff Kaiser was pitching for Cleveland. A real somebody stepped up: Jays' slugger Fred McGriff.

Back in Texas, Milligan swung hard and launched a go-ahead homer for the O's. Olson then retired the Rangers in order, including standouts Harold Baines and Ruben Sierra, to secure the 4–2 win. For a moment, it seemed the O's may pull closer to Toronto.

In Cleveland, though, McGriff hit a ground ball that found a hole between first and second. Nelson Liriano and Lloyd Moseby scored, giving Toronto a 7–5 lead. Frank Wills started on the mound for Toronto in the bottom of the sixteenth. Wills was a spot starter and middle reliever who would appear in only twenty-four games for Toronto on the season. But the three Indians hitters he was due to face were not club stalwarts either and he retired them in order to secure another win for Toronto.

Less than an hour earlier, the O's faced the prospect of moving within a half-game of Toronto or falling two and one-half games back. Instead they remained one and one-half games behind. All the drama of late Saturday night baseball in September changed nothing in the AL East race.

The next day, though, was September 10. The Rangers earned that 8–1 win over Baltimore while Toronto secured that 5–4 victory over Cleveland, pushing the O's two and one-half games behind. It marked their biggest deficit since they were three games back May 8, when they stood 13–17 and we considered that an achievement. The O's were hardly fading, but Toronto was surging. Only seventeen games remained in the season as the O's returned for their final homestand.

That day, September 10, will be forever etched in my memory. Things were about to change very suddenly and dramatically—more impactful immediately than even the failing health of my grandmother and beloved pet, and the nascent anxiety disorders I was trying to ignore. There was no more denying it, no matter how hard I tried: sixth grade was going to start and I was going to a new school without my friends. I would have to wear nice clothes, nice shoes. I would have to get up earlier. Hell, after a couple of weeks of lounging since we returned from the beach, I would have to get up in the morning . . . period.

Mom and I attended the Landon orientation for new students on campus. We headed to my homeroom, where a bombastic, fortyish, muscular, bearded white man with piercing blue eyes greeted us. "My name is Sandy. Welcome to Landon School," he bellowed.

I was intimidated instantly.

I met Chris, a skinny kid from Landover, and Pat, a heavyset kid whose father was also a doctor. Both were friendly. I found out that Neal, the only kid I knew at Landon from those baseball seasons, was in another class. I did notice that Adam, one of the Kiwanis kids, was in my class. At least I knew *of* somebody in my class.

"Mom," I called out, pointing to his name on an assigned desk, "I actually know this kid."

"Good!" she responded, a hint of relief reflected in her voice as she forced a smile.

The next day was the first day of my school year. I had no idea what I was walking into, but I knew I did not like it before I even got there. Mom made me pose for a picture before my ride arrived, so

I know I wore a striped light blue button-down shirt tucked into baggy, very wrinkled khaki pants. I did not smile for the photos. I looked exhausted. The school year had not even started yet.

On the ride to school, I sat in the back of my carpool scouring the *Post* sports section quietly. I read coverage of the Cowboys' NFL season-opening 28–0 loss at New Orleans. It was the first game for Dallas under new coach Jimmy Johnson, the first career start for rookie quarterback Troy Aikman. The *Post* printed a black-and-white photo of Johnson standing on the field with Saints veteran coach Jim Mora, chatting before the game. New Orleans seemed like a much surer bet to one day win a title with their coach. But there was a lot that I misread that fall.

After a few hours of class, we finally made it to recess. That was one thing about the new school that was not different from Ritchie Park. Only now, instead of being guaranteed I would be one of the top picks as we chose sides for a football game, I had to prove myself all over again.

I stood among a group of other sixth-graders as two were anointed captains, stepping a few feet in front of the rest of us and eying us keenly like well-dressed pieces of candy. Their decisions over the next couple of minutes could determine whether they would taste victory or defeat over the next half-hour and would affect our self-confidence for much longer. A few other kids got picked ahead of me, which did not surprise me given that the captains didn't know me.

Neal was not around but my new classmate Adam was. He was among those chosen first. Now about half the rosters had been selected, leaving about a dozen of us still standing there, anxiously waiting to hear our names called. I saw Adam whisper into the ear of his team's captain, his eyes fixed on me. I felt relief consume my body. "Okay," the boy called out, pointing at me: "I'll take you."

I exhaled and walked briskly over to my team.

The next morning I grabbed the sports section and was relieved to see the O's had beaten the White Sox the night before. Next to the game story I found another Boswell column, titled "No Time to Put Dreams Away, Orioles."

"The Orioles returned last night to Memorial Stadium for one final homestand that threatens to be turned into a wake. This is no time for the Orioles, trailing Toronto by two games with sixteen to play after beating the White Sox last night, to think about reality. They have been ignoring it since opening day when they won in spite of Roger Clemens. Instead, the Orioles need to remind themselves that if they keep bearing down and flying right, just as they have been for the past excellent month, they might still shock the world."

Hey, why not? Later in his career, after he had become an elite pitcher, Schilling joked of the perceived "mystique and aura" of pitching in postseason games at Yankee Stadium: "Those are dancers in a nightclub." Then he went out and helped Arizona beat New York in the World Series.

But now he and the other young O's needed to build such resilience and confidence, and fast. Otherwise the 1989 Baltimore Orioles would never be remembered with the mystique and aura that they deserved (unless somebody one day came along and wrote a popular book about them.)

"The Blue Jays aren't that big and they aren't that bad. They are just a good, yet frequently erratic team that's hot now but will probably cool off just in time to scare itself to death the last week of the season. That is, if the Orioles stay on their heels," Boswell wrote. The O's have "just been tested in the fire for the past month and they passed their examination splendidly. . . . Starting on August 11, the Orioles had to face their three closest pursuers within the span of four series. In each of those showdowns, the Orioles played a game in which they could have been knocked out of first place. They won all three."

"Next, the Orioles had to face their second-toughest road schedule of the season—nineteen games in eighteen days, sixteen of them on the road," Boswell continued. The O's, he added, went a respectable 11–8 over that span. "So, add it up. From August 11 through September 10, the Orioles faced all their chief foes head-to-head, then hit the road for a dog-days marathon. They went 19–11—better than .600 baseball. How much do we expect of this team? They're playing exactly like a bona fide clutch pennant contender. Despite the fact that, to be painfully candid, the Orioles are a mediocre team that has barely outscored the league for the year."

The O's had some factors working in their favor over Toronto, Boswell noted: their staff was rested and healthy, with Ballard, Milacki, and Harnisch "in the best form of their [albeit short] careers." Adding McDonald to Olson and Williamson only fortified a bullpen "comparable to any in baseball," he argued.

"For the past six weeks, the Orioles have been as injured as any contender, surviving without home run leader Mickey Tettleton, No. 2 RBI man Craig Worthington, platoon rookie Steve Finley, and second baseman Bill Ripken," he wrote. "Now they're back."

And of course, the Blue Jays carried the weight of their 1985 and 1987 collapses. "The Orioles should remember two things: Their foe is mortal," Boswell wrote. "And what's at stake is a kind of baseball immortality."

The O's were also buoyed by being back home after so much time on the road. They were greeted by two regions that still believed, still madly in love with these overachievers. Radio and TV stations played a new song that had become the team's slogan—"Why Not?"— and banners bearing those words were hung around the stadium. Fans posted signs in the outfield calling themselves "Brady's Bunch," "Phil's Phlock," and "Gregg's Groupies."

Tettleton returned to the starting lineup for the first time in over a month against Chicago and his homer keyed the 6–3 win Monday night. Even when the O's lost the next two to Chicago, they caught a break when Toronto lost three straight at .500 Minnesota. Baltimore was within one and a half games of first again as the weekend approached.

Baltimore next hosted Kansas City, which was only three and one-half games behind Oakland in the AL West. Like the O's, the Royals were scheduled to close the season against their nemesis, with a three-game set at Oakland over the season's final weekend. Both teams needed this series badly.

In the opener, Milacki scattered eleven hits while holding the powerful Royals to two runs, then Olson retired three straight to close it out in the ninth. Five different O's drove in runs, including Worthington, whose two-out single in the bottom of the sixth broke a 2–2 tie as Baltimore cruised 5–2.

But that night Toronto and Jimmy Key beat Cleveland and their ace Swindell, maintaining their one-and-a-half-game lead.

The next night was truly wild. A rain delay led to a 9 p.m. start in Baltimore and the O's held a 5–3 lead after seven. But in the eighth Williamson gave up a run and was pulled with runners at the corners and one out. Olson relieved him and struck out Kurt Stilwell, but future Hall of Famer George Brett singled to center, scoring Willie Wilson and tying the game.

Up stepped all-star Bo Jackson, enjoying his best season as a Major Leaguer. Brett was at first, Kevin Seitzer at second. Olson worked the count to 2–2, then fanned Jackson swinging. Whoever was left among an announced crowd of forty-five thousand rejoiced, as Olson walked toward the dugout fuming.

Baltimore needed to respond. In the bottom of the eighth, Milligan walked with one out, then advanced to third on a Sheets single. It was now around midnight as Finley pinch-ran for Sheets and stole second, but Worthington struck out.

With two out now, Melvin stepped up. He was only batting because of Tettleton's injury and because Anderson pinch-ran for Quirk in the bottom of the seventh. Robinson had no choice but to let Melvin hit; he had no backup catchers left for the ninth and perhaps beyond. Melvin promptly dropped a fly ball into left, scoring both Milligan and Finley. Baltimore led again, 7–5.

After giving up a double and walk to start the top of the ninth, Olson got Bill Bucker to ground into a fielder's choice, retiring Danny Tartabull at second. Olson then induced Wilson to hit a grounder to Gonzales at second. He fielded it cleanly and flipped to Cal Ripken, who finished off a game-ending double play by firing to Milligan in time to beat the speedy Wilson.

It was past midnight when the game ended, but the O's had managed to avoid losing ground to Toronto. The Jays defeated

Cleveland 3–2 in eleven innings that afternoon, only when consecutive errors by Cleveland defensive replacements allowed the Blue Jays to score the winning run. Baltimore remained one and a half games back.

Dave Johnson was set to face Royals ace Brett Saberhagen, gunning for his twentieth win, the next afternoon in the series finale. Toronto planned for Stottlemyre to pitch against Bud Black in their series finale. Twelve games still remained in the season—nine until the final weekend in Toronto.

That morning, my father and my brothers were out getting breakfast and grocery shopping when I woke up. After years of tagging along for this almost weekly ritual, on this day (and nearly every Sunday thereafter in middle school) I slept in.

I awoke and showered in time to watch the NFL pregame show, made myself breakfast, and scooted to our living room for the 1 p.m. Washington Redskins–Philadelphia Eagles tilt. Along with the New York Giants, the 'Skins and Eagles were expected to battle for the NFC East division title. The Redskins had opened up a 20–0 lead in the first half when Michael arrived home to join me, and we flipped between that game and the Orioles' game, a one thirty-five start.

The Royals cruised, jumping to a 7–0 lead in the sixth when Home Team Sports cut to a shot of a boy about my age holding a makeshift sign that read: "Redskins score?" An HTS reporter responded: "It is getting tighter: 30–28 Washington in the fourth quarter."

I felt my stomach churn. The big early lead and a 30–14 advantage at halftime had seemed like locks. Now it was wide open. Michael had disappeared. I could not stomach it to watch, even as the Redskins were driving. Fortunately, my father was running on a treadmill in the basement, with the volume loud enough for the neighbors to hear. When I heard the announcer call out a touchdown, I raced downstairs and saw the replay of Redskins receiver Art Monk completing a 43–yard catch-and-run from quarterback Mark Rypien to put Washington up 37–28.

Only a few minutes remained in the game, yet I still felt uneasy. It felt like a storm was brewing inside my stomach. My fingertips and toes were clamming up and I could barely breathe. It was like that afternoon in Hebrew school so many months ago.

Sure enough, the Eagles quickly drove and scored a touchdown. Just over two minutes were still left. As I sat in the living room, I briefly flipped over to NBC to watch the AFC game, but I could not help but switch back to the Redskins game. Coming back from the two-minute warning, the Redskins had the ball near the red zone. All they had to do was hold onto it, run some clock and they would win. But on the first play after the timeout, running back Gerald Riggs fumbled. My heart sank as I saw the Eagles recover, then return the ball deep into Redskins territory. The Eagles quickly scored another touchdown and, for the first time all day, they led, 42–37.

Still, almost a full minute remained. But my pounding heart and the massive sensation of fear coursing through my body told me this would not work out well. Sure enough, a Rypien pass was deflected and intercepted. It was Washington's sixth turnover of the day.

Just like I had been when I missed out on the first round of baseball all-star selections in June, I was emotionally tested. Again I did not respond well. I was furious, on the verge of tears that I struggled to hold in. I was really straining now. It felt odd. I had never cried over any game before—as a fan or a player—despite some devastating rec baseball losses such as the postseason defeat to Optimist in June. *What is wrong with me?* I wondered. Only when I joined some friends and other neighbors to play pickup football down the street a few minutes later did the intense emotions disappear.

I hoped they would never return.

Back to baseball season. Around the same time as the 'Skins' loss, the Royals polished off a 7–0 win in Baltimore. Meanwhile in Toronto, the Blue Jays walked off the visiting Indians in extra innings for the second straight game. With one out in the bottom of the tenth and the bases loaded, McGriff lashed a single to left, scoring outfielder Glenallen Hill to give Toronto a 2–1 victory.

The Orioles fell two and one-half games behind with only eleven to play. They took Monday off and prepared to host Detroit, with Toronto hosting a three-game set against Boston starting Monday.

That fall marked the first fall or spring season I was not signed up for any organized sports outside of school since I was a kindergartener. I had stopped playing soccer in fourth grade and aged out of the Rockville Football League's flag division after fifth grade. So my father approached me one afternoon late that summer with an idea: play baseball in the fall. I could play on a team with my old Ritchie Park chum Dave and a few other kids I knew, honing my skills for the upcoming spring season, he said.

Any other year I probably would have taken him up on his offer. But, adjusting to a new school and less sleep right as puberty was setting in, I was too exhausted even by the prospect of another organized activity. Between piano lessons, Hebrew school, the paper route, and my extra math classes, I had trouble finding time to even do my homework (and I frequently did not). Plus, I now had to rise about a half-hour earlier to start my school day. Just as I was starting to need more sleep, I was getting less of it. Middle school is cruel (and stupid) like that. Another organized activity, especially one that would cut into sleep on Sunday mornings, seemed like too much—even playing baseball.

My father walked away from me in the living room after his second or third attempt failed. "Alllllll riiiiight," he said, projecting his voice in the all-too familiar tone signifying he disagreed with my decision.

My baseball dreams were slightly stunted, but I was relieved. Besides, I would still be playing an organized sport that season—every day right after classes ended in school. In a shocking move, Mom allowed me to play football at Landon. I had always wanted to play organized tackle ball, and badly, but I had not even broached the idea with her in the past.

When our flag season ended the previous fall, Mark, our head coach and Ross' father, addressed us right after our final game. About fifteen elementary schoolers knelt on the sideline and perched our heads up as he spoke while our parents hovered nearby. "Fifth-graders," he said, addressing roughly half our team after a win, "nice way to go out."

A couple of us expressed mild surprise; we had not yet considered that this would likely be our final organized football game. Football was a huge part of our lives; we played almost every day at recess and often on weekends. But there was something special about playing organized ball under the lights, with our parents and siblings watching.

"This was your last game," Mark continued, "unless you can convince your mothers to let you play tackle." I heard chuckles all around us. Nodding to the fact that many of us were the spawn of Jewish mothers, he concluded, "So good luck with that."

Nearly a full year later, though, I needed a break. My parents were forcing me to attend an all-boys private school where I had to wear uncomfortable clothes and adjust to a very different student population. I was terrified and could easily become miserable without an organized team to distract me. Plus, Landon forced every student to play a sport and I was well over soccer and disinterested in cross-country (the other fall options). Knowing my frustration and fear as the school year started, Mom gave me one. It was one of the few times in my childhood when my parents put my mental health above my physical health.

I was elated when Mom told me I could continue playing football. While most of my friends were still attending classes together and developing better social skills in coed public school, I could at least take out my frustrations about not being with them on some unsuspecting new classmates while playing organized tackle football.

We were divided into two divisions by weight and I was assigned to the lighter league. Following a few days of instruction-heavy practices, the coaches chose captains to pick our squads and play an intramural season. Neal was one of the captains and poached me around the fourth or fifth round.

Neal assembled a strong team; we would go undefeated in the regular season. Our team was so deep, there was no place for me at any of the key skill positions. That was fine with me, though. I was assigned to start at end on offense (a hybrid tight end–receiver position). On defense, despite my lithe sub-eighty-pound frame, I started at defensive tackle.

"Defensive tackle?" my father responded, when I told the family over dinner one night. "At your size?"

Mom's eyes bulged. She had watched enough football to know what a tackle did.

"It's okay," I responded, not sharing their worry at all. "Nobody is that much bigger than me. Plus they taught us how to hit today out of a three-point stance and I was nailing people."

Despite my frame, I soon learned that I had advantages over other kids. I knew the game well and I was quick. I could throw off offensive linemen by looking them straight in their eyes or flinching and, after a few plays, I could anticipate a quarterback's cadence, jump the snap count, and fire into the backfield.

That is essentially what I did during our first game. My excitement built all day. Finally the school day ended and the game started. As my father watched from the sidelines on this warm, sunny Friday afternoon, I frequently nailed ballcarriers in the backfield. I relished the contact, and the sound of pads colliding and air wheezing out of a running back when I squared him up and pile drove him into the ground. It was more satisfying than playing pickup ball—maybe because helmets obscured the looks on my opponents' faces when I hit them and I did not yet know most of them well, negating any empathy I had when I typically played with friends and neighbors.

Afterward my parents greeted me along the sideline. My father was wearing dark Ray-Ban sunglasses, the croakies fastened to them flapping around the back of his neck. I could see him beaming as I walked steadily toward him, staring directly at him and smiling widely myself.

Maybe this new school would not be so bad after all, I thought—as long as it was me hurting other kids and not the other way around.

As our football season continued, I was still trying to adjust to my new surroundings—and a body that kept changing in seemingly strange ways.

We had another game on a sunny Friday afternoon that September and my father was coming again. This time I was not as excited as I had been before the season opener; now I was weary about playing well instead. With his busy work schedule, my sick grandmother, and two other kids to look after, these contests had become the only father-son time we got away from the rest of my family anymore.

After school I jogged with my classmates to the locker room in another building on the sprawling campus. I quickly ripped off my school clothes and donned my football gear—including a jockstrap and cup over my underwear, followed by tight-fitting white football pants. I jogged to the field with a few other kids and met our coaches there, who instructed us to run a few laps to warm up.

As I started running, it hit me. Maybe it was the anticipation of a game that forces one's adrenaline to rise, maybe it was the pressure of playing my father's favorite sport in front of him. Whatever it was, my attention was suddenly jerked from the game and warm-ups to what was going on inside my pants. Despite being engulfed by the cup, briefs, and football pants, my penis had suddenly and severely sprung into action. I had a full-on puberty boner and it radiated painfully.

I tried to ignore it, to run and prepare to play. But it was not going away. I could not recall anything like this ever happening before. The closest comparison I could come up with was when Brett made us all laugh by pointing out that Ross had a boner as he stood on the diving board at the pool early in the summer. But that had not lasted long, and Ross did not seem to be in any pain.

What is this? I wondered as I kept running, turning a corner on a lap. Panic gripped me: *What if this doesn't go away before the game starts?*

And Dad left work to come watch me, and I won't even be able to play because something is wrong with my dick?!

What if it never goes away?

Why is this so painful?

That pain and erection lasted only another minute or two. By the time we were done running and started focusing on the game itself, I no longer noticed it. Nobody said anything either, so I somehow avoided public embarrassment. I felt tremendous relief.

But humiliation would soon become an almost daily ritual as I struggled to fit in at my new school. Even football could not protect me from a school culture that possibly inspired the novel *Lord of the Flies*, especially as my anxiety disorders and puberty really set in. I was a long way from my Ritchie Park days of only a few months earlier.

Fortunately, for that first month of school, I still had a baseball division race to distract me. While the 7–0 loss to Kansas City on September 17 had dropped Baltimore two and one-half games behind Toronto with only eleven to play, the Jays were no longer surging. After going 29–11 from the end of July through September 10, they split their next six, including the two walk-off wins against middling Cleveland.

Toronto's consistent but small lead was due to both teams failing to play their best ball in September, when they often matched each other's daily results. After Toronto seized the division lead on September 1, their advantage oscillated only between one and two and one-half games for the next sixteen days. "Right now the Blue Jays and Orioles seem equally tight. And both are in the same scary place—a team batting slump," Boswell wrote in the *Post* that week. "The Blue Jays will be reminded of their past constantly. Will they repeat it? Or learn from it?"

The O's acted as if all the pressure was on Toronto: "If we haven't gotten nervous yet, there's no reason to be nervous now," Olson told the *Post*.

But in addition to struggling at the plate, the O's were short on starting pitching and their bullpen was tiring. After returning to the majors in early July and looking strong for two months, Harnisch failed to last past the sixth inning in his first three September starts. The O's skipped his next start and, with an extra day off that week, briefly used a three-man rotation.

Schilling did not make another start for the season after the clunker against Cleveland. He was only used sparingly, appearing in three other September games and only in middle relief. Despite Robinson's earlier promise of using McDonald in key situations out of the bullpen, McDonald only pitched four more times in September after his debut, usually in blowouts.

Robinson instead rode his trusted horses in relief, especially Olson and Williamson. On September 19, Williamson retired ten straight Tigers to close out a win. He entered the game in the sixth with two on and two out and Baltimore leading 5–2, retiring Mike Heath on a flyout to right. Then he stayed in the game, throwing forty-three total pitches even as the O's led 6–2 going into the ninth. Olson hit sixty season appearances in the September 16 win over the Royals. The way Robinson was using them, neither would be fresh for the final weeks of the regular season—or postseason if Baltimore qualified.

Still, while it appeared the O's may not outright seize the division, it remained possible Toronto could blow it. From September 7 to September 20, Jays starters went a combined 1–5. McGriff entered a series at Milwaukee September 22–24 mired in an eight-for-forty-nine slump, Mookie Wilson four-for-thirty-five.

What's more, on Monday, September 18, the O's won a coin flip awarding them home field for the divisional tiebreak game to be played Monday, October 2, if necessary. That week the O's also won three of four against Detroit and the Yankees to pull within one game of Toronto, which dropped three of five against Boston and Milwaukee.

The Jays nearly lost four of five and the division lead during that stretch, narrowly avoiding a three-game sweep at home against the Red Sox. Just as they had against Cleveland, though, the Jays benefited from an opponent's gift in extra innings on Tuesday night. Toronto trailed by a run in the thirteenth but loaded the bases with two outs. Liriano, a light-hitting twenty-five-year-old, faced reliver Greg Harris, who got ahead of him 0–2. Liriano then hit a deep fly ball to right, which outpaced Red Sox outfielder Danny Heep and bounced before the wall, scoring two to give Toronto a walk-off 6–5 win.

The O's had already wrapped up that 6–2 win at home over Detroit earlier that night and were watching the end of Toronto-Boston in the clubhouse. Their reactions there and elsewhere, as documented by the *Post*:

As Liriano stepped up to the plate, one Oriole yelled at the TV: "Choke! Pop it up! Then smash your bat on the plate."

Another Oriole claimed he was listening so intently on his car radio as he drove away from Memorial Stadium, he missed his highway exit and drove several miles into Pennsylvania before realizing it.

Hemond and his son listened in their car while sitting in the stadium parking lot. When Liriano won the game, both got out and slammed their doors.

The next day as they arrived at the ballpark to face Detroit again, a few O's ripped Heep for pulling up shy of the wall, preserving his body instead of making a concerted effort to catch Liriano's fly. The ball nearly bonked him on the head as a result. "Don't be afraid to put up your glove, Danny. Something might land in it," Hickey joked. "But then you might bump the wall."

Hemond was asked how many Orioles outfielders could have caught the ball. "Tough play," he said. "At least five." He was not joking.

That victory gave Toronto three wins in extra innings in a week. Even as they struggled, the Jays kept finding ways to avoid giving up the division lead. In fact, it had been one month since the O's had won the same day that Toronto lost. So the O's had not made up a full game on the Jays since mid-August, going from two and one-half games up to two back over that span.

The next day, though, Baltimore thrashed Detroit 9–2 while Boston pounded Toronto 10–3. The O's were now only one game back, the closest they had been in two weeks. "They've got to be wondering, 'What does it take to get rid of these guys?' " Milligan said. "They better beat us with some big club, because we're not going away."

The O's then split the first two games of a weekend series against the Yankees, while Toronto split two games with Milwaukee. So the O's were still sitting just one game back when another Boswell column was published in the *Post* before Sunday's games. He was feeling bullish. "When the Orioles go to Toronto for the final three games of the season and, after that, if they should go into postseason play, they will have one significant advantage," he wrote. "Nobody really knows them. Or how good they are. Or how much they've grown. This is a team that has gotten better all season and only slumped for two awful weeks when Olson—now as vital a player as Cal Ripken—was injured and ineffective during the season's roughest road trip [in July]. . . .

"Baltimore's second-line pitching is erratic and using Tettleton at designated hitter robs a marginal lineup of a much-needed bat. However, with off days protecting their Achilles' heel on the mound, the Orioles have reached a point where they are just about as good— on talent, not magic—as any contender in baseball."

That Sunday the O's played their final home game of the season, while the Blue Jays were in Milwaukee. They were both early after- noon starts, as was the Redskins' game at Dallas. That set up a perfect afternoon to lounge and watch sports, then play pickup football or baseball in my neighborhood before the sun set.

But instead I was stuck at my cousin's house. In my Dockers. We were celebrating Rosh Hashanah early with family. Mom wanted me to dress up a bit for the occasion, so she pulled a pair of khakis out of the closet that morning. "Wear these today."

I was incredulous. It was bad enough I had to wear Dockers on the weekdays. "Why do I have to wear nice pants on the weekend?!"

"Just put them on!"

In addition to having to wear khakis on a Sunday, I also missed most of the Orioles' and Redskins' games that day. The O's lost 2–0, before more than fifty-one thousand at Memorial Stadium. Ballard took the loss despite holding New York to seven hits and two walks. Fortunately Toronto lost too, 8–3.

After the O's loss, much of the sellout crowd stayed to give the team a three-minute standing ovation as they returned to the field, with many fans wearing "Why Not?" shirts. "You never heard such cheering on a day the home team lost," according to the Post. Fans hoped to return for the tiebreaker and the postseason. For the moment, all they knew was the O's had six games left to make up at least one game on Toronto, and they were all on the road.

"This isn't going to be your last game, is it?" one fan asked an usher.

"Let's hope not," he replied.

Losing two of three to a Yankees squad that had been eliminated from playoff contention marked a missed opportunity. But even this series produced a highlight that reinforced how plucky these O's were: During a 10–2 win Saturday, I watched from my living room as Jefferson sped for home while a throw came to New York catcher Don Slaught. Jefferson slid wide of Slaught's attempted tag, but also wide of the plate and about six feet past it.

The umpire gave no signal.

Jefferson stood up and eyed Slaught, who still cradled the ball in his mitt and stood between Jefferson and the plate. Slaught lunged at Jefferson, who sidestepped him, dropped to his knees and touched the plate safely. "I remembered my shadowboxing days in the Bronx," Jefferson said afterward. "That's us. We find any way to score."

There was only one week left in the season. The O's had not faded, as most pundits predicted. They only needed a decent showing that week in a three-game series at Milwaukee to set up the showdown for the division crown the following weekend in Toronto.

I could barely wait. But a full week of sixth grade at a school I was beginning to loathe stood before me first.

Hanging with a sickly Freddy, 19. Both his life and my childhood were running low on time.

Chapter 9

LATE SEPTEMBER: THE AUTUMN OF MY CHILDHOOD

B efore the Toronto series began, I had to get through another full week of school and afterschool activities—only to have Rosh Hashanah and all the associated family hubbub then coincide with the series. My patience must have been fraying. So was Mom's, as I soon found out.

Having a brother seven years younger than me had always been a blessing. When Tyler was a baby and toddler, I studied his every move, taught him how to catch a nerf ball and swing a large plastic baseball bat, read to him, and more. He believed everything Michael and I told him, and we were usually careful not to violate that trust.

By the fall of 1989, though, even my relationship with my baby brother was starting to change. With Mom gone much more caring for my grandmother and with me now in middle school, I resented having to watch him so often. Within a year, I would be ignoring him despite being charged with babysitting him while my parents were out—inviting friends over to watch porn on the Spice Channel in our basement instead. (Mine was a quick, slippery slide into rebellious adolescence.)

One day during this last week of September, with religious services coming up, Michael and I decided to scare him a bit. "The youth services are awful," we said. "They even fart in your face." While the first statement was mostly true, the second was about as documentable as most of the Bible stories they taught us in Hebrew school.

By the day of services, though, Tyler was thoroughly brainwashed. As Mom tried to get him ready, he protested. Loudly. He threw such a fit that Mom eventually gave up on getting us to services on time. She left my father to try to rally him, ordering Michael and me to pile into her station wagon immediately. Her stare and shouting momentarily frightened me and permanently halted our *Tecmo Bowl* game, as we tossed the controllers down and quietly marched into the car with our heads down.

As the eldest, I instinctively took the front seat; it may have been the only time in our entire childhood that Michael did not fight me for "shotgun." I buckled up, bowing my head and praying for once that we could get to shul quickly.

But throughout the ten-minute drive, Mom kept turning her head from the road to stare directly at me as she let rip: "We spent all week getting him ready! Me, Dad, his preschool teachers, everyone!" Her voice then rose another octave as she delivered her point: "And then you and your brother take FIVE GODDAMN MINUTES and just RUIN EVERYTHING!"

Mom had yelled at me before, but rarely and never to this extreme. I barely recognized this monster. She was a far cry from the woman who had consoled me from the same seat a few months earlier, when I was initially left off the all-star team. Her eyes bulged as she ranted about a fairly innocent prank. On its surface, it was frustration over our manipulation of Tyler, sure, but also likely worry about the health of MomMom Flick and Freddy, concern over how I was fitting in at a new school, and exhaustion from juggling it all mostly on her own while my father worked long, unpredictable hours.

It was usually my father who flew off the handle unexpectedly, but as much as that got to me, at least I knew it would happen sometimes and Mom would usually calm him down. Now Mom was blowing up too. I felt a bit guilty about messing with Tyler. But mostly I was upset that my most supportive ally—who had laughed at my high jinks for years—seemed to no longer appreciate them.

As I sat next to her quietly, looking away from her for the rest of the ride, I did not understand why.

Mom's tirade was only part of a long week and much longer month, with the climax being the O's-Jays series. Even in hindsight, the month seemed to last forever.

Some of my behavior that fall is on me, but much of it can be attributed to being separated from my friends and starting the new school—and not just any new school. Landon's culture at first shocked and confused me; it took quite a while for me to adjust and I never felt comfortable there. This school change, in addition to my hypersensitivity and all the new personal issues I had been suppressing since late spring, made every little slight feel like a big deal as I tried to roll with the new school year.

When Steve told me about the first school dance of the year at Julius West, I felt left out and sensed I had missed some crucial social signpost. "All the guys chanted 'New Kids suck!' when they [the DJ] played 'Hangin' Tough!' " he smiled, pantomiming the chant as we rode our bikes through the neighborhood the next day.

Meanwhile, despite enjoying playing organized tackle football, my experience at Landon overall got off to a very rough start. Sandy, my homeroom teacher, scared me. Some kids mocked my love of baseball (and not lacrosse) and protruding lower lip (They called me "dip lip"; I had no idea what they meant). I got Cs on math tests, a C on a history report when my paternal grandmother refused to tell me much about living through the Great Depression, and a C on an English test that had my father chewing me out as I teared up in the living room. The message was clear: My parents were not paying private school tuition for me to mess around anymore. But I still wanted to mess around.

One morning, I was standing at the urinal in the bathroom at school when one of my classmates walked up behind me and yanked my pants down to the ground. I felt humiliated when I heard other kids in the bathroom laughing behind me, but I kept my composure, finishing my piss before bending down to lift my pants back up. As I walked out of the bathroom, one of the kids asked me why I wore Jockey underwear. I froze. *Why does he care?* I wondered. There seemed to be no limit to what tidbits some of my new classmates hunted and pecked for while looking for excuses to pick on me.

In hindsight these constituted seemingly harmless pranks and teasing (especially compared with what I experienced and saw over the next few years at Landon), and I was far from the only kid there to get picked on that year. But as a new kid trying hard to fit in, they stung. And being a new kid at school was new to me, after six years of fitting in fine at Ritchie Park. It soon got to the point where I hated school – even more than Hebrew school.

I still had football. And the O's, at least for a little while longer. At some point they would both end, though. What then? I had no idea.

As the last week of September began, the AL East race featured two teams sporting records that would have eliminated them from competition in each of the other three divisions. But it was attracting a lot of national attention nonetheless. The other divisions were all but wrapped up. Only complete meltdowns would prevent Oakland and San Francisco from winning the West divisions, while the Cardinals had just a tiny chance of catching the first-place Cubs in the NL East.

Fans and media were thus focused mostly on the Orioles and Blue Jays, including longtime baseball writer Peter Gammons, a staff writer with *Sports Illustrated*. "In a divisional race that has defied convention from the beginning, it somehow makes sense that the race would end in Canada at a twenty-first-century stadium with a movable roof and a Hard Rock Cafe just beyond right field," Gammons wrote.

"Robinson and pitching coach Al Jackson have masterfully manipulated what amounts to a four-man pitching staff: Jeff Ballard and rookie Bob Milacki starting, Mark Williamson in the middle, and Olson closing. Robinson has had to juggle the third and fourth spots in the rotation; from August 17 through Sunday, Baltimore was 16–4 with Ballard and Milacki starting, 5–11 with anyone else."

Meanwhile, Gammons noted: "Toronto entered the final week in first place and as the favorite to win the division title for one reason: its pitching staff, especially its talented bullpen."

However, an earlier *Sports Illustrated* feature on the Blue Jays noted: "The Jays have been touted as the 'most talented team in the division' every year since winning the AL East in 1985. And every year since, they've come up short."

Gammons concluded: "The Blue Jays will have to outpitch not only the demons of seasons past but also a team from Baltimore that won't beat itself and has nothing to lose."

The O's played like that team on Monday night in Milwaukee. Harnisch reemerged, holding Milwaukee to one run over six innings as the O's rolled to a 5–1 lead keyed by four straight hits in the third. Williamson pitched with the flu, retiring five Brewers without allowing a run. He and Olson combined to retire eight of the last nine Brewers to close out a 5–3 win.

Around the same time, Key and Henke were combining to shut out the Tigers in Detroit, 2–0. The Blue Jays maintained their one-game edge in the standings, snapping a two-game losing streak. Five games remained in the season and just two until the final weekend.

The next night it appeared that Toronto might stretch its lead. The O's fell 7–3 in Milwaukee; Johnson struggled, giving up four earned runs in four and two-thirds innings.

Meanwhile in Detroit, Toronto built a 3–1 lead heading into the bottom of the ninth against a Tigers team that had already lost one hundred games. Duane Ward started the ninth on the mound for the Jays, now just three outs away from a two-game division lead with only four games to play.

Then the Blow Jays reemerged. Ward struck out the first batter, but Scott Lusader reached first on a throwing error by Ward. Matt Nokes drew a walk on a full-count pitch and Ward hit Doug Strange. The Tigers had loaded the bases without a hit.

Gaston brought Henke in to close the game. No dice. Gary Pettis broke his bat but singled to right-center, tying the game and moving Strange to second. Alan Trammell, who had been key in helping the Tigers steal the division from Toronto precisely two years earlier (including a walk-off single in the season's penultimate game), then broke his bat too. But he looped a fly ball that fell in left-center. Strange raced home with the winning run and Toronto's division lead miraculously stayed at one game.

"They don't look like a team in a pennant race," Brewers manager Tom Trebelhorn said of Toronto after the game from Milwaukee, after playing the O's. Perhaps he was merely hoping so. It seemed everyone outside Toronto was rooting for the Jays to blow the division to the upstart O's.

Wednesday night was far less dramatic. Toronto jumped out to a 3–1 lead and scored five in the ninth, blasting Detroit 8–1.

In Milwaukee, the Brewers loaded the bases in the first against Milacki with two out. Up stepped Sheffield, who lifted a fly ball to right-center. Fortunately, Devereaux flew over from center and made a running catch, keeping the game scoreless. That was Baltimore's only scare of the night.

In the fifth Tettleton smashed a changeup from Jerry Reuss over the wall in left. The three-run shot gave the O's a 3–0 lead and broke a one-for-seventeen slump that had dropped Tettleton to sixth in the order. The homer was only the fourth for the O's as a team in sixty innings. "I've been in one of those streaks where you start to wonder if you're ever going to get another hit. I wasn't even thinking home run. I was trying to hit the ball hard somewhere. That has been enough of a challenge here lately," Tettleton said.

Milacki settled down after the first, and Hickey and Williamson relieved him to close out a 4–0 win.

Williamson entered the Milwaukee finale with the O's already up 4–0 in the eighth and threw twenty-two pitches to retire six

Brewers. It was an efficient outing, but more strain on a tiring arm. At least the O's did not have to throw Olson, who would now be somewhat fresh for the weekend showdown in Toronto. Then there was the continued brilliance of Milacki. He improved to 9–4 since the All-Star break and was averaging seven and one-half innings pitched over his previous eleven starts.

Baltimore remained a mere one game back heading into the season's final series—just as Detroit had been one game back of Toronto entering the season-closing three-game set in 1987.

Against Toronto, Ballard was scheduled to start on Friday and Milacki on Sunday. Harnisch was set to be Saturday's starter. Milacki would pitch on three days' rest, skipping the struggling Johnson.

"It's exciting," Robinson said. "You understand what's at stake and each player gets to deal with his nervousness or whatever he feels. But you have to think of it as kind of an honor. How many times do you get to finish a season like this?"

The O's would need to take two of three in Toronto, then win the tiebreaker in Baltimore on Monday to seize the division. Or they could just sweep the Blue Jays in Toronto. The bottom line: they had to beat the more talented, deeper Blue Jays head-to-head three times within a few games and most of those games would be at SkyDome.

"For 159 games they've been baseball's sweetest success story— not only one of the game's most amazing turnaround teams, but a squad of rookies and youngsters playing regularly for the first time," the *Post* wrote. "If they haven't already been pulled from that cocoon —and indications are, they haven't—they will be this weekend when the national spotlight will focus on baseball's last unsettled divisional race."

"I don't think our young kids know what's going on yet," said Brian Holton, a member of the Dodgers when they won the championship a year earlier. "I'm nervous enough for all of them, but I don't think they even understand what's going on. I guess that's good. Maybe you have to go through it once or twice to understand it."

Both clubs had Thursday off as they traveled to Toronto. Many O's fans made the trek, showing up in bright orange shirts and hats to witness what we hoped would be a fitting cap to this magical season.

They are playing Toronto the last three games, of all teams, I thought, knowing the schedule had been set well before the season started. *It was meant to be. This is how we will win it—beating them head-to-head, at their stadium, on national TV.*

The Jays had the edge on paper. They had the division lead, however slim, and were playing at SkyDome, where they had been dominant since it opened. Toronto only needed to win two of four games.

But Baltimore had Orioles Magic. Boswell took stock in a column published in the *Post* the morning of the first game, Friday, September 29. "The Orioles are the most amazingly improbable team of overachievers in their league since the 1967 Boston Red Sox—the Impossible Dreamers. These Birds want to tie a ribbon around their glory, make it a unique story that will outlast their careers and be told when they're old men. Sad to say, runners-up get forgotten," he wrote.

The O's were essentially in the position of playing the last four games of a five-game series after losing the opener, he noted. "What does recent history tell us about five-game series when a team is down a game and must play three of the last four on the road? Since divisional play began in 1969, there have been seventeen such post-season scenarios. Thirteen times, the team in the Blue Jays' position has won. Four times, the team in the Orioles' hole has come back to win."

"Both teams are healthy with all pitchers ready and rested. No excuses. However, the Orioles have caught three minor breaks. Rookie Pete Harnisch, who has the best stuff among Orioles starters, rediscovered his form on Monday (a one-hitter through six innings before faltering) and gives Baltimore a semicredible starter on Saturday against tough Jimmy Key.

"Also, Toronto has its rotation out of whack with veteran lefties John Cerutti and Mike Flanagan unrested and will start young Todd Stottlemyre, with an 11–14 career record, against Orioles ace Jeff

Ballard (18–8) on Friday. Finally, Dave Stieb, who does not prefer three days' rest, would pitch Sunday—on three days' rest—against Bob Milacki, who seems to love such a four-day rotation (6–1, 2.24 ERA)."

But: "Anybody Toronto chose for a Monday playoff would be favored over anybody Baltimore could offer," he added.

The O's had hung in despite clear talent and production disadvantages. O's hitters were twelfth in batting in the AL, while their pitchers were last in strikeouts and had allowed the second-most hits. "No wonder the Orioles have outscored their foes by only twenty-two runs," Boswell quipped.

But Baltimore statistically was the AL's top defensive team and had drawn the second-most walks, placing them fourth in runs scored (the same amount as Oakland). "They still remain essentially mysterious, even after you've jiggled every number and unearthed every hidden strength and praised their gumption and even granted that several Orioles are more talented than their reputations."

The series would mark only the twelfth time in twenty-one seasons since the MLB playoff format had expanded that a series over the season's final weekend would decide a division race.

To add to the series' appeal, that week a Toronto newspaper reported controversial news that left many wondering just how badly MLB wanted the O's and Jays to play for the division that final weekend. Bobby Brown—not the '80s crooner, but the AL president—had written George Bell a letter shortly after an incident in Cleveland about two weeks earlier. "I am aware that the Jays are in the final stages of a tough pennant race, and to lose your services would cripple them considerably," he wrote. "In my opinion, threatening an umpire with physical violence is an offense that could merit a suspension. Considering the circumstances, however, I am going to warn you that this cannot occur again." So instead of suspending Bell and removing him from the Jays lineup, Brown merely fined him a thousand dollars.

In the two weeks after the incident, the Jays won three games in which Bell had multiple hits, including the eleven-inning win over Cleveland on September 16 and thirteen-inning win over Boston on September 19. By the time the letter leaked, however, there was nothing the O's could do about the nonsuspension and the games Toronto may have lost without Bell. They could only prepare to face Bell, an MVP candidate and the Jays' cleanup hitter.

The *Post* published Richard Justice's game preview on the front of the paper Friday, after he filed from Toronto the night before: "A playoff atmosphere. You play for opportunities like this, and since you don't get many of them, you want to take advantage of it," Cal Ripken told him. Indeed, it had been six years since Ripken had played in a game of this magnitude—the last one being the final game of the 1983 World Series.

Nearly the entire O's roster has been turned over since then, much of it throughout 1989 alone. Of the ten players who started opening day for Baltimore, only four remained regulars all season.

Yet here they were, so close to becoming the first team in MLB history to go from worst to first in their division/league in one season. "They represent a team that, in a lot of people's eyes, can't lose no matter what the scores are this weekend," Justice wrote. "No matter what happens to the Orioles this weekend, they've been the game's sweetest story in a season in which scandals involving Pete Rose (gambling) and Wade Boggs (feuding with management) and the death of Commissioner A. Bartlett Giamatti have dominated many of the headlines."

Meanwhile Toronto had everything to lose and knew it. "When we're playing the games, it doesn't seep into the brain," said Lloyd Moseby, a Blue Jay regular in both 1985 and 1987 as well. "But when there's no game, that's all you read in the paper. We get no peace."

One other nugget that Justice included perhaps foreshadowed the series opener: Holton was nervous, he said from the locker room. "A few feet away, Olson was tugging on a sweatshirt and agreeing."

" 'He's nervous,' " Olson said. " 'The last couple of days he's jumped on me a dozen times. Maybe he's making me nervous. When I went in that game Monday night [against Milwaukee], I started thinking, 'Hmm, blow this game, blow a season.' You can't start doing that. We've had fun all year, and there's no reason to stop now.' "

Game 1, Friday night

"Jeff Ballard," said the play-by-play man for the network TSN Canada, "is dominating the Blue Jays." Indeed he was. Ballard was unfazed by the game's significance or the pressure of playing before a record crowd of nearly fifty thousand packed into an enclosed SkyDome.

The roof had been closed before the opening pitch even though the sky was clear and temperatures hovered around sixty degrees. Toronto officials cited the temperature and a forecast calling for a slight chance of rain, the *Post* later reported. O's brass noted that Toronto was 11–0 with the roof closed and 21–20 with it open.

No matter . . . for a while. Through seven innings Ballard shut out the Jays, stranding seven runners and scattering five hits. As usual, Ballard had help. Despite playing shallow in center to cut off would-be singles in the cavernous SkyDome outfield, Devereaux ran down a few long flies near the warning track.

On offense Toronto played like the Blow Jays we knew and loved. "If there is some fundamental error, either of judgment or execution, which the Blue Jays did not commit, it escapes the mind. One got picked off first. Another wandered off second and was trapped. Yet another got confused and belatedly tried to steal second; he was thrown out by yards to kill a rally," Boswell wrote after the game. "Five times in the first seven innings, the Blue Jays got men into scoring position. . . . None of them scored."

But the Orioles left several men on themselves, including leaving the bases loaded in the fourth, and still led just 1–0 after seven on the strength of the Phil Bradley leadoff homer.

Then it happened: the eighth inning. Few O's fans who saw this game will ever forget this frame. While it is not as indelible in baseball history as, say, the tenth inning of Game 6 of the 1986 World Series between the Mets and Red Sox, it swung a memorable season and leaves an imprint on my memory more than thirty years later.

The O's seemed poised to stretch their lead and put the game away. In this frame four O's would hit the ball hard off Jim Acker and Tettleton would walk. Cal Ripken led off by smashing a drive deep to left, but Wilson caught up with it in time to make the catch. Orsulak then smacked a ground ball right back up the box for a solid single. Finley ran for him; Robinson planned for Finley to replace Orsulak in the field too, offering the O's more speed to extend their lead on the bases and better defense to help maintain it.

Baltimore had a 76 percent win probability as Milligan stepped up, according to *Baseball Reference*. What unfolded was one of the most critical at bats of the season—and an all-time, largely forgotten gaffe. On a 2–2 count Milligan drove an Acker pitch that landed deep in the right-center field gap. Rightfielder Glenallen Hill cut it off just before the warning track, but he was far from his cutoff man, second baseman Manny Lee.

Finley seemed to recognize that Milligan's shot would not be caught off the bat, sprinting toward second base as the ball zoomed into the outfield. As Finley approached second, however, the Jays' experience trumped the Orioles' inexperience. Lee and Fernandez, who had been positioned in double-play depth with the pitch, mimed turning two, pretending to toss the ball to each other.

Two years later, in the 1991 World Series, Twins middle infielders Chuck Knoblauch and Greg Gagne would employ the same trick to slow Braves outfielder Lonnie Smith and almost certainly cost Atlanta the go-ahead run. That play is well-remembered in baseball lore because Smith could have put Atlanta up 1–0 in the eighth inning of Game Seven, a game the Braves would eventually lose 1–0 in extra innings.

That the Finley-Lee-Fernandez play has been essentially forgotten is probably only because this game did not decide a championship and neither the Jays nor O's went on to win the World Series. But would the play settle a division title?

Seeing the veterans pantomime a double play, the rookie Finley slowed as he approached second. He did not slide to break up the double play as if he believed them fully, but he did not round the base in full stride either. He simply froze. Finley then restarted, rounded second and quickly approached third. By then Hill had retrieved the ball and made an accurate throw to Lee, now standing in short right-center. With only one out, third base coach Cal Ripken Sr. held Finley at third.

Milligan chugged into second with a standup double, but the score remained 1–0. "Fernandez and Lee made a great play," the TSN announcer said, "and may have saved the Jays a run."

The O's still had the makings of a big inning. Acker walked Tettleton intentionally to load the bases, setting up a double play and a force at home. Juan Bell ran for Tettleton, giving the O's a better chance at breaking up the double play but removing Tettleton's bat from the lineup for the night. In the top of the eighth, the O's were going all in. Toronto drew Kelly Gruber and Fred McGriff in at the corner infield spots, with Fernandez and Lee again stationed at double-play depth.

Worthington, the RBI machine, came up. Acker jammed him on a 1–1 pitch and the right-handed Worthington pulled a grounder toward the hole. Gruber moved to his left, toward the ball and Fernandez, who was charging in. A double play was out of the question, with Bell motoring to second. The Jays could either go for the speedy Finley at home or take a likely second out at first, which would concede a run.

In roughly a second, the swift Fernandez called off Gruber, fielded the ball cleanly with his backhand and fired to catcher Pat Borders. His throw was slightly offline, forcing Borders to vacate the plate—and the force out—to corral it.

Finley did not hesitate this time, taking off the moment he saw the ball hit the ground and flying toward home and a potential 2–0 lead. Finley slid feet first toward the plate as Borders caught the ball, reaching back to tag Finley. High-angle replays from the TSN broadcast show Borders appearing to tag Finley on his back just as his foot touches the plate. Did he ever tag him? Did the tag beat his foot?

Home plate umpire Al Clark thought so, calling Finley out. In the days before instant replay, the O's had little recourse. Perhaps they thought Finley was indeed out, because neither Finley nor Robinson argued the call. Still, they had been inches away from taking a 2–0 lead with still only one out and the bases loaded. Now the bases were still loaded, but there were two outs and they still only led 1–0. It was maddening.

Devereaux stepped up, his face expressionless as he chewed a glob of bubble gum against his cheek and swiftly strode to the plate. Devereaux was aggressive, lacing the first pitch on a line to center. For a moment it appeared again that the O's would extend their lead, perhaps by two or even three runs if the ball got over the head of Moseby.

But Moseby was in good position and snared the liner, retiring the side.

So, despite hitting four balls on the nose, forcing a walk, and hitting a soft grounder in between infielders with the bases loaded and one out, the O's somehow did not score a single run in the inning. This team that had scratched together so many close victories over nearly 162 games by executing in these situations had again largely executed (with the exception of Finley's mistake). But the baseball gods had not done them any favors. It was not fair to anyone associated with the O's—especially Finley, who had kickstarted this magical season with his amazing catch on Opening Day.

As I watched the inning conclude from the foot of my parents' bed, my father and I simultaneously yelled, "Dammit!"

With that, Mom made me go to bed. We had services in the morning and it was well past ten, so I did not protest this time. Instead I flipped off my bedroom light and lay on my stomach vertically across my bed, facing toward the hallway. I could see a blurry reflection of the game on my parents' bedroom window and hear the broadcast fairly well.

Fuck sleep. Fuck being rested for a youth service regarding some religion I cared less and less about every year. Baseball was essentially my religion now anyway. I was not missing the end of this game.

My heart was pounding. Toronto still had six outs to work with and needed only a single run to tie. Instead of a seemingly sure insurance run giving them some leeway, now a mere mistake could cost the O's this game.

As the bottom of the eighth began, Olson was still indeed having fun, playing with several Teenage Mutant Ninja Turtles action figures he had strategically placed on top of the bullpen wall. He smiled and joked with teammates, standing as he anticipated a call if Ballard faltered.

Wilson began the frame by singling to center and was forced out at second on a McGriff grounder. McGriff reached first, with veteran utilityman Tom Lawless pinch-running for him. With the right-handed Bell and Gruber due up, Olson replaced Ballard. The southpaw's career year had yielded one more strong start. Now it would be up to his teammates to see if he would get to start again this season, likely in Game One of the ALCS four days away.

Olson had saved twenty-seven games on the season despite not earning the closer's role until May. He was often so dominant, he would be named AL Rookie of the Year and finish twelfth in AL MVP voting. He had not been charged with a single run in twenty appearances dating to July 31, blowing just one save opportunity over that span. Despite often throwing a curve ball that ended up well outside the strike zone, he had only issued one walk over his previous eight and two-thirds innings, spanning eight outings.

His task tonight began with retiring the rest of the Blue Jays' murders' row to escape the eighth. Or perhaps just Bell, a good candidate to ground into a double play on one of those low breaking balls.

But, on Olson's first pitch, Lawless stole second. Lawless took off again on a hit-and-run, advancing to third on a Bell groundout to short. Gaston was not playing scared, despite his club's history of doing so in big games.

With two out now, Olson faced Gruber. He fired a heater by him and then a curve for strike two. The count was 1–2. One more strike and the O's would be out of the inning with the lead intact.

Quirk, who had started the game presumably to provide another lefty bat against Stottlemyre, was still catching with the Toronto starter long gone. Melvin, who had more experience catching Olson, remained on the bench. Quirk set up outside against the right-handed Gruber and called for another breaking ball. Olson fired.

The ball quickly shot down toward the ground to Quirk's right. Quirk barely moved laterally and the ball got away from him, bouncing toward the backstop. Lawless easily dashed home with the tying run.

I heard my father scream from down the hall: "Goddaaaaaammmmmmmit!"

This was how games sometimes got tied late during one of our rec league contests. But this was not supposed to happen in the majors, unless you were the cursed 1986 Red Sox.

Olson, with such pinpoint control of his hook all season.

Quirk, who had transformed himself into a serviceable catcher.

Quirk, whom Robinson must have considered the best defensive option among the four catchers on the O's active roster that night (though Tettleton's injury left Melvin and Hoiles as the only viable other options.)

Quirk, who was only on the team because Tettleton had suffered that injury in August, the O's could not find a better option to acquire then and they deemed the twenty-four-year-old Hoiles (a September call-up) not ready for meaningful playing time.

"One curveball. One curveball in the dirt. One curveball that an old brainy catcher, already released by three teams this season, could not block. Is that what a season comes to—after seven months and nearly two hundred games?" Boswell posited. "If a game could be declared a forfeit on aesthetic grounds, then the Blue Jays would have lost before this one ever reached its turning point."

Alas . . .

Would a healthy Tettleton have blocked it? Melvin? Hoiles?

"I should have blocked it," said Quirk. "Olson's supposed to throw that curveball there. . . . I've blocked that same ball before."

"It kicked up," said Quirk, "because I didn't go out and get it."

Holton, also a curveball specialist, disagreed: "He's not really right to take the blame. I don't think he could have blocked it."

Some questioned whether Olson should have thrown a curve at all, with a runner on third and two out. A 1–2 count afforded him a few pitches to otherwise retire Gruber. How about a high fastball?

As the O's prepared to resume the game, I could not ignore the dancing blurry blue-and-white figures and the massive sound of the Toronto crowd emanating from the TV. My stomach sank as I sensed the worst. Baltimore had hit four balls hard in their half of the eighth but failed to score an insurance run. Toronto had a mere single in the bottom of the eighth but had plated the tying run.

Olson being Olson, he recovered to fan Gruber swinging on a 3–2 pitch to end the inning. Quirk spiked the ball on the turf after he caught it, then angrily threw off some of his catcher's gear in the dugout.

The Orioles went 1-2-3 in the top of the ninth, with Robinson neglecting to pinch hit for the light-hitting Quirk. Olson also retired Toronto 1-2-3 in the bottom of the ninth, with Gaston seeming to hedge his bet by leaving the overmatched Lee in to fly out, but pinch-hitting veteran Ernie Whitt for Borders.

Gaston opted to have Duane Ward start the tenth on the mound and Cal Ripken promptly greeted Ward with a single off the fingers of his pitching hand. Only after the Jays' medical staff and Gaston examined Ward did Gaston remove him and send out the oft-dominant Henke. There could be no save situation with Toronto the hosts in extra innings, yet Gaston had held back Henke from this crucial hold scenario. Now he was forced to use his ace closer anyway.

Henke instantly took control. Finley and Sheets, hitting respectively for Orsulak and Tettleton because of the eighth-inning changes, popped out and struck out swinging. Milligan fanned in between them, as Ripken became the eleventh Oriole left on base in the game. Baltimore had not scored a single run in nine innings.

In this battle of elite closers, Olson's tenth was shakier as he faced six batters. With runners at second and third and one out, rookie John Olerud stepped up. A hit, error, sacrifice fly or another pitch that got away would give Toronto the win. Olerud swung at the first pitch and hit a fly to center. But Devereaux caught it shallow enough to keep pinch-runner Junior Felix from tagging up at third. After Olson intentionally walked Bell to load the bases, Gruber came up again and worked the count to 2–2. On his thirty-ninth pitch of the night, Olson got Gruber to hit a grounder to Billy Ripken, who fielded it cleanly and made the throw on the run to Milligan in time to end the threat.

As he arrived in the dugout, Olson calmly high-fived teammates as he looked them in the eyes. We were on to the eleventh.

At some point around this time, early adolescence defeated me and I passed out, missing the end of the game. I awoke the next morning, gathered the *Post* from the end of our driveway, and saw the game had ended too late for that edition. It felt like my heart had descended to my crotch as I wondered who had won.

My father was already up, so I deduced that the game could not have lasted as long as the Caps-Islanders playoff game in April 1987, which set a then-NHL record by going four overtimes and ended close to two a.m. My father had slept in the next morning after watching all the overtime action.

I flipped on *SportsCenter* and eventually saw it: in the bottom of the eleventh, the light-hitting Lee rewarded Gaston by grounding a ball the other way into the hole between Cal Ripken and Worthington. The hit came with one out off Williamson, who had replaced Olson to start the frame. Liriano ran for Lee, took off on a hit-and-run and advanced to second on a groundout by Whitt—the man Gaston had sent into the game to replace Borders.

There were two out now. Robinson and his staff had a choice: face Felix with first base open, or walk him and face Moseby with runners on first and second. They went with the latter option. A few scouts sitting in the press box shook their heads, but Robinson was incredulous after the game: "It sets up the force at any base," he said. "It makes it easier to get an out."

What he did not say was that Moseby was hitting .219 on the season, would finish the year with just forty-three RBI in 572 plate appearances and had a history of choking in big moments. Felix, a .250 hitter that season, was a rookie who carried none of the baggage of the 1985 and 1987 collapses that Moseby did.

Moseby suddenly got clutch, however, blasting a Williamson offering over Bradley's head and off the left-center field wall, easily scoring Liriano. SkyDome erupted. Toronto now led the division race by two games with only two to play. "It's a huge win, probably the biggest in Blue Jays history," Moseby said in the locker room after the game.

"I thought whoever won this game would have a big emotional lift. We're fortunate it was us," Gaston said.

For a team that had just lost such a crucial game in excruciating fashion, the O's did not seem too down in the clubhouse after the game, reporters noted. "My gut feeling is we're still going to win," said Holton. "We've been coming back against the odds all year long. Why change now?"

"We win tomorrow, then we go into Sunday just like we wanted," Olson said. "I'll be ready tomorrow night. I'm not going to back down now."

Of course, the next game was not at night. It was scheduled for the following afternoon and Olson had just thrown thirty-nine pitches. Would he even be available for the biggest game of the season?

After watching ESPN's breakdown of the bitter loss, I turned my attention to the next game. I too felt hopeful—if not simultaneously terrified—as I tuned in for the 2:30 start of Saturday's game after returning from services.

It was a beautiful fall afternoon, the sun shining through our living room window as the thirty-something, teenaged-looking Bob Costas led off NBC's coverage. The camera showed a toddler sporting an Orioles cap during the opening montage. "And even this young fan knows the Orioles must win the last two games of this series to force a tie atop the standings and a one-game playoff," Costas said.

I had my doubts. But to me, part budding realist but still part dreamer, that scenario also seemed very possible.

Why not?

Game 2, Saturday
Unlike Friday, Toronto seemed to have a decisive edge for this game on paper, with the momentum from the previous night's win compounding a short turnaround and Key on the mound. Although he had posted an uneven 1989, the left-hander was a veteran former

All-Star who would finish the season leading the AL in fewest walks issued per nine innings. He also was the losing pitcher in the 1987 season finale, giving him a chance at redemption nearly two years to the day of that loss.

Meanwhile, one omen seemed to favor the O's, but another favored Toronto. First, the good sign: the weather—clear and crisp, with skies matching the Jays' blue trim—and perhaps the media reports after Friday night's roof closure induced the Blue Jays to keep the roof open Saturday.

Then the bad, almost inexplicable, sign: as if losing in such crushing fashion Friday night was not enough, Harnisch stepped on a nail while walking back to the hotel afterward. When he arrived back at SkyDome for the game Saturday, he could not even step on the affected foot. The incredulous right-hander had to be scratched from his start.

Instead, Baltimore turned to Johnson. Told just hours before the game that he would start, this rookie who had been called up from the minors only two months earlier and had lost five straight starts was now charged with saving the O's magical season—on three days' rest. "It was, well, a surprise," he said later.

Somehow he was up to the challenge. Without fanning anyone, Johnson held Toronto to one run on only two hits through seven innings. During one stretch, he retired eighteen of nineteen Toronto hitters—albeit with Bradley, Jefferson, and Devereaux often chasing down drives in the outfield gaps. "He got the Blue Jays on a mixture of high sliders and fastballs that he moved in and out, up and down. He got fourteen of his eighteen outs on flies to the outfield," according to the *Post*.

Key, however, was not ready for his redemption song. Baltimore put Friday night behind them early on, taking a 3–1 lead through four on RBI hits by Cal Ripken, Milligan, and Bradley.

Baltimore still led 3–1 when Hulett led off the seventh with a double. Bradley stepped up and hit a routine grounder to short, with Hulett taking a chance and racing toward third. Fernandez threw to Gruber, who tagged Hulett as he slid into the bag on another bang-bang play. If he is called safe, the O's will have runners at the corners with nobody out. If he is called out, the O's will have a runner on first with one out.

The umpire calls Hulett out.

Replays seem to show Hulett sliding under a high tag from Gruber, but again there is nothing the O's can do to change the call. Again, they don't even argue. They can hardly blame an umpire for a bang-bang call on a baserunning mistake. Hulett tried to advance to third with nobody out on a grounder hit to the shortstop—the gifted Fernandez, who led AL regular short-stops in fewest errors that season. A team that is only alive for the postseason so late in the season because they have played sound baseball all year perhaps deserved to give up a runner in scoring position for this glaring error in judgment. Again, the baseball gods have punished the O's.

But they take mercy on Toronto. When Jefferson steps up next, the Jays make a mental error of their own. Bradley bluffs a steal, forcing the Jays to cover second. Both Fernandez and the second baseman Liriano sprint to cover, leaving gaping holes in the infield. Jefferson hits a soft liner—right up the middle. The ball goes straight to the out-of-position Liriano, who makes the catch as Bradley retreats to first to avert a double play. Fernandez walks over to Liriano, briefly instructing the young infielder before they return to their positions.

When Bradley then tries to steal second on a 1–2 count to Cal Ripken, now with two out, a high pitch gives Whitt a jump on the throw down. His toss is accurate and nails Bradley, ending the Orioles' threat.

The O's have wasted another opportunity to essentially ice a game in this series. The Jays only have two hits and nearly have given the O's another run (or more) with a poor defensive play. But they still trail only 3–1, not much of a deficit for their potent lineup against a tiring Johnson and a gassed bullpen needing to secure nine more outs together.

But, just when it seems the Jays have gained some momentum, Johnson and the O's defense move through the bottom of the seventh without faltering. Johnson issues a walk and, with two outs, Gruber lofts a drive to deep right-center. But Devereaux sprints over and makes another running catch look routine, saving at least one run.

Alas, the O's 3-4-5 hitters—Cal Ripken, Milligan, and Worthington—go down 1-2-3 in the top of the eight against Jays reliever Frank Wills. It marks the fourth straight scoreless inning that Wills, hardly one of Toronto's top bullpen arms, pitches in relief of Key, who was pulled after the fourth.

By now I had moved to the kitchen, watching earnestly with Michael. With it being Rosh Hashanah and approaching five o'clock, we needed to leave for my aunt's house soon. Mom was well aware, the most important Major League Baseball game of our young lives be damned: "Boyyyyyyzzz! Half-hour! We can't be late," she called down from her room directly up the eight carpeted stairs.

My aunt on my father's side was always late for family gatherings. Now we could not be late to her house? Just this one time? I wasn't leaving until the game ended, so I sat in a kitchen chair and fixed my eyes on the TV. Michael dutifully went upstairs to change. I looked at my fading, dirty white-and-red Nike sneakers sitting in the corner of the room by the door and considered myself ready to go.

Then it happened: the bottom of the eighth.

It took me thirty years to muster the courage to even try to watch this frame of this game again. When I finally did rewatch it as a forty-something man during the pandemic, it felt just as painful as when I saw it live. Writing about it was only slightly less jarring.

The bottom of the eighth seemed innocuous to start. Toronto's bottom of the order led off against Johnson, who had been nearly flawless. But Johnson walked the leadoff man, Liriano, on four pitches, often missing his spots badly. After throwing eighty-one high-leverage pitches on three days' rest, and with four straight lefty or switch-hitters coming up, he was pulled.

Johnson paced the dugout by himself as Robinson turned to the lefty Hickey. NBC's broadcast team supported the move, noting Hickey would face the left-handed bats and force the switch-hitters to turn around and bat from their weaker sides.

But on a full count, Hickey walked the switch-hitting Lee. With two on now and still nobody out, he went to 2–1 against the lefty Moseby. "I felt good, I just couldn't focus in on the plate," Hickey said later.

Robinson again made a move. This time he turned to Williamson, who had thrown thirteen pitches and taken the loss less than twenty-four hours earlier after pitching a lot already in September. Robinson eschewed the well-rested, less trustworthy arms of McDonald and Schilling. He also ignored a gassed yet eager Olson, and the rested Schmidt, Holton, and Mark Thurmond. None of those veterans had been as effective as Williamson during the season. But Holton had pitched well in four postseason games for the Dodgers in 1988. And, along with Friday night, Saturday marked the biggest games in Williamson's uneven career.

After consulting with Jackson, Robinson made up his mind. Like the rest of us, he then sat and helplessly watched as Wiliamson faced five Toronto batters. Eventually Olson and another reliever got up and threw in the bullpen. Would it be too late?

First Moseby successfully laid down a sacrifice bunt, moving the runners to second and third with one out. Then Wilson, like Lee the night before, hit a grounder the other way that found a hole between Ripken and Worthington. Liriano scored and Rob Ducey, running for Lee, advanced to third. Toronto now had the tying run at third and the speedy Wilson, representing the go-ahead run, at first. There was only one out.

I must have had another panic attack. I could barely breathe, my hands were getting clammy, and it felt like a velociraptor was tearing up my stomach. The crowd at SkyDome was deafening, anticipating the runs needed for a division title in this very frame.

To compound matters, the heart of the Jays order came up next. McGriff drew the count to 2-2. Then he lashed a Williamson pitch to right that fell in front of Finley. Ducey scored; Wilson scooted to third. There was still only one out, the game was tied, and SkyDome was really loud now (even with the roof open).

The noise pissed me off. So did the Jays' celebration in front of and inside their dugout. I felt hopeless. Yet I kept watching, unable to leave the room or cover my eyes even as I sensed hope abandoning me. I felt an overwhelming sense of dread that this miraculous season, this marathon that I had invested in so much emotionally, was about to come crashing down—possibly with the very next pitch.

What then? How could I possibly deal with losing this potential miracle that I had clung to for months? Especially as my world was morphing around me so much, so fast—too much, too fast for me to handle or even acknowledge. The O's had aided my denial by providing distractions almost daily, feeding my innocent belief not only in sports miracles but in so many other aspects underpinning my mostly carefree childhood. Only a few months earlier I had tried to prevent Mom from selling an old "He-Man" toy. Now I was trying to act tough in a hypermasculine middle school. What if a key distraction and romantic, childish notions suddenly disappear with one pitch in a baseball game? Are eleven-year-olds equipped to handle that? Especially my hypersensitive, panic-saddled version of an eleven-year-old?

Robinson stuck with Williamson and he got a first-pitch strike on Bell. Then he fired and Bell struck, lifting a fly ball deep to right. George fuckin' Bell: the guy who almost certainly should have been suspended earlier in September but was not because the AL president did not want to interfere with a division race. The crowd roared as Wilson raced back to third to tag up. Finley caught it, but his throw was nowhere near on time to get the speedy Wilson, who slid home with the go-ahead run. The crowd exploded.

So did my heart, as my head sank into my hands.

The Jays had been outhit 9–4 and trailed nearly all day. They looked like they would surely need to wait until Sunday for another shot to clinch the division, against the red-hot Milacki and a rested Olson. Now they were only three outs away and had one of the game's top firemen ready to close.

I could feel myself starting to crack. I had not cried when the Redskins had blown that game to the Eagles two weeks earlier, even as I felt something fierce building inside of me. I had not cried when I was separated from my friends and sent to a new school, nor when I was bullied at that school. I had not even cried about the illnesses of my grandmother or beloved pet. Even though this all deeply upset me.

But now, again, the feelings were there and they were rapacious—the same feelings I experienced during that Redskins game and when I had received the bracelets in that Hebrew school gift swap some nine months earlier. Dread, panic, fear. It was as if the end of the Orioles' season would eminently lead to my own death.

It was almost time to go to my cousin's house. Fortunately, my father had joined me to watch the game and was not ready to leave either. We watched in stunned silence as Williamson retired Fernandez on a groundout to Cal Ripken to end the eighth. But Baltimore, which had begun the frame up by two, now needed a run just to tie the game. They had merely three outs to work with.

Gaston did not hesitate to bring in Henke this time. With his goggles, intense and soulless expression, and an unbroken-in hat that appeared as if a silly child had placed a sky blue square on top of his head, he looked like a robot sent from the future that SkyDome represented to vanquish our heroes.

It would be a future I have not enjoyed as much as my first eleven years, a future I still have some trouble accepting at times.

Henke had thrown twenty pitches the night before, but that did not faze him. Tettleton led off. He worked the count to 3-2, but went down looking at a nasty Henke forkball around the outside part of the plate. The pitch seemed to fool him as the crowd roared louder now.

I sank a bit lower into my chair and pondered covering my eyes. Still, they fixated on the small kitchen TV, the volume turned way up. I still held out some hope.

Orsulak hit for Devereaux and grounded out to Gruber. Baltimore was down to their last out and had nobody on base.

"Their Cinderella season," Costas said, "may be coming to an end."

Sheets pinch hit for Melvin. If you remember Larry Sheets, you may recall he hit thirty homers only two seasons earlier and played six full seasons in the majors largely as a power bat for hire. Robinson and everyone attached to the Orioles were hoping for one thing and one thing only. Like the Mighty Casey, Sheets was swinging for the fences. The game, a season, two major metros areas—a childhood largely untested—all rested on his broad shoulders.

Sheets fell behind 1–2. Then, with the crowd roaring even louder, Henke threw a fastball and struck Sheets out swinging.

The crowd noise now seemed to be in person, it was so loud. It seemed intrusive and unnecessary to me as I struggled to accept the suddenness of this loss. In less than twenty-four hours, the O's had gone from being on the verge of validating their miracle season with a division title to losing two gut-wrenching games and being eliminated from the postseason.

I bowed my head and covered my eyes with my hands. After a few moments, I could not hold it in anymore—no matter how much I had been told that big boys don't cry. I could feel tears welling up in my eyes and rolling down my cheeks. It was like missing the first All-Star game cut all over again. The intense feelings that I had been bottling up for weeks, maybe months, and especially that afternoon, poured out of me. Pretty soon I was whimpering as I struggled to hold in more tears. Within a minute or two, I got the tears to stop flowing. But my emotions were still raw: sadness, despair, now some anger too.

Nobody in my family seemed to notice. At some point they all gathered in the kitchen and ushered me out the door. I don't remember anyone comforting me, not even Mom, even though the tear residue was still sparkling on my cheeks and lips. We had an important religious holiday celebration to tend to and my parents were not going to be very late just because their son was having a breakdown over—what must have appeared to them at least—a mere baseball game.

No matter that I hated going to this aunt's house and I cared approximately one-thousandth as much about my religion as I did about baseball. There would be no time that night for me to reflect on what had just happened, no time to start processing what I had just experienced: my first broken heart and essentially the end of my sweet childhood.

It would be thirty years until I processed this moment to any real degree, after rewatching both games and discussing the emotions they brought back up with a therapist. (The first time I rewatched the games, I had to stop after the seventh innings. It took me months to lay down again, fire up YouTube, and rewatch the play from the eighth inning onward.)

And so a pattern was born. If it was not an important religious holiday preventing me from processing deep emotions, it would be a test or a piano recital or whatever else life threw at me as I was continuously pushed until I eventually pushed myself just as hard. This trend would well outlast my adolescence.

That evening, as I got into the back seat of Mom's station wagon and sat next to Tyler in his car seat, I was on my own with my thoughts. I said nothing, staring down at my favorite size-eleven sneakers that seemed way too big for the rest of my thin frame and replaying the events of the past twenty-four hours throughout the ten-minute drive.

When we got there, I saw my cousin Melissa. Now a sweet-natured sixteen-year-old, she had been doting on me at least since we collaborated on our own Smurfs books when I was about six. She greeted me with a big hug as always. "Hi Ry, what's up?"

"Fuckin' Williamson," I muttered, struggling to get even that much out as tears again welled up in my eyes and a lump reemerged in my throat.

"Huh?"

I have no recollection of the rest of that night. I'm sure apples and honey were consumed, prayers were chanted, family served brisket and kugel for dinner. My cousins and brothers and I probably sped away from the table after dessert and played Nintendo or watched college football or played football in the front yard in the dark.

Three decades later, that I can recall so many details about that year but none from that night says something about what must have been going on in my head. It was over, that much I suspect I considered. I must have been struggling to process not only the O's loss but also the losses of my nurturing elementary school and daily time with my closest friends, my airtight bond with Mom, my natural fearlessness and optimism before the anxiety disorders had set in. No to mention the impending losses of my beloved grandmother and cat. Now forced to confront all these issues as a key distraction linking me to my childhood was ripped away, it must have shocked my system.

Is this analysis a bit hyperbolic? Possibly. But a couple of years of stimulating my memory to recall the events of 1989—via daydreaming, talking with Mom and friends, looking at old photos and videos, and writing—have not returned any other memories from that night to the front of my mind beyond hugging Melissa.

Back in Toronto the O's did not handle the defeat much better. Hickey called it "a kick in the stomach." Several players sat stunned in the dugout as Toronto celebrated in front of them. "I was happy to get the chance to pitch, but I'm disappointed we didn't win. Seeing the Blue Jays jump around on the field after winning is tough," Johnson said.

Robinson waxed poetic. "I'm very proud of these guys," he said. "I'm disappointed we didn't win. We all are. But this club couldn't have played any better."

(Really? With all the men left on base? The Finley baserunning miscue? The Olson breaking ball that Quirk could not block? Scoring just four runs combined in two games? They did not play badly, but they really could not have played any better?)

"There's no World Series game that was ever as exciting as these two," Cal Ripken Jr. said. "I feel fortunate to have been a part of it. You leave the field and know this is what you played the whole season for."

But, to me, still not over losing in the playoffs of my own rec league season three months earlier, they had played the whole season not just for the chance to compete for the division title, as Ripken suggested. They had played to win it. It was not the ending I felt I had been promised by the tales of the Miracle on Ice or Miracle Mets.

Justice made sense of the nonsensical in the *Post*, filing from the SkyDome press box just after the game. "The Baltimore Orioles were pushed from the American League East race for good this afternoon, on the next-to-last day of a season that could have been scripted by Disney and staged in a Magic Kingdom," he wrote.

"In the end, the Orioles lost, not because they were one of baseball's youngest contenders ever, but one of its thinnest. . . . The worst of the Orioles was an offense that was a couple of bats short and a bullpen that was Gregg Olson, Mark Williamson, and no one else.

"They came here having blown four leads in the eighth inning or later all season. But they blew a 1–0 lead in the eighth inning on Friday and a 3–1 lead in the eighth tonight," he added. "Williamson (10–5) was charged with both losses, but that was more a tribute to the fact that he was willing to take the ball even with what he admitted 'was nothing. My stuff isn't too good right now.' "

"Yeah, I was tired, but that's bull," he added. "I just made bad pitches. I hung a change-up to Wilson and McGriff hit a slider that didn't move."

One hanging change-up, one flat slider, and—on Friday—a breaking ball in the dirt, across two measly innings spanning twenty-four hours, had wrecked 159 full games of near bliss over almost six months. Nobody had told me "that's baseball" yet. (Except more or less for that jackass Optimist coach from the spring, whom I despised too much in that moment to listen to.)

Now I knew. I would never be fooled again.

The next day the front of the *Post* greeted us with the following headline: "Orioles Wince at What Got Away, but Hold Heads High; Pain of Close Losses in Toronto Assuaged by Season's Singular Accomplishments."

A Boswell column followed, but neither his prose nor praise of the O's' stunning season could assuage the pain that I felt. "A baseball team cannot play much better than the Orioles have for two games here in the SkyDome—and still lose," he wrote. "For the second straight game, the Orioles, with a dozen players barely wet behind their Major League ears, played to their highest expectations—showing flawless and sometimes spectacular defense, fiercely determined finesse pitching, and consistently heady play."

But it did not matter—not to a hardened scribe, not to a formerly sweet-natured eleven-year-old boy. Both of us were still having trouble comprehending this loss. "What if catcher Jamie Quirk had blocked that pitch (Friday), prevented the run and Olson—who still has not allowed a run since July—had completed the save?" Boswell wrote, closing his column. "Then Williamson would have been fresh this afternoon. Were the Orioles really just one pitch away from winning both of these games?"

More than three decades later, that remains a startling question: Were the 1989 Baltimore Orioles really just one pitch away from completing the most miraculous regular season in modern baseball history (up to that point)?

We will, of course, never know. They posted the best one-season turnaround since the 1946 Red Sox, going from fifty-four to eighty-seven wins. They set the all-time record for fielding percentage in a season, .986. But it did not matter. The Orioles' season was over. That much I knew as I read Boswell's column.

What I did not yet know: an era of my life was, too. Boswell's column ran on the first of October. Summer—summer break especially—was long over. The year had exactly one-quarter left. So did the decade and the packaged black-and-white view of the world that American culture had been selling to middle class suburban kids for the duration of my conscious childhood (for starters: Russia bad, USA good).

The world had already started changing drastically earlier that year; now that movement seemed to accelerate from my vantage point. In a couple of weeks a major earthquake interrupted the World Series, killing a few dozen and injuring a few thousand. A few weeks after that, the Berlin Wall collapsed. Nelson Mandela would be freed from a South African prison within months. As a sixth-grader at a new, more demanding school, I was charged with comprehending these major world events as vociferously as I had ignored Tiananmen Square, the George H. W. Bush inauguration, and the sudden death of Giamatti, the baseball commissioner, earlier in 1989.

There had been months of baseball, to play and to watch and to otherwise consume. But not now. Now I had to read—actually read and not skim—nonsports articles from adult newspapers and magazines about these events. I had to start trying to understand a larger world that I preferred to ignore. I had less time for *Blades of Steel* and *Tecmo Bowl*, more time dedicated to boring, educational computer games in school. To save myself socially, I had to ditch the New Kids for the Fresh Prince (okay, so there were some wins that fall.)

That day, October 1, I sat for a bit on the living room couch, flipping between the Redskins' game at New Orleans and a now-meaningless Orioles season finale in Toronto. What I had anticipated as being a division-deciding game instead featured both teams largely emptying their benches. Juan Bell started for the O's—a cruel reminder that if Baltimore had just picked up a little more in the Eddie Murray trade . . .

The Redskins edged the Saints 16–14 when Morten Andersen, the Saints' all-pro kicker, missed a short field goal in the final minutes. My father yelped, but I could scarcely feel any joy. There would be another 'Skins game the following week and for several weeks after that. The Caps would kick off a new season later that week. In November, I would rejoin some of my Ritchie Park friends on our rec basketball team and in March more of them on our baseball team. With Steve living so close by, we still saw each other almost daily. So there would be some normalcy in my world as so much changed.

But not yet. First, I had to make some sense of this magical, yet tragic, Orioles season before I could move on. Their season, which had started so long ago that when pitchers and catchers reported, I was in the middle of fifth grade at my old elementary school, goofing off and playing endless hours of recess games with friends . . . that was over.

There would be another baseball regular season starting in a few months, involving many of these same players on the O's, but there would never be another 1989 Baltimore Orioles.

Not for me.

In Baltimore, the O's were greeted like champions. On Sunday night, they landed at BWI Airport just after eight, where about three thousand fans greeted them with banners including "Thanks for a

Super Year," "Comeback Kids," "Thanks, O's," and "O, Well." Fans chanted "Let's Go O's" as Cal Ripken and others addressed them.

Robinson thanked them. "Next year, we'll bring it all home," he said.

It was raining, hard.

The front of the *Post* sports section provided an epilogue as I greeted it the next morning, stuffing it in my bookbag for the ride to school. The newspaper printed the AL East standings: atop read "Toronto 89–73," followed by "Baltimore 87–75." After school I pulled the section out again and stared at it for several minutes, while sitting on my bedroom floor. Freddy limped into the room, curled up on a loose piece of notebook paper lying on the floor and stared at me as I wondered to myself, *The Orioles' season is over? They finished second?*

Yes, it was and they did. There would be no division title, no playoff series against the mighty A's. There would be no more watching *SportsCenter* in the morning to find out if the O's had won on the West Coast the night before, no more bedtime prayers answered by Tim Freakin' Hulett, no more flipping open the sports section daily to read about this beloved team.

It seemed so unfair. I had been watching sports for a few years now, but had never followed a season and a team as closely as I did in 1989. Before 1989, I had been too young to stay up until the end of most night games, too distracted by Tyler's mesmerizing growth, too obsessed with new Nintendo games and making mix tapes, too squirrely to sit long enough in front of the TV to really get invested in a team like I did that season.

Much of that changed in 1989. By then I possessed a rapidly evolving understanding of the game, appreciating the strategy to such an extent that I eschewed the popular *Strat-O-Matic* game and tried to create a more sophisticated simulation. It was no longer enough for me just to play on a team with my friends: I now needed to excel or at least help our team win. The games—my own and those featuring the Orioles—took on vast significance. That spring and summer and early fall, it was not that I wanted to but I had to play and consume baseball whenever possible.

The tragedy is 1989 may have been the only year I could fully indulge that desire, that sweet, innocent MO. It came and went so quickly. Over the following springs and summers, there would be so much more homework, family tragedies and personal heartbreak, and powerful anxiety disorders fully emerging to prevent me from immersing myself in any team as I had the 1989 O's. Not even the Redskins' pursuit of an undefeated season and championship in 1991 got as much of my attention.

I tried diving into the 1990 and 1991 Orioles seasons with the same emotional intensity, but the O's finished below .500 both seasons, MomMom Flick was getting very sick and—toward the end of the 1990 season—PopPop Eddie was also diagnosed with cancer and died within a couple of months. (MomMom Flick made it another year, somehow hanging on to see my Bar Mitzvah and Brad's high school graduation).

Mom was affected deeply by these losses, as well as my disappearance into a deep adolescent funk that lasted until I was about sixteen. ("It was like a gremlin inhabited your body," she told me years later.) She did her best to hide her grief and other deep feelings from my brothers and me and usually succeeded, but it eked out in seemingly odd ways at strange times. Mom and I spent much of the next few years feuding about minuscule shit—from the winter afternoon when I was twelve and threw a jacket at her after she told me I needed to wear it while playing pickup football, to the day in high school when she tried to stop me from going to a Dave Matthews Band concert in Richmond and I threatened her.

I did not handle losing my grandparents or my changing relationship with Mom well either (not to mention my other burgeoning issues). I went through nasty kleptomania and pyromania phases in middle school. I almost completely stopped confiding in Mom after losing my trust in her ability to help fix my problems during tumultuous sixth- and seventh-grade years.

In the spring of 1989, I would sometimes stretch out vertically on my stomach, laying on my parents' bed at night and reading *Sports Illustrated* or the *Post* sports section while Mom rubbed my back and read the rest of the newspaper. We often talked to each other in a soft, sweet tone—when my friends were not around.

A year later, over one weekend I snapped at her when she filmed me trying (unsuccessfully) to heave an adult-sized bowling ball down the lane, and again when she zoomed in on me watching friends play basketball on our driveway instead of filming our two-on-two tournament, as I had instructed her.

My sudden, sometimes frosty behavior was not reserved just for Mom. Soon after the 1989 O's season ended, I stopped crying entirely, and this lasted until well into adulthood. It was a defense mechanism I subconsciously developed mostly to stop the bullying, a mechanism I could not shake even years after the bullying ended. Several women over the years accused me of being cold and distant; they were right.

This new behavior and a vastly different phase of my life started in earnest that fall, around the time the O's failed to deliver on the promise of that epic season and lost two gut-wrenching games in Toronto.

But I did not acknowledge any transitions as I stared at the newspaper that Monday afternoon. Instead, we all quickly moved on. There was another big Jewish holiday a week later, football practices, piano lessons, Mom's frequent trips and calls to check on MomMom Flick. Nobody in our family grieved the O's loss beyond that Monday, not even me. That day I went to school, football practice, and then Hebrew school, as usual, shoving a couple of Tastykake cupcakes in my mouth after practice for the usual pre-Hebrew school sugar rush on a half-empty stomach.

The 'Skins' win the day before, especially Andersen's shocking miss, was the main topic of conversation in all three settings of this Redskins-mad town that day. The 'Skins had always belonged to DC, at least since before my grandparents even moved there.

The Orioles? After 1989, nearly two decades after DC had lost a second Major League team to relocation, they did too. They were the closest team, planning to move even closer when the new Camden Yards stadium would open in a couple of years at the southern tip of downtown, conveniently for Washingtonians. And they had won our hearts.

But their season was over and everyone else was moving on, so I had too as well. Even if I was far from ready to do so.

Reading box scores in the Washington Post sport section at Bethany Beach in Delaware, August 1988, in between throwing around a baseball and body-surfing. My childhood may have perished, but its spirit lives on.

NO JOY IN ROCKVILLE

"When he was six, he believed that the moon overhead followed him. By nine he had deciphered the illusion, trading magic for fact. No tradebacks."
—Pearl Jam, "I'm Open," 1996

Later that week, as we delighted in watching the Jays get hammered by Oakland in the ALCS, the O's began making offseason news. On Tuesday, Ballard had surgery to remove bone chips from his pitching elbow. Surgeons determined he would have to return later to have a bone spur removed from the same elbow. " 'He'll be ready far before spring training," Hemond said. "He just had the elbow cleaned up. . . . I've seen a lot of pitchers have this kind of thing done."

The elbow had been bothering him since midseason, yet he had pitched well through it as he strived to help the O's win the division. But did that effort help derail his career? Ballard had just turned twenty-six, starting thirty-five games, earning eighteen wins and posting two hundred–plus innings in his career year. His last two starts were clutch and dominant, even if they ultimately did not yield wins.

For the rest of this career, though, he won a combined thirteen games while making forty-four starts over four seasons. Baltimore let him leave as a free agent after the 1991 season and his career ended with him coming out of the bullpen for the Pirates in 1994. He never posted an ERA below 4.86 for a season again after 1989. Any hope of returning to form was shattered when he broke his neck in a car accident in January 1995.

"Between [the surgeries], the lockout [before the 1990 season], and the [labor] negotiations, my rehab did not go as it should have and I was just awful in 1990," he told author Ron Snyder years later. "I was even worse in 1991 because my mechanics were all messed up after the surgery. It took me years to get those mechanics back, which happened right before the accident."

Meanwhile, Traber, Sheets, Quirk, Moreland, and Schmidt were likely to leave Baltimore that offseason, the *Post* reported. They all did. None excelled elsewhere, though Quirk returned to Oakland and played sparingly in the 1990 and 1992 postseasons. Traber never played in the majors again, while Moreland retired. Schmidt signed with the Expos as a free agent after the season and lasted parts of three more seasons in the majors. Working exclusively out of the bullpen as he had for much of his career, he saved thirteen games for Montreal in 1990, but barely pitched in 1991 or 1992.

Schilling and McDonald would get every opportunity to nail down rotation spots in 1990, while the O's would likely acquire a few new players, according to reports. But Hemond and Robinson expected most of the club's nucleus to return.

In the offseason, the O's indeed signed power-hitting designated hitter Sam Horn from Boston and traded Sheets to Detroit for utility infielder Mike Brumley—who promptly did not even make the team. Otherwise they did nothing else to replace their outgoing players, hoping their young players would continue improving.

The Orioles opened the 1990 season with a lot of optimism and won their season opener in eleven innings again, but started 35–45. Yet the AL East stunk again and, when a sleepaway camp director announced to us over breakfast one morning that Baltimore had swept four from the White Sox and were within four and one-half games of first in late July, I was sure they would make another run at the division. They finally reached .500 on August 3, when a 14–1 win over Kansas City kept them four and one-half games out with a full one-third of the season to play.

But Baltimore's shortcomings in talent and experience shone down the stretch much more in 1990 than in 1989. In addition, with Ballard and Tibbs unable to bounce back from their injuries and Harnisch and Milacki taking steps back, the O's lost twenty-two of their next twenty-nine and finished the season below .500, eleven and one-half games out of first. They were virtually eliminated just as the NFL season started, like we had been accustomed to seeing for a few years (besides 1989).

Eventually much of the nucleus formed in 1989 helped lead contending teams in 1992 and 1993. Milligan, Devereaux, the Ripken brothers, Orsulak, Milacki, Olson, McDonald, and Anderson were all regulars on those teams, which fought Toronto again well into September—but fell short of the division crown again both times. The O's then radically altered their roster after the 1994 season was halted by a strike in August.

By the time the O's returned to the playoffs in October 1996, after a thirteen-year drought, I was a freshman in college arguing about umpires' calls with Indians fans over greasy mozzarella sticks and jungle juice throughout a taut four-game series against Cleveland. (Albert Belle batted just three-for-fifteen in the series, while Cory Snyder had been traded away by the Indians after the 1990 season.)

In the ALCS against the Yankees, Jimmy Key again started a critical game against Baltimore. This time he was stellar, winning Game Three to give New York a 2–1 series lead they would not relinquish.

At eighteen, I chased away this loss not by staring at a newspaper or crying, but by ripping bong hits of shwaggy weed and pounding Meister Bräu beer and Jim Beam whiskey. Whatever emotions that were bubbling to the surface were quickly suppressed. (But, still, fuck that kid who turned a Derek Jeter flyout into a game-tying homer in Game One of that ALCS.)

By 1996, only Cal Ripken and Anderson remained consistently from the 1989 roster, though Devereaux and Billy Ripken rejoined Baltimore before the season after departing earlier. That 1996 club was managed by Davey Johnson, whose last full season managing the Mets came in 1989, with Murray returning in a late-season trade from Cleveland.

Wither the rest of the 1989 Baltimore Orioles?

In a move that should be noted prominently in some *Baseball Hall of Shame* book as among the worst trades in baseball history, Harnisch, Finley, and Schilling were dealt after the 1990 season for Glenn Davis, a power-hitting thirty-year-old first baseman with Houston. Davis would post three awful seasons in Baltimore, never slugging more than thirteen homers after hitting at least twenty in each of the previous six seasons.

Schilling became a Hall of Famer, albeit only after Houston gave up on him too. Finley and Harnisch enjoyed long careers often on contending clubs, with Finley joining Schilling on the 2001 Arizona Diamondbacks World Series champions. That team's regular first baseman was Mark Grace, whose rookie card had undergone little change in value since 1989 due to a baseball card market that was well over-saturated in the late 1980s and 1990s.

I will argue you to the death that the O's would have captured either the 1992 or 1993 division crown (or both) had they not made this trade. A Finley-Devereaux-Anderson outfield with Harnisch as the fourth or fifth starter behind Mike Mussina, McDonald, and Rick Sutcliffe would have given Baltimore a great chance, even if Schilling needed another trade to wake him up (as has been well-documented).

Meanwhile Worthington, like so many on the 1989 team, never played that well again. He hit below .230 and socked a combined twelve homers from 1990–1991. Baltimore traded Worthington to San Diego after the 1991 season, and he would never be a regular again.

Olson saved at least twenty-seven games every year between 1989–93 for Baltimore, then left in free agency for Atlanta. He pitched for eight more seasons, but lost his closer role until a comeback 1998 season in Arizona. He was never an All-Star again after 1990. It could be argued that his rookie season was his best—it was certainly his most memorable.

Williamson continued to be Olson's setup man for a while, pitching out of the bullpen for five more seasons with Baltimore.

Dave Johnson pitched for a couple more seasons and then was out of baseball. After 1989, he never pitched in a meaningful late-season game again. He certainly made the most of his only opportunity.

Bradley was traded on July 30, 1990, to the White Sox, for the power hitting Ron Kittle. The O's were only four games out of first when they moved Bradley; before August ended, they were more than ten games out. Bradley never played in MLB after that season, when he was thirty-one.

Tettleton played only one more season in Baltimore. After he regressed to a .223 average and just fifteen homers in 1990, Baltimore traded the thirty-year-old to Detroit for reliever Jeff Robinson, replacing him with the rising Hoiles at catcher. Tettleton played six more full seasons with the Tigers and Rangers before retiring in 1997, hitting more than thirty homers and driving in more than eighty runs four times. He finally played in the postseason with Texas in 1996.

Jefferson spent two more years in the majors as a platoon player for three teams.

Friends and I used to randomly rehash the 1989 O's season, especially on long road trips during college breaks and our early twenties. Adam, struggling to drive around dawn as we zoomed across I-70 in Maryland one late May morning circa 1999, turned to me as I sat shotgun, "Base, help me stay awake. Talk to me about the '89 O's."

We always recalled Ballard as the most tragic figure in their story. The legend for years was that he started 5-0 in April and was poised to become the next great Oriole hurler when he took that line drive to the neck. Then he was never the same.

That tale of course doesn't stand up. But the mythology surrounding him does. Ballard was the Icarus of the 1989 Baltimore Orioles. His sudden, fleeting ascension to the top of the majors for one season before literally crashing was always one of the first developments that came to our minds whenever we thought of the team. He was an unexpected phenomenon in a season full of them, a shooting star that gave fans hope, made us believe that these Orioles—picked to finish last by nearly everyone and early in a rebuild—could actu- ally win a seven-team division one season after losing more than one hundred games. And that they could do it with a roster full of cast- offs, rookies, and Cal Ripken.

Ballard defeated some of the league's top aces and did not waiver even after being hit by that drive or after suffering a midseason swoon. His performance often mirrored the club's. He won nine games by June 5 as the O's soared to the top of the division—then notched just two wins over his next thirteen starts, as the club fell from the sky and seemed headed for a reality check by early August.

Then, just as most experts and fans were counting both out again, Ballard and the O's rebounded. He won seven of nine starts between August 17 and September 20, as the O's stayed in contention with Toronto until the season's final weekend.

In what would be the final meaningful start of his career, he held the mighty Blue Jays down that Friday night, shutting them out for seven innings. The O's led 1–0 when Olson replaced him, so he could have easily been awarded a win with a division race on the line. Considering that context, it was one of the great starts in Oriole history.

Ballard's fall after the season also mirrored the Orioles' struggles in 1990 and 1991. And no player on that team was more synonymous with my own struggles over those years, as the promise of much of 1989—viewed through the lens of an optimistic, goofy preteen boosted by caring friends and a fully present mother—was crushed by adolescence, serious untreated anxiety disorders, an awful fit at a new school, family tragedies, and a growing breach between me and Mom. By 1992 I may still have been an avid Oriole fan and baseball junkie, but I was well on my way to becoming the cynical Washington Nationals fan that I am today.

Since 1989, I have admired and cheered for greats such as Mussina, Cal Ripken, Anderson, Max Scherzer, Bryce Harper, and Juan Soto. But there never has been, nor will there be, another Jeff Ballard for me. After the events of 1989 and the years immediately following, there never could be.

So if you have made it this far, you must be wondering what happened to some of the "characters" from my world in 1989. Somehow, some way, we are all still kicking and I remain friends with many of them. Our early bonds must have been that strong.

Ross lives in Oakland and works in marketing. Brett started a charity and still lives in the DC area. Adam runs a musician management company in LA. Steve is a Realtor in the DC area. Michael works in finance in New York, while Tyler is an allergist near LA. They both visit DC with their families, though not often enough for Mom. Brad is a contractor living in the DC area.

My parents are retired and still live in the house they raised us in. My father plays golf, draws, and cooks, while Mom attends adult education classes, plots vacations, still helps her kids deal with our problems, and spends as much time as possible with her grandchildren.

In Baltimore, Oriole Park at Camden Yards indeed opened in 1992. Situated within walking distance from Inner Harbor and much of downtown, it led to an explosion in attendance and interest in the team, especially in a Washington area still lacking its own club.

My father got partial season tickets for the first couple of seasons—lower level!—and often took my brothers and me. While we missed out on attending a Caps playoff game in 1989, I vividly recall him, Michael, and me standing in the concourse waiting out a rain delay during a critical O's-Jays game in late September 1992. Not even he cared that we would be severely sleep-deprived the next day at school.

The Nationals arrived in DC from Montreal in 2005. I had briefly moved back to the area by then, after spending four years in St. Louis for college and a few years working as a newspaper journalist in small cities. I had given up on my dream of being a pro athlete later in middle school and launched my journalism career as a sportswriter, interning at *The Baltimore Sun* and *Newsday* during two summers in college. After years of playing, watching, and otherwise consuming baseball, here I was covering the majors up close. I felt like I was on the verge of reaching a new dream.

But it was sometime between when O's starter Scott Kamieniecki told me to buzz off in the locker room at Camden Yards, and when I watched an over-the-hill Mets infielder named Carlos Baerga gorge on a postgame spread in the bowels of Shea Stadium, that any idolatry I had for pro athletes completely disappeared. I would no longer hang over dugouts hoping for Cory Snyder's autograph, or anyone's.

By 2005, I was more interested in news and business reporting, features, and column writing. The subjects hardly mattered. I was only back in DC for about fifteen months, securing a master's in journalism from the University of Maryland before moving to Charlotte for another reporting job.

But I was around long enough to catch the entire 2005 season, the first Major League season in my hometown since 1971. The Nats' manager that year: Frank Robinson. These Nats, like the '89 O's, were picked to finish last by most observers. These Nats, like those O's, were in first place at the All-Star break. Washington actually went 50–31 over the first half of the season.

Mmmmaybe . . . I thought.

Nah, I immediately corrected myself. *They're just not good enough.* I no longer believed in miracles; that had been dashed some sixteen years earlier and then buried by years of adolescence and early adulthood.

I was right. These Nats also missed the playoffs. They fell apart much more quickly than the 1989 O's, finishing 81–81.

I had learned from the folly of youth, so this collapse hardly bothered me. Three days after the Nats' final game that season, though, Alexander Ovechkin made his debut for the Caps. It took a while, but the Caps finally won their first Stanley Cup, led by the superstar forward. My tears during their banner-raising ceremony in October 2018 marked the first time I had cried over a sporting event since that late September day in 1989 when I watched a fried Mark Williamson fail to retire several Blue Jays, as the raucous SkyDome crowd pierced my newly pubescent ears—and soul.

I decided to become a sportswriter in eighth grade after writing a couple of stories for our student newspaper, per an English class unit. I stuck with the dream until I felt the hours and deadline stress were no longer worth it, especially in the last days of limited WiFi access on many college and high school campuses. I converted to more serious journalism in my mid-twenties and stuck with the profession full-time on and off for the next fifteen years. That lasted until overcovering the COVID-19 pandemic as a medical journalist directed by greedy corporate bosses killed much of my passion for journalism . . . and literally made me sick, with daily panic attacks interrupting my work.

The profession sometimes broke my heart, always jeopardized my relationships and finances, and often had me questioning why I had pursued it. Being a journalist, then, for me was not unlike rooting hard for your favorite baseball team that ultimately lets you down.

I sometimes wonder if my life would have turned out better had the O's won the division in 1989—my own "Mr. Destiny" story. In some alternate universe where they did, I have just passed down my sacred division champions T-shirt to my oldest nephew and have spent considerably less time and money on therapy over the last few years—because the O's triumph extended my faith in miracles and helped give me a rosier outlook throughout a difficult adolescence, the Great Recession, the pandemic, and health problems.

But that's not how it played out. Instead, I like to think the events of spring, summer and, especially, fall 1989 started preparing me to withstand all the trials my life has since presented. Why not?

Plus: Would I have written this book had they won? I doubt it.

I conceived of the idea around 2006. I was in my late twenties, feeling established in my career and confident about my looks and social skills. I made women laugh and proffer me attention with my encyclopedic memory of old school rap lyrics and by regaling them with stories of the filthy, goofy boy I used to be. But I only started writing this book in the summer of 2008—as a work of fiction—hoping to leverage the seasonal drop in my workload as a staff writer with the

Charlotte Observer. I researched the season, jotted down memories, and crafted a few short chapters to start.

But the book never felt right as fiction, and a few months later, the Great Recession hit Charlotte hard, eventually costing me my job and my home. In the summer of 2009, I thought about starting the writing part over as a memoir and pursuing a career as a writer. Instead, I opted for what I thought was a safer route and started applying to doctoral sociology programs, aiming to become a research professor.

I put the book down. For quite a while.

I knew I would come back to it at some point; I just had trouble locating that point. Sometimes I didn't because I did not have the time and energy. Other times I buried myself in new pursuits—curse the hours I spent on dating apps and many of the ensuing dates— rather than writing the book.

It took the pandemic to persuade me to pick up this project again. This time I had no choice. I knew that if I did not write this book then, when there was little else to do during my free time, it would never get done. Writing much of this also provided a welcome respite from reporting on the pandemic; I went from five long days of focusing on saddening, infuriating topics to spending a few hours on the weekend revisiting what I initially found to be a happier, more social time. I also spent hours viewing old family photos and videos and talking with Mom, unearthing other memories that worked their way into the narrative—even the awful developments that I discovered shaped 1989 for me as much as the good times. Looking at the box scores of key games on *Baseball Reference* also dislodged some buried gems in my mind.

Something also intrinsically drove me to write this to completion this time, and to do it as a memoir. It was a similar force as the one that hatched this idea in the first place and got me to spend hours working on it in 2008 and 2009. That force was far more powerful this time. It felt as if I had to tell my story, and quickly. The fear of being judged publicly for being such a sensitive, anxious preteen— which had nudged me to start this project as fiction—barely even registered anymore.

So I fucking wrote it, finally. I did it for myself first, my friends and family second. If the whole lot of you never got the chance to read this because no publisher was wise enough to pick it up, I would have been okay with that. I think.

Maybe not.

Because I also am sharing my story for everyone who was forced to grow up before they were ready, who feels like their childhood was suddenly ripped away against their will by adults who may have been well-meaning, but had their own agendas too.

I hope my story and the tale of the 1989 Baltimore Orioles jive with you. Baltimore's season played out along with the end of my own childhood and transition into adolescence in real time. For a few months, a bunch of kids went out and played ball. They had fun and were successful, winning a lot of games against teams with superior talent. Then the pressure ratcheted up, with the season nearing its end and more experienced teams closing in on them. They were forced to grow up in a hurry to achieve their goal. They tried. Hard. They fought until the very end, but they came up short.

And, like much of my experience during adolescence, I think it was largely the adults who let the O's down. Ultimately, the O's lost for many reasons: because Toronto was more talented and much deeper, and because on paper the O's should have only won eighty-three games, according to *Baseball Reference*. But they also lost because Robinson made key mistakes and refused to trust inexperienced arm talent to help a tiring bullpen, Hemond failed to land much hitting at the trade deadline, Moreland then underachieved, Schmidt fell apart, even Cal Ripken slumped at the plate down the stretch. And of course, the aging Quirk failed to block a rookie's explosive curve ball that fateful night, and an umpire blew a critical call the next day when the veteran Hulett committed a cardinal baseball sin.

To say the kids on the team were not quite ready for the very grown-up pressure of a division race is largely folly. Finley's baserunning gaffe and Olson's arguably wild pitch aside, my research found little evidence of the regular youngsters on this team making mental mistakes or failing to perform in August and September. Plus, had Tibbs not gone down for the season in July and Tettleton not been injured in August, would the last weekend of the season even have mattered? What if the AL president had suspended George Bell instead of merely fining him?

The kids deserved to win the division that year, simply put. So it is bittersweet to note some of them never enjoyed strong seasons again, never got the chance to compete for a postseason spot in a September race again. Baseball was cruel like that in the days before postseason expansion. It's fair to conclude that many of them overachieved in 1989, that the innocence of youth and lack of expectations allowed them to flourish for one magical season, that the expectations that always follow early-career success were probably too much for some of them to handle.

And me? I also deserved better. I have never been close to the same person as I was before and during 1989. I will never recapture that innocence as I cluelessly rollicked toward adolescence—when I expected nothing more of myself than keeping an eye out for my brothers and avoiding too much trouble at school; collected baseball cards thinking they would one day help pay for a nice single-family house; and still thought my mother was a perfect, totally unflappable human being.

I lived a mystical, uneven first three quarters of that year, one I could never forget even if I took an Olson fastball to the cranium. It hardly matters that the O's did not win the division. Rarely since have I reached the top of my own profession or achieved unexpected lofty goals. The 1989 O's helped prepare me for such disappointments. In the end, with all the lessons their season taught me (including the excruciating late-season defeats in Toronto), perhaps it was better for me, at least, that they did not win.

Fruit Loops tosses and dramatic walk-offs and believing in miracles can only last so long. I was lucky I got to experience one season full of all that . . . and more.

Why not?

The End

Frozen in Time: Posing with my brothers on a bunk bed at sleepaway camp, sporting my Orioles hat and another Nike shirt. When this picture was taken in mid-July, the O's were several games ahead of the AL East field and I was mere weeks past elementary school.

ACKNOWLEDGMENTS

Thanks to Aaron McFarling, whose suggestion that we watch the documentary *Orioles '89 Why Not?: The Story of The 1989 Baltimore Orioles* one night after work some time in 2003 helped spark my idea to one day write about their season.

Thanks to everyone who read at least part of a book draft and offered feedback, including: Kent Babb, Steve Gormley, Brett Meyers, Ross Yader, Adam Harrison, Mark Kawar, Mary Jacoby, David Grandouiller, Mom, and anyone I may have missed. Thanks especially to Steve for corroborating some scenes and for reminding me of the correct amount of money Mom gave me after that garage sale. I had forgotten you were even there that day. Thanks to others who undoubtedly hit "control-F," skimmed sections of the book for their name, then gave me a thumbs up to proceed—even if they could not remember the scenes they are in. Thanks to Diana Rodriguez Wallach for advising me on how to shape, publish, and market this book. Thanks to other friends, especially Amy Polishuk, whose sincere intrigue about this book let me know that I wasn't (too) crazy for writing it.

Thanks to members of the DC Writers' Salon who helped me drastically improve this book with your thoughtful feedback during numerous workshop sessions. Thanks to editors and reporters Lisa Hammersly, Dave Cowan, McGregor McCance, Adrianne Flynn, Jim Asher, Ralph Berrier, Aaron McFarling (thanks again, Stampy!), Greg Esposito, and others who have taken an active, personal interest in my writing over the years. Thanks to Mike Sager for taking a chance on this project and for helping jumpstart my journalism career.

Finally, thanks Mom. For reading a polished draft and offering extensive feedback—including strong suggestions that I remove some especially gross scenes. For digging up family photo albums and videos and recounting what I was like as a preteen, helping me flesh out the book details. For giving me your blessing to publish this, even if you preferred that I didn't. For helping me construct an important scene entirely from your memory. And especially for revisiting a difficult time in both of our lives. You have never stopped doing things for me—or your other children, nieces and nephews, and now grandchildren.

Love, always.

LIST OF SOURCES

Berkowitz, Steve. "Orioles' Milacki Beats Rangers' Ryan, 5-2." *Washington Post*, August 6, 1989.

Boswell, Thomas. "Bad Baseball," *Washington Post Magazine*, March 26, 1989.

Boswell, Thomas. "Revival on 33rd: Heady," *Washington Post*, June 1, 1989.

Boswell, Thomas. "Birds Are of a Feather." *Washington Post*, June 30, 1989.

Boswell, Thomas. "There's Joy in Birdland," *Washington Post Magazine*, July 9, 1989.

Boswell, Thomas. "Olson: The Closer as the Start of Something Big." *Washington Post*, July 19, 1989.

Boswell, Thomas. "Little Belief Goes a Long, Long Way." *Washington Post*, August 23, 1989.

Boswell, Thomas. "No Time to Put Dreams Away, Orioles." *Washington Post*, September 12, 1989.

Boswell, Thomas. "Blue Jays Try to Bust Some Ghosts." *Washington Post*, September 16, 1989.

Boswell, Thomas. "The Beauty of Baseball: The All-Consuming Pennant Race." *Washington Post*, September 22, 1989.

Boswell, Thomas. "Orioles Can Contend They're Not Just Lucky." *Washington Post*, September 24, 1989.

Boswell, Thomas. "One Great Race Deserves One-Game Playoff." *Washington Post*, September 26, 1989.

Boswell, Thomas. "First 159 Just Game 1 in Best-of-5." *Washington Post*, September 29, 1989.

Boswell, Thomas. "Nightmarish Ending Haunts Dream Season." *Washington Post*, September 30, 1989.

Boswell, Thomas. "Orioles Wince at What Got Away, but Hold Heads High." *Washington Post*, October 1, 1989.

Brennan, Christine. "Orioles' Luck Evens Out." *Washington Post*, July 20, 1989.

Carey, John. "For the Orioles, Less Is More – It's First Place." *Business Week*, July 10, 1989.

Gammons, Peter. "A Flight to the Finish." *Sports Illustrated*, October 2, 1989.

Gammons, Peter. "Oh, What a Relief It Is." *Sports Illustrated*, October 9, 1989.

Gildea, William. "Orioles Stay in the Air on a Wing and a Prayer." *Washington Post*, August 11, 1989.

Gildea, William. "Orioles Take a Bow." *Washington Post*, September 25, 1989.

Gildea, William. "Improbable Heroes Come Home to Cheers of 3,000 Soggy Fans." *Washington Post*, October 2, 1989.

Gladwell, Malcolm. "Feathering Their Nest." *Washington Post*, July 17, 1989.

Hackett, Darren C. "There's Joy in Birdville as Fans Flock Back." *Washington Post*, June 10, 1989.

Justice, Richard. "37,204 at RFK Stadium See Orioles' Last Tuneup," *Washington Post*, April 3, 1989.

Justice, Richard. "Orioles Win Opener in 11th Inning, 5-4," *Washington Post*, April 4, 1989.

Justice, Richard. "Only Finley's Injury Lessens Orioles' Joy," *Washington Post*, April 5, 1989.

Justice, Richard. "Major Legue Owners Approve Orioles Sale," *Washington Post*, April 19, 1989.

Justice, Richard. "Orioles' Milacki Faces 27, Wins Three-Hitter," *Washington Post*, April 24, 1989.

Justice, Richard. "For Orioles, It's Fun Being Different," *Washington Post*, April 30, 1989.

Justice, Richard. "Orioles Top Mariners as Ballard Goes 5-0," *Washington Post*, May 1, 1989.

Justice, Richard. "Orioles: The Secret of Their Success," *Washington Post*, May 26, 1989.

Justice, Richard. "Tettleton's 13th Homer Lucky for Orioles, 8-5," *Washington Post*, June 1, 1989.

Justice, Richard. "Orioles Draft McDonald 1st, Likely to try Him This Season," *Washington Post*, June 6, 1989.

Justice, Richard. "16-3 Win 8th in Row for Orioles," *Washington Post*, June 6, 1989.

Justice, Richard. "Young Orioles Blithely Turn Respectability Into an Art Form," *Washington Post*, June 8, 1989.

Justice, Richard. "Weston Arrives in Time to Save Orioles." *Washington Post*, June 19, 1989.

Justice, Richard. "Tettleton a Bona Fide All-Star; Orioles' Ballard Left Off Team." *Washington Post*, July 7, 1989.

Justice, Richard. "Orioles' Margin All but Gone." *Washington Post*, August 2, 1989.

Justice, Richard. "Johnson's Home; Orioles Grateful." *Washington Post*, August 9, 1989.

Justice, Richard. "Orioles' Rookie Johnson Named Player of Week." *Washington Post*, August 15, 1989.

Justice, Richard. "Orioles and McDonald Have a Deal: $950,000 Over Three Years." *Washington Post*, August 19, 1989.

Justice, Richard. "Orioles Patch Holes, Remain Organized." *Washington Post*, August 29, 1989.

Justice, Richard. "Orioles Sink into 2nd on 10-1 Loss." *Washington Post*, September 2, 1989.

Justice, Richard. "Notebook; Blue Jays Might Yet Reward Patient Wisdom of Gillick." *Washington Post*, September 3, 1989.

Justice, Richard. "Orioles Drop 2 Behind with 9-0 Loss to Indians." *Washington Post*, September 7, 1989.

Justice, Richard. "Miracle Rookies Could Keep the Orioles Flying for Years." *Washington Post*, September 19, 1989.

Justice, Richard. "Orioles Win, Set Up Toronto Title Series." *Washington Post*, September 28, 1989.

Justice, Richard. "Orioles' '89 One for Books." *Washington Post*, September 29, 1989.

Justice, Richard. "Blue Jays Shove Orioles Into Tight Spot, 2-1." *Washington Post*, September 30, 1989.

Justice, Richard. "Reality Finally Catches Up with Orioles, 4-3." *Washington Post*, October 1, 1989.

Justice, Richard. "Johnson Steps Forward With a Surprise Effort." *Washington Post*, October 1, 1989.

Justice, Richard. "Orioles Savor Season's Success, Begin Making Preparations for the 1990's." *Washington Post*, October 3, 1989.

Justice, Richard. "Notebook; Ballard Has Surgery to Remove Bone Chips." *Washington Post*, October 12, 1989.

Justice, Richard. "Robinson Named Manager of Year." *Washington Post*, October 14, 1989.

Keplinger, Steve. *The Comeback Kids: A Fan Relives the Amazing Baltimore Orioles 1989 Season*. Publishers Place, 1989.

Kornheiser, Tony. "Orioles and Robinson: When You're Hot..." *Washington Post*, July 11, 1989.

Kornheiser, Tony. "Mets of Old Mirror Orioles Anew." *Washington Post*, July 20, 1989.

Maske, Mark. "Bautista's Return Helps Orioles Past A's, 4-2." *Washington Post*, June 18, 1989.

Maske, Mark. "Orioles Break Losing Streak." *Washington Post*, July 29, 1989.

Lidz, Franz. "For the Birds," *Sports Illustrated*, May 2, 1988.

Lidz, Franz. "Birdland," *Sports Illustrated*, September 11, 1989.

Sell, Dave. "Hulett's The Hero This Time." *Washington Post*, September 5, 1989.

Snyder, Ronald. *A Season to Forget: The Story of the 1988 Baltimore Orioles*. Sports Publishing, 2019.

Wulf, Steve. "O You Beautiful Birds," *Sports Illustrated*, June 19, 1989.

Yardley, Jonathan. "For O's in '89, the Magic Number Is 98." *Washington Post*, September 4, 1989.

"Sunny Days at the Stadium." *Washington Post*, July 20, 1989.

Baseball Reference

Orioles '89 Why Not?: The Story of The 1989 Baltimore Orioles, distributed by the Baltimore Orioles Management.

ABOUT THE AUTHOR

Ryan Basen was an award-winning reporter with the *Charlotte Observer* who has written features for the *New York Times*, the *Washington Post*, and the *Baltimore Sun*. He is the author of several non-fiction books aimed at preteens and has coached youth and high school baseball. Basen attended college at Washington University (St. Louis) and earned a master's degree in journalism from the University of Maryland. He lives in Washington, DC.

ABOUT THE PUBLISHER

The Sager Group was founded in 1984. In 2012 it was chartered as a multimedia content brand, with the intent of empowering those who create art—an umbrella beneath which makers can pursue, and profit from, their craft directly, without gatekeepers. TSG publishes books; ministers to artists and provides modest grants; and produces documentary, feature, and commercial films. By harnessing the means of production, The Sager Group helps artists help themselves. For more information, please see www.TheSagerGroup.net.

MORE FROM THE SAGER GROUP

The Swamp: Deceit and Corruption in the CIA
An Elizabeth Petrov Thriller (Book 1)
by Jeff Grant

Eat Wheaties: A Novel
by Michael Kun

#MeAsWell
by Peter Melhlman

Death Came Swiftly: Novel About the Tay Bridge Disaster of 1879
by Bill Abrams

High Tolerance: A Novel of Sex, Race, Celebrity, Murder... and Marijuana
by Mike Sager

Miss Havilland: A Novel
by Gay Daly

The Orphan's Daughter: A Novel
by Jan Cherubin

Lifeboat No. 8: Surviving the Titanic
by Elizabeth Kaye

Into the River of Angels: A Novel
by George R. Wolfe

See our entire library at TheSagerGroup.net

THE SAGER GROUP

Artifex Te Adiuva

www.ingramcontent.com/pod-product-compliance
Lightning Source LLC
Chambersburg PA
CBHW030406130626
46549CB00004B/1648